Petar Cholakov

ETHNIC ENTREPRENEURS UNMASKED

Political Institutions and Ethnic Conflicts in Contemporary Bulgaria

ibidem-Verlag
Stuttgart

Bibliografische Information der Deutschen Nationalbibliothek
Die Deutsche Nationalbibliothek verzeichnet diese Publikation in der Deutschen Nationalbibliografie; detaillierte bibliografische Daten sind im Internet über http://dnb.d-nb.de abrufbar.

Bibliographic information published by the Deutsche Nationalbibliothek
Die Deutsche Nationalbibliothek lists this publication in the Deutsche Nationalbibliografie; detailed bibliographic data are available in the Internet at http://dnb.d-nb.de.

Cover picture:
photo collage by Petar Cholakov.
Top left—the former leader of the MRF, Ahmed Dogan (© Vladimir Petkov via Wikimedia Commons. Licensed under CC BY-SA 2.0, s. https://creativecommons.org/licenses/by-sa/2.0/deed.en);
Top centre—remembering the victims of the conflict in Katunitsa during a procession in 2013, the slogan reads: "We are not going to forgive, we are not going to forget" (© Petar Cholakov);
Top right—the leader of the Ataka party, Volen Siderov (© Иван via Wikimedia Commons. Licensed under CC BY-SA 4.0, s. https://creativecommons.org/licenses/by-sa/4.0/);
Bellow, the "cliché of multiculturalism" at the centre of Sofia (see section 1.1 of the book): centre left—the Orthodox Church "St. Nedelya" (© Petar Cholakov);
centre right—Catholic cathedral "St. Joseph" (© Petar Cholakov);
bottom left—the mosque "Banya Bashi" (© Petar Cholakov);
bottom right—the Sofia Synagogue (© Petar Cholakov).

∞

Gedruckt auf alterungsbeständigem, säurefreien Papier
Printed on acid-free paper

ISSN: 1614-3515

ISBN-13: 978-3-8382-1189-3

© *ibidem*-Verlag
Stuttgart 2018

Alle Rechte vorbehalten

Das Werk einschließlich aller seiner Teile ist urheberrechtlich geschützt. Jede Verwertung außerhalb der engen Grenzen des Urheberrechtsgesetzes ist ohne Zustimmung des Verlages unzulässig und strafbar. Dies gilt insbesondere für Vervielfältigungen, Übersetzungen, Mikroverfilmungen und elektronische Speicherformen sowie die Einspeicherung und Verarbeitung in elektronischen Systemen.

All rights part of this publication may be reproduced, stored in or introduced into a retrieval system, or transmitted, in any form, or by any means (electronic, mechanical, photocopying, recording or otherwise) without the prior written permission of the publisher. Any person who does any unauthorized act in relation to this publication may be liable to criminal prosecution and civil claims for damages.

Printed in the EU

Soviet and Post-Soviet Politics and Society (SPPS) Vol. 189
ISSN 1614-3515

General Editor: Andreas Umland,
Institute for Euro-Atlantic Cooperation, Kyiv, umland@stanfordalumni.org

Commissioning Editor: Max Jakob Horstmann,
London, mjh@ibidem.eu

EDITORIAL COMMITTEE*

DOMESTIC & COMPARATIVE POLITICS
Prof. **Ellen Bos**, *Andrássy University of Budapest*
Dr. **Ingmar Bredies**, *FH Bund, Brühl*
Dr. **Andrey Kazantsev**, *MGIMO (U) MID RF, Moscow*
Prof. **Heiko Pleines**, *University of Bremen*
Prof. **Richard Sakwa**, *University of Kent at Canterbury*
Dr. **Sarah Whitmore**, *Oxford Brookes University*
Dr. **Harald Wydra**, *University of Cambridge*

SOCIETY, CLASS & ETHNICITY
Col. **David Glantz**, *"Journal of Slavic Military Studies"*
Dr. **Marlène Laruelle**, *George Washington University*
Dr. **Stephen Shulman**, *Southern Illinois University*
Prof. **Stefan Troebst**, *University of Leipzig*

POLITICAL ECONOMY & PUBLIC POLICY
Prof. em. **Marshall Goldman**, *Wellesley College, Mass.*
Dr. **Andreas Goldthau**, *Central European University*
Dr. **Robert Kravchuk**, *University of North Carolina*
Dr. **David Lane**, *University of Cambridge*
Dr. **Carol Leonard**, *Higher School of Economics, Moscow*
Dr. **Maria Popova**, *McGill University, Montreal*

FOREIGN POLICY & INTERNATIONAL AFFAIRS
Dr. **Peter Duncan**, *University College London*
Prof. **Andreas Heinemann-Grüder**, *University of Bonn*
Dr. **Taras Kuzio**, *Johns Hopkins University*
Prof. **Gerhard Mangott**, *University of Innsbruck*
Dr. **Diana Schmidt-Pfister**, *University of Konstanz*
Dr. **Lisbeth Tarlow**, *Harvard University, Cambridge*
Dr. **Christian Wipperfürth**, *N-Ost Network, Berlin*
Dr. **William Zimmerman**, *University of Michigan*

HISTORY, CULTURE & THOUGHT
Dr. **Catherine Andreyev**, *University of Oxford*
Prof. **Mark Bassin**, *Södertörn University*
Prof. **Karsten Brüggemann**, *Tallinn University*
Dr. **Alexander Etkind**, *University of Cambridge*
Dr. **Gasan Gusejnov**, *Moscow State University*
Prof. em. **Walter Laqueur**, *Georgetown University*
Prof. **Leonid Luks**, *Catholic University of Eichstaett*
Dr. **Olga Malinova**, *Russian Academy of Sciences*
Prof. **Andrei Rogatchevski**, *University of Tromsø*
Dr. **Mark Tauger**, *West Virginia University*

ADVISORY BOARD*

Prof. **Dominique Arel**, *University of Ottawa*
Prof. **Jörg Baberowski**, *Humboldt University of Berlin*
Prof. **Margarita Balmaceda**, *Seton Hall University*
Dr. **John Barber**, *University of Cambridge*
Prof. **Timm Beichelt**, *European University Viadrina*
Dr. **Katrin Boeckh**, *University of Munich*
Prof. em. **Archie Brown**, *University of Oxford*
Dr. **Vyacheslav Bryukhovetsky**, *Kyiv-Mohyla Academy*
Prof. **Timothy Colton**, *Harvard University, Cambridge*
Prof. **Paul D'Anieri**, *University of Florida*
Dr. **Heike Dörrenbächer**, *Friedrich Naumann Foundation*
Dr. **John Dunlop**, *Hoover Institution, Stanford, California*
Dr. **Sabine Fischer**, *SWP, Berlin*
Dr. **Geir Flikke**, *NUPI, Oslo*
Prof. **David Galbreath**, *University of Aberdeen*
Prof. **Alexander Galkin**, *Russian Academy of Sciences*
Prof. **Frank Golczewski**, *University of Hamburg*
Dr. **Nikolas Gvosdev**, *Naval War College, Newport, RI*
Prof. **Mark von Hagen**, *Arizona State University*
Dr. **Guido Hausmann**, *University of Munich*
Prof. **Dale Herspring**, *Kansas State University*
Dr. **Stefani Hoffman**, *Hebrew University of Jerusalem*
Prof. **Mikhail Ilyin**, *MGIMO (U) MID RF, Moscow*
Prof. **Vladimir Kantor**, *Higher School of Economics*
Dr. **Ivan Katchanovski**, *University of Ottawa*
Prof. em. **Andrzej Korbonski**, *University of California*
Dr. **Iris Kempe**, *"Caucasus Analytical Digest"*
Prof. **Herbert Küpper**, *Institut für Ostrecht Regensburg*
Dr. **Rainer Lindner**, *CEEER, Berlin*
Dr. **Vladimir Malakhov**, *Russian Academy of Sciences*

Dr. **Luke March**, *University of Edinburgh*
Prof. **Michael McFaul**, *Stanford University, Palo Alto*
Prof. **Birgit Menzel**, *University of Mainz-Germersheim*
Prof. **Valery Mikhailenko**, *The Urals State University*
Prof. **Emil Pain**, *Higher School of Economics, Moscow*
Dr. **Oleg Podvintsev**, *Russian Academy of Sciences*
Prof. **Olga Popova**, *St. Petersburg State University*
Dr. **Alex Pravda**, *University of Oxford*
Dr. **Erik van Ree**, *University of Amsterdam*
Dr. **Joachim Rogall**, *Robert Bosch Foundation Stuttgart*
Prof. **Peter Rutland**, *Wesleyan University, Middletown*
Prof. **Marat Salikov**, *The Urals State Law Academy*
Dr. **Gwendolyn Sasse**, *University of Oxford*
Prof. **Jutta Scherrer**, *EHESS, Paris*
Prof. **Robert Service**, *University of Oxford*
Mr. **James Sherr**, *RIIA Chatham House London*
Dr. **Oxana Shevel**, *Tufts University, Medford*
Prof. **Eberhard Schneider**, *University of Siegen*
Prof. **Olexander Shnyrkov**, *Shevchenko University, Kyiv*
Prof. **Hans-Henning Schröder**, *SWP, Berlin*
Prof. **Yuri Shapoval**, *Ukrainian Academy of Sciences*
Prof. **Viktor Shnirelman**, *Russian Academy of Sciences*
Dr. **Lisa Sundstrom**, *University of British Columbia*
Dr. **Philip Walters**, *"Religion, State and Society"*, *Oxford*
Prof. **Zenon Wasyliw**, *Ithaca College, New York State*
Dr. **Lucan Way**, *University of Toronto*
Dr. **Markus Wehner**, *"Frankfurter Allgemeine Zeitung"*
Dr. **Andrew Wilson**, *University College London*
Prof. **Jan Zielonka**, *University of Oxford*
Prof. **Andrei Zorin**, *University of Oxford*

* While the Editorial Committee and Advisory Board support the General Editor in the choice and improvement of manuscripts for publication, responsibility for remaining errors and misinterpretations in the series' volumes lies with the books' authors.

Soviet and Post-Soviet Politics and Society (SPPS)
ISSN 1614-3515

Founded in 2004 and refereed since 2007, SPPS makes available affordable English-, German-, and Russian-language studies on the history of the countries of the former Soviet bloc from the late Tsarist period to today. It publishes between 5 and 20 volumes per year and focuses on issues in transitions to and from democracy such as economic crisis, identity formation, civil society development, and constitutional reform in CEE and the NIS. SPPS also aims to highlight so far understudied themes in East European studies such as right-wing radicalism, religious life, higher education, or human rights protection. The authors and titles of all previously published volumes are listed at the end of this book. For a full description of the series and reviews of its books, see www.ibidem-verlag.de/red/spps.

Editorial correspondence & manuscripts should be sent to: Dr. Andreas Umland, Institute for Euro-Atlantic Cooperation, vul. Volodymyrska 42, off. 21, UA-01030 Kyiv, Ukraine

Business correspondence & review copy requests should be sent to: *ibidem* Press, Leuschnerstr. 40, 30457 Hannover, Germany; tel.: +49 511 2622200; fax: +49 511 2622201; spps@ibidem.eu.

Authors, reviewers, referees, and editors for (as well as all other persons sympathetic to) SPPS are invited to join its networks at www.facebook.com/group.php?gid=52638198614
www.linkedin.com/groups?about=&gid=103012
www.xing.com/net/spps-ibidem-verlag/

Recent Volumes

172 Maria Shagina
Joining a Prestigious Club
Cooperation with Europarties and
Its Impact on Party Development in Georgia, Moldova, and Ukraine 2004–2015
With a foreword by Kataryna Wolczuk
ISBN 978-3-8382-1084-1

173 Alexandra Cotofana, James M. Nyce (eds.)
Religion and Magic in Socialist and
Post-Socialist Contexts II
Baltic, Eastern European, and Post-USSR Case Studies
With a foreword by Anita Stasulane
ISBN 978-3-8382-0990-6

174 Barbara Kunz
Kind Words, Cruise Missiles,
and Everything in Between
The Use of Power Resources in U.S. Policies towards Poland, Ukraine, and Belarus 1989–2008
With a foreword by William Hill
ISBN 978-3-8382-1065-0

175 Eduard Klein
Bildungskorruption in Russland und der Ukraine
Eine komparative Analyse der Performanz staatlicher Antikorruptionsmaßnahmen im Hochschulsektor am Beispiel universitärer Aufnahmeprüfungen
Mit einem Vorwort von Heiko Pleines
ISBN 978-3-8382-0995-1

177 Anton Oleinik
Building Ukraine from Within
A Sociological, Institutional, and Economic Analysis of a Nation-State in the Making
ISBN 978-3-8382-1150-3

178 Peter Rollberg, Marlene Laruelle (eds.)
Mass Media in the Post-Soviet World
Market Forces, State Actors, and Political Manipulation in the Informational Environment after Communism
ISBN 978-3-8382-1116-9

179 Mikhail Minakov
Development and Dystopia
Studies in Post-Soviet Ukraine and Eastern Europe
ISBN 978-3-8382-1112-1

180 Aijan Sharshenova
The European Union's Democracy Promotion in Central Asia
A Study of Political Interests, Influence, and Development in Kazakhstan and Kyrgyzstan in 2007–2013
With a foreword by Gordon Crawford
ISBN 978-3-8382-1151-0

To my daughter Elena

Contents

List of Figures and Tables 9

Abbreviations 11

Introduction 17

1. An Institutional Approach to Ethnic Conflicts 29
   1.1 The debate — institutionalists and their opponents 29
   1.2 A historical "autopsy" — explaining the demise of SFRY .. 38
   1.3 The Bulgarian ethnic models 45
   1.4 Contemporary challenges to ethnic relations 52
   1.5 Strength of state institutions and ethnic conflicts 59

2. The Role of Political Parties 75
   2.1 The contemporary party systems in Bulgaria 76
       2.1.1 Bipolarity (1990–2001) 76
       2.1.2 Polycentrism, populism, and nativism
              (2001 until present) 82
   2.2 MRF — electoral support and ideology 93
   2.3 The Bulgarian PRR 103
       2.3.1 Representatives 105
       2.3.2 Origins, ideology, development 108
       2.3.3 The PRR and the Bulgarian ethnic model 112
       2.3.4 A glimpse into the future of the PRR 116
   2.4 Roma, crime and politics 121

3. Channeling Ethnic Conflicts 141
3.1 The integration policies of Bulgarian governments after 1989 143
3.2 The legislation and the judicial system 161
3.2.1 General framework for analysis 161
3.2.2 The PADA 163
3.2.2.1 *Purpose and concept* 163
3.2.2.2 *Scope* 165
3.2.2.3 *Genuine and determining occupational requirements* 166
3.2.2.4 *Positive action* 167
3.2.2.5 *Minimum requirements and protection of rights* 168
3.2.2.6 *Burden of proof and victimization* 169
3.2.2.7 *Dissemination of information and social dialogue* 170
3.2.2.8 *Equality body* 172
3.2.2.9 *Compliance and sanctions* 174
3.3 Discrimination against Roma ethnic group: case studies 176
3.3.1 Segregation 176
3.3.2 Use of excessive force by the police and lack of effective investigation 180
3.3.3 Hate crimes 184

Conclusion: A Story about Garbage Trucks 189

References 199

List of Figures and Tables

Figures

1. Discrimination against Roma 53
2. The scope of state functions 61
3. Strength of state institutions and scope of state functions 62
4. Comparison between six states in 2013, based on WGI (Graph View) 69
5. Votes for the MRF in the elections for BNA, 1991–2014 87
6. Fears of the MRF voters 101
7. Votes for the main PRR parties 104
8. Votes for Ataka, NFSB, and MRF in the parliamentary elections (2005, 2009, 2013, 2014) 113
9. Social distances (2016) 118
10. Social distances (2008 and 2016) 118
11. Criminal activities among the main ethnic groups—thefts ... 122
12. Criminal activities among the main ethnic groups—robberies 123
13. Criminal activities among the main ethnic groups—premeditated murders 123
14. Criminal activities among the main ethnic groups—batteries 124
15. Criminal activities among the main ethnic groups—rapes ... 124
16. Social distances. "Do you agree or disagree with each of the following statements?" 144

Tables

1. Main ethnic groups in Bulgaria since 1878 46
2. Main sources of income for Roma households 54
3. Comparison between six states in 2013, based on WGI 67
4. Control of corruption in six states in 1996, 2003, 2008, 2013 68
5. Ethnic profile of the political parties in the Bulgarian
   National Assembly in 2009 96
6. Crimes and Roma suspects 127
7. Number of complaints lodged with the Commission for
   Protection Against Discrimination per year 173
8. Use of force by the Bulgarian police by years 181

Abbreviations

Abbreviations of political parties and organizations

Abbreviation in English	Full name of the organization in English	Abbreviation in Bulgarian	Full name of the organization in Bulgarian
ABR	Alternative for Bulgarian Revival	АБВ	Алтернатива за българско възраждане
ASP	Alternative Socialist Party	АСП	Алтернативна социалистическа партия
BAPU	Bulgarian Agrarian People's Union	БЗНС	Български земеделски народен съюз
BAPU "Nikola Petkov"	Bulgarian Agrarian People's Union "Nikola Petkov"	БЗНС "Никола Петков"	Български земеделски народен съюз "Никола Петков"
BAPU "United"	Bulgarian Agrarian People's Union "United"	БЗНС "Обединен"	Български земеделски народен съюз "Обединен"
BDF	Bulgarian Democratic Forum	БДФ	Български демократичен форум
BEL	Bulgarian European Left	БЕЛ	Българска евролевица
BNRP	Bulgarian National Radical Party	БНРП	Българска национално-радикална партия
BNU	Bulgarian National Union	БНС	Български народен съюз
BSDP	Bulgarian Social Democratic Party	БСДП	Българска социалдемократическа партия
BSP	Bulgarian Socialist Party	БСП	Българска социалистическа партия

DLP	Democratic Labor Party	ДПП	Демократична партия на труда
DOST	Democrats for Responsibility Solidarity and Tolerance	ДОСТ	Демократи за отговорност свобода и толерантност
DROM	Movement for an Equal Public Model	ДРОМ	Движение за равноправен обществен модел
FF	Fatherland Front	ОФ	Отечествен фронт
IMRO-BNM	IMRO-Bulgarian National Movement	ВМРО-БНД	ВМРО-Българско Национално Движение
MBC	Movement "Bulgaria of the Citizens"	ДБГ	Движение "България на гражданите"
MRF	Movement for Rights and Freedoms	ДПС	Движение за права и свободи
NCPPI	National Committee for Protection of Peoples' Interests	ОКЗНИ	Общонароден комитет за защита на националните интереси
NFSB	National Front for the Salvation of Bulgaria	НФСБ	Национален фронт за спасение на България
NMSP	National Movement for Stability and Progress	НДСВ	Национално движение за стабилност и възход
ODS	United Democratic Forces	ОДС	Обединени демократични сили
OLJ	Order, Legality, and Justice	РЗС	Ред, законност и справедливост
PPFD	Peoples' Party "Freedom and Dignity"	НПСД	Народна партия "свобода и достойнство"
PROUD	People for Real, Open and United Democracy	ГОРД	Гражданско обединение за реална демокрация

PU	People's Union	НС	Народен Съюз
TNLMB	Turkish National Liberation Movement in Bulgaria	ТНОДБ	Турско национално-освободително движение в България
UBNL	Union of Bulgarian National Legions	СБНЛ	Съюз на българските национални легиони
UDF	United Democratic Forces	СДС	Съюз на демократичните сили
UDF Center	Union of the Democratic Forces "Center"	СДС "Център"	Съюз на демократичните сили "Център"
UFD	Union of Free Democrats	ССД	Съюз на свободните демократи
UNPP	United National Progressive Party	ОНПП	Обединена национално прогресивна партия
UNS	Union for National Salvation	ОНС	Обединение за национално спасение
UYNL	Union of Youth National Legions	СМНЛ	Съюз на младежките национални легиони

Other important abbreviations

Abbreviation in English	Full name in English	Abbreviation in Bulgarian	Full name in Bulgarian
BHC	Bulgarian Helsinki Committee	БХК	Български хелзинкски комитет
BNA	Bulgarian National Assembly	НС	Народно събрание на Република България
CEC	Central Electoral Commission	ЦИК	Централна избирателна комисия
CPAD	Commission for Protection against Discrimination	КЗД	Комисия за защита от дискриминация
ECHR	European Convention on Human Rights	ECHR	Европейска конвенция по правата на човека
ECtHR	European Court of Human Rights	ЕСПЧ	Европейски съд по правата на човека
FYROM	Former Yugoslav Republic of Macedonia	–	–
GSI	Global Slavery Index	–	–
NAP-DRI	National Action Plan for the pan-European Initiative "Decade of Roma Inclusion"	НПД-ДРВ	Национален план за действие по инициативата "Десетилетие на ромското включване"
NCCEDI	National Council for Cooperation on Ethnic and Demographic Issues	НССЕДВ	Национален съвет за сътрудничество по етническите и демографските въпроси

NCCEII	National Council for Cooperation on Ethnic and Integration Issues	НССЕИВ	Национален съвет за сътрудничество по етническите и интеграционните въпроси
NCEDI	National Council on Ethnic and Demographic Issues	НСЕДВ	Национален съвет по етническите и демографските въпроси
PADA	Protection against Discrimination Act	ЗЗД	Закон за защита от дискриминация
PRR	Populist Radical Right	–	–
SAC	Supreme Administrative Court	ВАС	Върховен административен съд
SANS	State Agency National Security	ДАНС	Държавна агенция национална сигурност
SFRY	Socialist Federal Republic of Yugoslavia	–	–
WGI	Worldwide Governance Indicators (World Bank)	–	–

Introduction

The relative ethnic peace which Bulgaria has enjoyed in the recent decades is among the few remaining bastions of national self-confidence. Amid bitter antagonism, bloodshed, and financial crises, which devastated many countries after the collapse of the Communist bloc, the sanctity of interethnic accord has, in general, been revered in Bulgaria. Its preservation is possible because the political system, despite its multiple drawbacks, is still able to tame the flashing sparks. Not only the limited comprehensive research on the topic but also the current affairs testify to the relevance of this book, dedicated to the role of political institutions in ethnic conflicts in Bulgaria after 1989. As I am writing these lines, Lyutvi Mestan, the leader of the newly formed ethnic party Democrats for Responsibility Solidarity and Tolerance (DOST),[1] states that the amendment of the Election Code,[2] which the majority in the Bulgarian National Assembly (BNA) approved on April 28, 2016, "is a continuation of the Revival Process."[3] The events in Katunitsa, Orlandovtsi, Garmen, and Radnevo indicate that the clashes and physical violence between Bulgarians and Romani, who remain subjected to social exclusion and marginalization, are on the raise. In addition, there are numerous other less visible and often ignored outbursts of hostility on ethnic grounds which happen on a daily basis. The issues discussed in the pages that follow are even more pertinent when we consider the international context. The principles and values on which the European Union (EU) is built are challenged by the constant migrant flow from Syria, Iraq, Afghanistan, and other

---

1   In Bulgarian—ДОСТ. Mestan was formerly the chair of the Movement for Rights and Freedoms (MRF, ДПС).
2   The amendments effectively reduced the number of polling stations in which the Bulgarian emigrants can vote abroad. The purpose of the legislative changes, which were initiated by the National Front for the Salvation of Bulgaria (NFSB), a populist radical right (PRR) party, was to reduce the weight of the ethnic vote, coming mainly from Turkey.
3   See "Mestan: the Election Code is a Continuation of the Revival Process" (2016).

failing states. At the same time, the increasingly menacing shadow of terrorism revealed its poisonous tentacles in the attacks in Madrid (2004), London (2005), Burgas (2012), Paris (2015), Brussels, Istanbul, Nice, Würzburg, Ansbach, Munich, and Berlin (2016).

The subject of this study is the way the political institutions manipulate the ethnic conflicts during the past 27 years. Political institutions are relatively durable and sustainable social groupings or structures operating under statutory or common rules and regulatory systems that are responsible for the political process (March and Olsen 2008: 3).[4] In *a narrow sense*, to them pertain the institutions forming the backbone of the state which are at the core of the political process and are empowered, whenever appropriate, to apply coercion—the parliament, the government, the judiciary bodies, the public administration, etc. In *a broad sense* to them must be added the political institutions-intermediaries[5] as well as the institutions that postulate the norms of social behavior such as the constitution and electoral law. In order to achieve optimal heuristic value *the analysis will be limited to the political parties, the parliament, the government, the judiciary, and the relevant legislative framework*. I will not dwell on the role of the presidential institution or the media. The impact of the tidal wave of migrants from failed states and the threats to national security posed by terrorism are also not going to be examined. Furthermore, I have purposefully not included a full-blown geopolitical analysis. This does not mean that, for example, the neo-Ottoman doctrine of the Turkish President Recep Erdogan and the hybrid propaganda, employed by the Kremlin and the traditionalist values defended by the Russian diplomacy, in the

---

4   "An institution is a relatively enduring collection of rules and organized practices, embedded in structures of meaning and resources that are relatively invariant in the face of turnover of individuals and relatively resilient to the idiosyncratic preferences and expectations of individuals and changing external circumstances. They are constitutive rules and practices prescribing appropriate behavior for specific actors in specific situations" (March and Olsen 2008: 3). A comprehensive guide to the study of political institutions is *The Oxford Handbook of Political Institutions*, see Rhodes et al. (2008).

5   They provide a link between the citizens and the state. To them belong political parties, professional and other organizations, interest groups, the media, etc. See Karasimeonov (1997: 16).

concept of "Conservative Revolution" which seeks natural allies in the populist radical right (PRR) and left parties in the EU,[6] are not relevant to this study (Koritarov 2016, Minchev 2016, Vasilev 2016). However, in order to make my task more realistic and manageable, I decided not to incorporate at length these issues in the project.[7]

I have also resisted the temptation to draw parallels between the Bulgarian case and the ethnic issues on the Balkan Peninsula as a whole or, even still, between the ethnic conflicts in this country and those in polities across Europe. At first glance, the reasons for such comparisons are compelling. For example, not unlike the ethnic formations in Bulgaria, the ethnic parties in the Former Yugoslav Republic of Macedonia (FYROM)[8] play a significant role in its political system.[9] To go even further, at present, journalists persistently bring forward the question of the rights of the "Bulgarian minority" in Albania; others, who discuss the dramatic events surrounding the Catalan independence referendum which took place on October 1, 2017, juxtapose the Revival Process in Bulgaria with the policies of "el Caudillo de la Última Cruzada y de la Hispanidad"[10] Francisco Franco (1892–1975) toward the Basques.[11] Although I am familiar with the ethnic relations in other Balkan countries, as well as the ethnopolitical issues in EU in general, I have to admit that I am by no means a pundit in all of them. The real danger

---

6   As openly stated by the former director of the Russian Institute of Strategic Studies, Vladimir Reshetnikov, for example. The pillars of this doctrine are the conservative values of the Christian Orthodoxy, anti-globalism, and nationalism. This "traditionalist ideology" maintains a strong opposition to the North Atlantic Treaty Organization and EU; see Vasilev (2016).

7   Naturally, whenever it was absolutely necessary, I provided and explored specific examples of the influence of Turkey, Russia, the EU, etc., on the ethnic relations and conflicts in Bulgaria.

8   The formations of ethnic Albanians, such as the Albanian Democratic Union for Integration, the Democratic Party of Albanians, the Besa Movement – Lëvizja Besa, etc.

9   According to the population census from 2002, approximately 64% are Macedonians, 25% Albanians, 3.8% Turks, 2.66% Romani, etc.

10 "The Leader of the Last Crusade and of the Hispanic heritage," one of the many titles of Franco.

11 For this comparison, see Indzhov (2017). For a general introduction to the politics of ethnic identity in the Balkans see, e.g., Limenopoulou (2004).

here is that, at the end, I could inadvertently open a can of worms. It could be detrimental to the project if I embark on the perilous journey of drawing such parallels throughout the book. For these reasons, the only in-depth comparison that I explore in detail is between the Bulgarian ethnic models and the former Yugoslav federation.[12]

I do not believe that conflicts are necessarily something "evil," or that they should be avoided at all costs. As it was famously pointed out by Ralf Dahrendorf, they may be beneficial to society (Dahrendorf 1959, 2007). The latter could not survive without both consensus and conflict.[13] In my view, however, conflicts become particularly dangerous and volatile whenever *they stem from politicized ethnic identity*[14] *coupled with unsuccessful attempts at their institutionalization*. My scientific curiosity has been provoked by such problematic cases and the consequences that they have for the Bulgarian political system and society. It is equally important to clarify (my take on) some other terms used in this study. Ethnic identity is the sense of belonging to a named human population with myths of common ancestry, shared historical memories, one or more elements of common culture, a link with a homeland, and a sense of solidarity (Hutchinson and Smith 1996: 4-6, Limenopoulou 2004: 2). A minority ethnic group is any ethnic group in a given society that forms an appreciable subsystem with limited access to roles and activities central to the economic and political institutions of the society (Shermerhorn 1996: 18). By "ethnic party," I understand a political party, the majority of whose constituents belong to one or more ethnic minorities. An "ethnic entrepreneur" is a person (typically a politician) who voices and uses the interests, everyday challenges, and fears of a particular ethnic group (or groups) in order to mobilize political support for a certain cause.

---

12   The other country to which I make a brief reference is the Republic of South Africa.
13   According to Dahrendorf, without conflict, there can be no consensus, and although consensus leads to conflict, conflict also leads to consensus. Of course, we should not forget that Dahrendorf's main unit of analysis was the class, and not the ethnic group. See Dahrendorf (1959).
14   See Section 1.1.

The structure of the project corresponds to the facets of the subject. *The first part* necessarily begins with an adjustment of "the optics" through which the analysis will be performed. In a dynamic and interdisciplinary field, such as the study of ethnic conflicts, there is a lot of controversy regarding the notions and methods of investigation. There are, as well, disagreements on the use and content of the conceptual apparatus. The advantages of an institutional approach to conflicts, which I use in this work, are illustrated mainly through the means of the exploration of the tragic demise of the Yugoslav federation. The study of ethnic relations in the Socialist Federal Republic of Yugoslavia (SFRY), the mistakes of the political elites in particular, is an invaluable lesson stimulating the better understanding of our own country. Using this study as a starting point of the analysis of the Bulgarian case, I then pinpoint the specifics of contemporary challenges in front of ethnic relations in Bulgaria. *The second part* examines the role of political parties both outside and inside the parliament. I trace the developments of the ethnic model in its interconnection with the first and the second party systems. I highlight the particularities in ideology, political support, and mobilization of the main ethno-political formation— the Movement for Rights and Freedoms (MRF), as well as of the representatives of the PRR. Last but not least, I discuss various case studies on Roma, crime and politics. *The third part* of the book is devoted to the integration policies of Bulgarian governments after 1989, especially those that are targeted toward Roma. I assess the role of the judicial system and the antidiscrimination legislation.

There is a plethora of explanatory concepts about the nature and causes of ethnic conflicts. The "classic" schools of thought are the primordialist (Geertz 1973), the instrumentalist (A. Smith 1986), and the constructivist (Anderson 2006). Scholars of ethnic conflict and civil wars have introduced theories that draw insights from all of these schools. Significant approaches, some of which are influenced or related to the three fundamental paradigms, are the institutionalist (Lijphart 1968, 1977, McGarry and O'Leary 1993, Crawford and Lipschutz 1998, Hechter 2000, Osipov 2013),[15] the environmental (or economic, which can be derived from, for example, Marxism), the ethnocultural (MG Smith 1969), and the theory of modernization (Horowitz 1985, Altermatt 1998).[16] An "army" of scholars has examined ethnic relations in Bulgaria: political scientists, sociologists, social psychologists, historians, ethnographers, economists, philosophers, and others. Nonetheless, there is a relative lack of comprehensive studies dedicated *entirely to the role of political institutions* for deterrence and/or incitement of ethnic conflicts during the last 27 years. Instead, these issues are discussed in chapters or sections of monographs and compendiums (e.g., Kertikov et al. 1990, Makariev 1999, 2017, Hopken 2000, Dimitrov 2001, Dronzina 2004, Mizov 2008, Engström 2009, Karasimeonov 2010, Zlatanova 2013) and, above all articles that highlight specific aspects of the problem, for example, the link between political parties and ethnic conflicts (Smilov 2006, 2007, 2008, Kabakchieva 2008, Todorov 2012), the Bulgarian ethnic models (Arsenova and Kertikov 2002, 2003, Mitev 2005, Bosakov 2006, Pamporov 2008, Geiselmann and Karamelska 2010), the integration policies targeting minorities (Grekova 2008, Gulubov 2008, Ivanov 2008, Rechel 2008), etc. For example, although the important recent book by Plamen Makariev — *The Public Legitimacy of Minority Claims* — explores the Bulgarian case as well, its scope is much more ambitious and broader[17] than the purpose of mine. Makariev's work is a study of public policies concerning the national minorities in Central and Eastern Europe. Furthermore, it analyses these policies through the means of political philosophy, in particular through the prism of "the Habermasian version of the theory of public deliberation and the model of deliberative democracy" (Makariev 2017: 9).

---

15 Some of the key "branches" of the institutional approach are the consociationalism, federalism, and non-territorial autonomy.
16 As I mentioned above, this work is guided by an institutionalist understanding of conflicts. A detailed account of this approach is made in Chapter 1.
17 See Makariev (2017).

Of importance for the better grasp of the questions that my work attempts to answer are studies of nationalism (Kabakchieva 2006), postcommunist politicization of the religious (Krasteva 2015), ethnic identity (Mizov 2003, Nedelcheva 2003, 2004, 2007, 2010, Bosakov 2004, Ahmed 2008, Nedelcheva and Topalova 2010) and ethnic relations (Mitev 1994, Zografova 1996, Genov 2004, 2005, Mantarova and Zaharieva 2007, Pamporov 2012), practices of controlled voting (Bezlov and Gounev 2012b, Stoychev 2016), economic dimensions of the Revival Process (Avramov 2017), public spheres in Bulgaria and Serbia (Dawson 2014), etc. An imposing amount of academic research illuminates the actions of political institutions in the conflicts that marked the breakup of former Yugoslavia and the constitutional crisis in Macedonia (Flere 1991, Vukovic 1997, Crawford and Lipschutz 1998, Hinkova 1998, Arsenova and Kertikov 2002, 2003, Todorov 2002, Dronzina 2004, Garabedian 2007, Detrez and Segaert 2008, Banchev 2009, Minchev 2009).

The precise meaning and place of the "Bulgarian ethnic model" in the political system has been a constant object of heated debates and discussions not only in the scientific community but also in the public sphere. In my opinion, although undoubtedly charged ideologically, the term is not void of content or a shallow description of a myth. In fact, several such models operated since the Liberation in 1878 (Arsenova and Kertikov 2002). Their apex has been in 1940s, when the decisive intervention of the institutions (the monarch, the parliament, and the Bulgarian Patriarchate) led to the Rescue of Bulgarian Jews from deportation (Bar Zohar 1998, Todorov 2001, Arsenova and Kertikov 2002). In my view, generally speaking, the model *aims to guarantee the rights and freedoms of all ethnic and confessional communities.* It has two elements, a dynamic one, as well as another which is much more stable. Its main building blocks are a legislative framework, which obviously changed through the years, and the specifics of Bulgarian political culture. *I believe that the model not only reflects the idiosyncrasies of the latter but also influences it. The essence of the Bulgarian ethnic model(s) is not merely a combination of policy measures or a modus operandi of particular institutions. In fact it could be independent of or even "act" against the normative framework which the state imposes on society.* This approach is confirmed by the fact that even during the Revival Process (1984–89),[18] Bulgarian Turks and Roma, "manifesting wisdom and understanding,"[19] accepted that this policy was not instigated or supported by the ethnic majority. Thus the amicable, neighborly relations between ethnic Bulgarians and minorities were, as a whole, preserved in spite of the discriminative and violent actions that the state undertook (Kertikov et al. 1990). The ambivalence of the term "ethnic model," a phenomenon of the political culture and an institutional mechanism for the integration of ethnic communities, is expressed as well in the political rhetoric.[20]

When they discuss the political system, most scholars do not perceive or outline an immediate threat to the nonviolent relations between the ethnic groups. During the first decade after the beginning of transition to a democratic political system, in particular, there was a consensus among mainstream political parties, on the necessity of preserving the ethnic peace. This tacit agreement is enshrined in the Constitution of Bulgaria from July 13, 1991, as well as in the legislation as a whole. Using the examples of Bulgaria and Macedonia, Jenny Engström claims that democratization can prevent violent conflict in ethnically divided societies (Engström 2009, 2014). Engström's analyses contain many indispensable insights into Bulgaria's road to democracy. However she does not compare the current ethnic model with its "predecessors." Engström paints an overly optimistic picture of the contemporary model that overlooks some of its important flaws, development, and deterioration.[21]

Many scientists and human rights activists hold that integration policies of Bulgarian government targeting minorities, especially those that relate to the Roma, failed to produce any significant outcomes (Grekova 2008, Rechel 2008). In addition to that, the ina-

---

18 Also known as "Process of Rebirth." I use the two terms interchangeably.
19 See Kertikov et al. (1990).
20 For a different take on the "Bulgarian ethnic model" see, e.g., Bosakov (2006).
21 I address these issues in my work.

bility of the state to combat crime has direct repercussions on ethnopolitics. The minorities, Roma and Turks in particular, are most vulnerable when it comes to the practices of control over voting (Stoychev 2016: 16, 25). Many political parties attempt to coerce and/or to manipulate constituencies to give them their unreserved support in the elections, but the ethnic formation MRF is a sui generis leader in these illegal practices (ibid.: 51, 54). Political parties work together with organized crime in order to place voters under control (ibid.: 24).

The analysis of the relationship between political institutions and ethnicity reveals that the state cannot be a source of ethnicity (Dronzina 2004: 136). In ethnically heterogeneous Balkan societies "ethnicity is a source of legitimacy of the state and a power resource"[22] (ibid.). The relatively stable proportions between the variables related to ethnicity[23] are conducive to the better accommodation of ethnic communities, even when the institutions are severely weakened and damaged, as was the case between 1992 and the spring of 1997 (Dronzina 2004: 134, 136). This conclusion, however, has been disputed by the PRR. In 2016, the presidential nominee of the United Patriots and leader of Internal Macedonian Revolutionary Organization (IMRO)—Krasimir Karakachanov—warned [24] about the dangerous "Islamization of Bulgaria" and the potential for it to transform into a "Gipsy State" (Offnews.bg 2016). In response to such fears, skillfully ignited by politicians, scholars point to the fact that, for example, Bulgarian Turks have been loyal to

---

22   Kosovo is a classic illustration of how demographic changes, combined with ethnic discrimination, invalidate the political institutions and lead to the emergence of a parallel institutional order. The situation in Macedonia is similar.
23   There is no drastic change in the ratio between Turkish and Bulgarian population—in 1892 the percentage of Bulgarian Turks was 17.21%, in 1910—11.63%, and today (according to the last census of 2011)—8.8%.
24   As he has done many times before that. The full name of the party is IMRO-Bulgarian National Movement. Here and below I refer to it as "IMRO." The name of this party established in 1991 is a reference to the Internal Macedonian Revolutionary Organization, a historic Bulgarian-established revolutionary political organization in the Macedonia and Thrace regions founded in the late nineteenth century.

Bulgarian state for decades (Arsenova and Kertikov 2002). The predominant majority of the ethnic Turks living in the country are Sunnis. Unlike Albanian Islamists in Kosovo, Macedonia, and Albania "most of them are not involved in large-scale criminal activities"; the MRF never had separatist ambitions nor it intended to make Bulgaria a "binational state"; Bulgarian Roma have relatively limited political claims — the problems and objectives that they voice are primarily economic (ibid.). For these reasons, the implementation of a "Kosovo scenario" on Bulgarian territory is highly unlikely (Arsenova and Kertikov 2002).

The beginning of the new millennium was marked by significant changes in Bulgaria's party system that had repercussions on the ethnic relations (Smilov 2007, 2008). PRR parties such as Ataka, which entered the political scene in 2005, bluntly defied the unwritten rules of transition and started a fierce crusade against the "privileges" of minorities (Smilov 2008: 50). At present the party system is in the stage of cartel, a situation that can be observed in many European countries (ibid.: 39–40). Caught in an ideological vacuum, more parties may decide to mobilize the electorate through radicalization of their messages. An extreme radicalization can take the shape of an acute attack on "human rights and the rule of law, especially the protection of minorities" (Smilov 2008: 41). The contemporary Bulgarian nationalism, according to some scholars, is not aggressive (Nedelcheva 2007: 113). It does not rely on the condition that proponents must identify with the state — the individual vision for Bulgaria (i.e., what the country represents) is in fact mostly limited to family values, friends, and birthplace (ibid.). However a retreat in the family life, a barricading, or entrenchment in the home space pose the threat of re-ethnicizing of nationalism — such a trend is observed mostly among Bulgarians and Turks and, to a lesser extent, among Roma (Kabakchieva 2008: 94). From this perspective, under such circumstances, other ethnic groups may begin to look "foreign" and "dangerous," and, ultimately, to become "enemies." This process can lead to the resuscitation of "traumatic nationalism of survival," which then will channel ethnic strife. Between 15% and 20% of Bulgarian citizens would support a patriotic party that bases its propaganda on constant reminders to the public of the glorious pages of Bulgarian history, the national ideals, and, possibly, a protectionist economic policy (ibid.: 94). Such a party would have to compete primarily with parties like GERB[25] and Bulgarian Socialist Party (BSP), whose electorates share such values. It would neither endanger the niche of aggressive nationalism, occupied by parties like the Bulgarian National Union (BNU), nor threaten the existence of Ataka, since the latter is concerned mostly with a criticism of corrupt elites and the injustices brought by the transition to democracy rather than with purely nationalistic goals and values (Kabakchieva 2008: 94–5).

Several *hypotheses* lie at the heart of this work. *The first is that the contemporary Bulgarian ethnic model is not a fixed political construct, as it is often perceived, but underwent significant developments in the last 27 years.* Thus far the political system is able to prevent the occurrence of serious ethnic conflicts. The integration measures undertook by the government notwithstanding, various studies bespeak that the social distances between the main ethnicities in Bulgaria are increasing (Pamporov 2008, 2016).[26] *The second hypothesis reads that the political system reflects the interests of minority ethnic groups in a mostly superficial way that typically not only does not exceed but is below the minimal standards. Many of the Roma, for example, live in conditions that are often indistinguishable from modern forms of slavery. The political institutions are unwilling to commit to tangible, real integration measures due to the resistance toward distributive justice which the predominant part of Bulgarians display when the target or the beneficiaries of such measures are minorities.*

The third hypothesis postulates that political populism thriving as a result of the impotence of the "old" ideologies and convergence of left and right can give birth to the greatest threat for ethnic peace. The low wages

---

25 The name of the political party GERB is not an abbreviation, the latter is a common misconception. However, the party, which was established in December 2006, emerged on the basis of a nonprofit organization with the acronym Citizens for European Development of Bulgaria, Граждани за европейско развитие на България – ГЕРБ (GERB).

26 For an analysis and overview of important studies on social distances, see Part 1.

and pensions, especially compared to the EU average, strengthen even further the iron grip of populists and ethnic entrepreneurs. The radicalization of nationalist rhetoric and the policies influenced by it deepen the sclerosis of political system, clogging the channels of political participation—which is a ramification of, for example, the attempt to limit the social benefits for minorities. The result is that new, fervent outbreaks of interethnic tension emerge constantly.

This book has the following *objectives*: to verify the hypotheses and to promote a better understanding of the essence of the Bulgarian ethnic model, its mechanism, its building blocks, and its advantages and vulnerabilities. In order to achieve these objectives, I have used the following *methods*: legal and political analysis of laws and regulations, a secondary analysis of statistical information, party programs, slogans, political messages, etc. The project reveals the way the institutions function and interact in resolving or instigating ethnic conflicts. It provides an assessment of the performance of these institutions and helps to map the dynamics and outline the possible stages in the development of the Bulgarian ethnic model. On the basis of the findings I make recommendations and formulate future scenarios for the development of political institutions and ethnic relations.

1. An Institutional Approach to Ethnic Conflicts

1.1 The debate – institutionalists and their opponents

The contemporary violent conflicts have numerous idiosyncrasies, which distinguish them from their predecessors. Today they are more often based on cultural differences; most of the time, unlike their predominantly interstate character in the past, their fires are burning within the borders of political communities (Ramsbotham et al. 2011: 5); they are marked with ferocity, which leads to a drastic increase in the number of victims of the civilian population.[27] The interethnic conflicts occur more often in or between the states that once belonged to the Communist bloc (on the territories of the former Soviet Union and the Balkans)[28] in comparison to the Western liberal polities,[29] but also in juxtaposition to other states with predominantly Muslim population, as well as to other less developed but well-consolidated democracies. Nowadays, more than ever, it is imperative to identify the causes of ethnic conflicts, which often predetermine the fate of entire nations. The institutional approach to these issues is part of the toolbox of a plethora of different theo-

---

[27] Approximately 14% of all casualties in the First World War were from the civilian population. They increased to 67% in the Second World War. After the Cold War and the collapse of the bipolar model of the international system in the 1990s (when the violent conflicts were of predominantly intrastate nature), the civilian deaths amount to approximately 90% of all victims (Crawford and Lipschutz 1998: 3).

[28] Of course, the differences between the former communist regimes themselves, in this regard, are very significant, a fact that further complicates the task of political analysts. For example, the dissolution of former Czechoslovakia, the "velvet divorce," was peaceful unlike the bloody end of Yugoslavia.

[29] I use here the term "Western" in its "civilizational meaning," in a similar fashion to Huntington (2011).

ries. In this work, I refer to concepts coined and supported by leading institutionalists (e.g., Crawford and Lipschutz 1998). It would not be possible to represent and submit to a critical analysis the institutional approach to the study of conflicts in its entirety. The answers, which this approach provides, might be best understood in the context of the debate with rival interpretations.

According to *the primordialists*[30] (Geertz 1973, Van Den Berghe 1978, Vanhanen 1991, Grosby 1994), "the centuries of accumulated hatred" between ethnic groups are rooted within the very essence of humans (Grosby 1994: 168). Ethnocentrism and racism are forms of nepotism, which assumed monstrous proportions. They have a tendency to favor the blood relatives at the expense of the others, because altruism and cooperation are genetically programmed to be triggered by the biological code of the common origin.[31] The moment the grip of government is weakened, people start to look for and find a mainstay in life in national identity or in what passes as such. Primordialism, however, fails to provide a satisfactory answer to the question why some ethnic groups manage to live together in a relative peace (e.g., Bulgarians and Turks after 1989, French and Germans in Alsace-Lorraine, and Muslim Malays and Chinese Christians in Malaysia). The main disadvantage of primordialism is that it ignores the fact that differences in cultural identity do not necessarily lead to conflict. For this reason, at the center of the institutional approach lies the understanding that *the conflict potential of the cultural, in particular, ethnic identity is unlocked only when it is politicized, that is when it becomes a criterion for discrimination and privileges in the struggle for the distribution of political and economic resources* (Crawford and Lipschutz 1998: 11). Primordialists do not recognize the role of state institutions in the management of conflicts: in fact, the government can appease the latter (e.g., it can channel groups' interests by means of legislative changes), legitimize, instigate, or even create and cultivate them.

---

30   Another notion used to describe this approach is "perennialism."
31   I am not going to examine in detail the different versions of this approach. For further details, see for example the analysis of Dronzina (2004), where she distinguishes between radical and moderate primordialism.

The security dilemma approach (Butterfield 1951, Herz 1959, Jervis 1976) sometimes referred to also as "the spiral model," developed by John Herz in his monograph *Political Realism and Political Idealism* (1951), offers an alternative explanation. Unlike primordialism, this approach accepts the importance of state institutions. When these institutions de facto cease to exist and anarchy prevails, security becomes a priority. Ironically, the measures that a group takes in this situation to ensure its safety (e.g., the development of new weapons and/or the modernization of the available arsenal and its expansion) provoke the fears of others. They now take similar actions, which are perceived as a threat by the first party. The result is, often, an arms race and a conflict escalation. In Herz's own words, the security dilemma is a structural notion in which "the self-help attempts of states to look after their security needs tend, regardless of intention, to lead to rising insecurity for others as each interprets its own measures as defensive and measures of others as potentially threatening" (Herz 1950: 157). The security dilemma describes the mechanism of this vicious circle, which leads to a higher risk of using violence. The problem with this approach, according to institutionalists, is that, in the first place, it was developed originally for the needs of the theory of international relations and (tacitly and erroneously) puts on the same footing the interactions between countries with those between groups (Crawford and Lipschutz 1998: 12). In the second place, it accepts not unlike the primordialists that groups have a priori incompatible political interests and therefore the only question is under what conditions their clash will become of violent nature. Third, the security dilemma approach naively paints and supports a one-dimensional image of the role of institutions as a "good shepherd," while their functions are much more complex. The institutions are guided by the "logic of the political game" (Levy et al. 1995) and, even if one of their tasks is to channel conflicts, they do not treat all conflicts equally. Institutions not only impose restrictions on the political actors, but can also provide incentives in order to influence political preferences. They could further prohibit discrimination and, instead, emphasize on competition between classes and ideologies or they could politicize ethnic identity. Fourth, Herz's approach does not explain why interethnic strife and violence sometimes rage in political systems with strong and, in general, legitimate institutions neither it outlines the reasons for the failure or the demise of the latter.

The approach of liberal democracy and free market (Fukuyama 1992, Bhalla 1994, Whitehead 1995) affirms that they contribute to the aggregation and representation of all interests in society, by replacing conflicts based on ethnic identity with these, which stem from (economic) interests. The logic of this approach is that democratic polities and institutions are steered by *individual* rights rather than those of social collectivities. It is the individuals who are protected by the law and have the right of political participation. Wherever there are religious or ethnic conflicts, they can be successfully regulated and/or resolved, if the organizational principles of the political system recognize the necessity of tolerance and social cohesion. The theorists of consociational democracy[32] (McGarry and O'Leary 1993, Lijphart 1968, 1977, 1994, 1999) and federalism (Stain 1968) support this view. Although this approach, which sees liberal democracy as a panacea for ethnic conflicts, is in its nature institutional, it is not unconditionally accepted even among the institutionalists. [33] One well-known theory, which embraces this approach, is Francis Fukuyama's concept of the "end of history" which was first formulated in an article for *National Interest* published in 1989.

Inspired by the "velvet revolutions" in Central and Eastern Europe, Fukuyama proclaims the triumph of liberal democracy. As an unlikely last stop in the "ideological evolution of mankind" and "last form of government," it marks the "end of history" because it cultivates optimal conditions for the realization of human "desire

---

32 Countries such as Belgium, the Netherlands (between 1917 and 1967), New Zealand, Switzerland, and others are often defined as consociational democracies in the scientific literature.
33 See Crawford and Lipschutz (1998: 12).

for recognition,"[34] scientific progress, and economic prosperity (Fukuyama 1992: xvii). It was, in a sense, "the VCRs [videocassette recorders] which actually won the Cold War" and led to the collapse of the communist regimes behind the Iron Curtain (Fukuyama 1992: xi, 98–108). One of the main arguments for the superiority of liberal democracy, according to the American political scientist, is that it forces the retreat of irrational forms of the desire for recognition such as nationalism; it soothes societies divided by ethnic cleavages and promotes consensus. The neoconservative project of Fukuyama was, however, met with considerable and, often, fierce criticisms. The "homogenizing," "integrating," and "pacifying" potential of the institutions of the liberal democracy is seen as particularly controversial. In response to Fukuyama, Samuel Huntington postulated the concept of the "clash of civilizations"[35] (Huntington 2011), while immediately after the terrorist acts of September 11, 2001, the American journalist Fareed Zakaria sarcastically declared "the end of the end of history."

Following the Hegelian Alexandre Kojève,[36] Fukuyama perceives the existence of the EU as compelling evidence that liberal

---

34 Recalling the three parts of the soul, which were famously described by Plato in *The State*, Fukuyama believes that "the desire for recognition" is intertwined with self-esteem which "arises out of the part of the soul called *thymos*" (Fukuyama 1992: xvii). The latter generates emotions like anger, shame, and pride. People, Fukuyama explains, "believe that they have a certain worth, and when others treat them as though they are worth less than that they experience the emotion of anger" (ibid.: xvii). Following Hegel, Fukuyama postulates that the desire for recognition and the emotions of anger, shame, and pride are crucial for political life. The desire for recognition can be truly fulfilled only in the liberal democracies. This desire can never be satisfied in the nondemocratic societies; thus, the vast majority living in the Communist bloc could only aspire and hope to receive for their efforts only such "goods" such as going on holiday to Bulgaria (Fukuyama 1992: 162–70).

35 According to Huntington, the spread of Western technology and mass culture does not necessarily make the world a smaller and friendlier place, because, as he notes with penetrating irony, the Western civilization is not the tasty Big Mac hamburger but Magna Carta (Huntington 2011: 76).

36 Alexandre Kojève (1902–1968), a Russian-born French philosopher, was a high-ranking civil servant, who worked on the construction of the European Community.

democracies can overcome national, ethnic, or cultural differences, and build a working supranational political system. *The Bulgarian case after 1989 seems to be particularly relevant for the viability of Fukuyama's project. The country, which is an EU member, is often held up as an example of a stable multiethnic polity.* The peaceful coexistence in close proximity in the center of the capital Sofia of four religious institutions (the Orthodox Church "St. Nedelya," the Catholic cathedral "St. Joseph," the mosque "Banya Bashi," and the Sofia Synagogue) is even referred to as "a cliche of multiculturalism" (Detrez and Segaert 2008: 55). Notwithstanding, European leaders such as Chancellor Angela Merkel, Prime Minister David Cameron, and President Nicolas Sarkozy announced the fiasco of the policies and ideas of multiculturalism, and Hungarian Prime Minister Viktor Orban defended the need to build an "illiberal state," because liberalism is the god that failed (Traub 2015). Furthermore, the events in front of the same mosque "Banya Bashi" in 2011 unequivocally indicate that the interethnic tensions in Bulgaria are on the rise. *I claim that the main thesis of Fukuyama cannot be supported because of its historicism and holistic zeal (in the sense of Karl Popper[37]). The institutions of liberal democracy in many cases are an effective means to control and overcome the tensions between ethnic groups. However, the economic inequalities caused by the policy of accelerated liberalization and the long-term effects of globalization can easily turn against the liberal political practices, undermining their foundations, while fanning and feeding the flames of ethnic conflict. This conclusion is supported by the analysis of the current Bulgarian ethnic model. In fact, Fukuyama himself, as we shall see, revised and reevaluated in his later writings the positions advocated in The End of History (Fukuyama 2004a, 2004b, 2006, 2012, 2013).*

Regardless of the many aspects of the institutional approach, we can outline several major points on which its proponents maintain relative consensus. They correspond to the questions raised in the debate with rival theories. First, as already mentioned, not the ethnic identity itself, but its politicization creates preconditions for conflict. Politicization traditionally became the path of colonization (as was, for example, in the Ottoman Empire through the institution

---

37 See Popper (1994, 2013).

of millet,[38] or in India, as part of the British Empire) or it was engineered within political systems by their elites (e.g., in the United States such a role had the segregation laws known as "Jim Crow," while in Russia similar function had the temporary regulations regarding Jews—also known as the "May" anti-Semitic laws, introduced by Emperor Alexander III, in 1882–1914). The political importance of cultural cleavages will be strengthened or even "invented"—artificially created where existing "faults" in society are legitimated by state institutions. In particular, economic discrimination and preferential status based on ascribed (ethnic, religious, etc.) signs make cultural identity politically significant (Crawford and Lipschutz 1998: 26). Conversely, second, the political relevance of identity may be reduced if it is sanctioned by those in power (ibid.: 18). The stronger and more legitimate the institutions, the greater their chances to weaken the political significance of differences or to transform the volatile tensions between groups into nonviolent competition (we observe this situation in Adjara, an autonomous republic within Georgia; Malaysia, where political parties operate on the basis of ethnicity; another example is South Africa after the abolition of apartheid).

Third, if the institutions are illegitimate in the eyes of groups deprived of access to resources, but still can, nonetheless, effectively exercise coercion, the discontent will be kept under control (e.g., the Georgians in Abkhazia, or South Africa before 1990). It follows that, fourth, when the repressive institutions are weakened or they collapse we can expect the eruption of interethnic strife (such

---

38 The official documents of the Ottoman Empire virtually do not contain ethnonyms. The population was classified on the basis of its religious affiliation. The legally recognized confessional communities or millets (from the Arab word "millah," which literally means "nation") were composed of Believers (who professed Islam) and infidels who had the right of self-government. Until the nineteenth century besides the Muslim millet, the main millets were the Rum millet, Jewish, Armenian, and Syrian Orthodox. Millets had autonomous administrative institutions (courts, schools, hospitals, etc.), which were located in specially designated areas (districts) in the cities and in the villages. Until 1861, when a separate Bulgarian Millet was formed, Bulgarians were part of the "Rum Millet" ("the Roman nation") or the Greek (Orthodox) community.

as the violent conflicts that accompanied or followed the dissolution of the USSR and Yugoslavia—in Bosnia, Kosovo, Chechnya, etc.). The collapse of institutions could be the result of the influence of internal or external factors, such as, in particular, the short-sighted economic policies or the negative effects of globalization.[39] Fifth, ethnic entrepreneurs will be facilitated in their actions and have more chances to mobilize support for their "programs" when the ethnic card was previously used by the eroded or nonexisting state apparatus; when minorities are, comparably, more affected than the rest of population by unfavorable economic conditions or liberalization; and when these "entrepreneurs" can offer political resources to the affected by the crisis[40] (e.g., Vladislav Ardzinba in Abkhazia, Slobodan Milošević in Serbia, and Franjo Tuđman in Croatia).

These guiding points in the interpretation of conflicts can be illustrated and confirmed by comparing the political institutions of Republic of South Africa (RSA) before and after 1991, when the system of racial segregation, the apartheid,[41] was abolished and denounced by the South African politicians. Racial segregation in South Africa already existed during the period of the Dutch and British colonial rule. Its foundations were laid in the seventeenth century. Apartheid became official state policy after the elections in 1948. It was conducted through several laws passed by the National Party, which were headed by Protestant priest Daniel François Malan (1874–1959). Legislation classified inhabitants into four racial groups—"black," "white," "colored," and "Indian." The last two groups were divided into several subclassifications.[42] On the basis

---

39 For further examples see the analysis in Crawford and Lipschutz (1998: 18, 22, 26).
40 See Crawford and Lipschutz (1998: 22, 26).
41 The term "apartheid" (Afrikaans) literally means "the state of being apart." The apartheid was defined as a crime against humanity in the Roman Statute of the International Criminal Tribunal, based in the Hague (Netherlands), which operates since 2002.
42 The main acts that established and maintained segregation were the Prohibition of Mixed Marriages Act (1949), the Population Registration Act (1950), the

of this "distinction," the residential areas were segregated.[43] Apart from the white the other racial groups were not represented politically. The "black people" were deprived of citizenship. The government segregated public transport, hospitals, schools, universities, etc. The marriages and sexual contacts between the races were prohibited. The apartheid was the subject of fierce resistance of the oppressed ethnic groups and placed South Africa in international isolation, but because of the effective power of the repressive state institutions, it was maintained for decades.

The analyses and evaluations of the contemporary political system of South Africa, after the abolition of apartheid, are contradictory. Thanks to the country's liberal constitution and, in particular, the positive role of the Commission for Truth and Reconciliation, initiated by President Nelson Mandela, the re-politicization of ethnic identity has so far been avoided. The role of ethnic cleavages as main generator of conflicts has been replaced, however, by fierce class polarization.[44] Although the RSA has been ranked fifth in Africa in terms of income per capita, nearly one-quarter of the population of 58.9 million is unemployed. The country, which has 11 official languages, is marked by growing xenophobia and violence against immigrants (Crush and Pendleton 2004). The political repressions have been resumed under the rule of the current president of South Africa and leader of the African National Congress – Jacob Zuma (Buccus 2011). These facts raise concerns for the future.

If the example of the apartheid in South Africa seems too distant or "exotic" compared to the situation in Bulgaria, one has to take a look at the Roma ghettoes and de facto segregated schools

---

Group Areas Act (1950), the Reservation of Separate Amenities Act (1953), and the Bantu Education Act (1953).

43   This is the so-called Bantu homeland system – the "bantustan" was a territory set aside for black inhabitants of South Africa and South West Africa (now Namibia). The bantustans were in many ways successors to the "reserves" that were established by the British colonial administration at the beginning of the twentieth century with the intention of segregating black South Africans from whites.

44   According to the World Bank, in 2009 the pre-tax Gini coefficient in South Africa was the highest in the world – 0.65. See World Bank (2009).

that continue to exist in the small Balkan state.[45] The following section, which examines the reasons for the painful decay and violent decomposition of Yugoslavia, provides a further, more detailed illustration of the institutionalists' approach to ethnic conflicts. The ethnic relations in this former neighbor of our country bare some striking similarities to the ethnic models operating in Bulgaria. I use the insights of the study of SFRY as a fundament of the analysis of the Bulgarian case.

1.2 A historical "autopsy" — explaining the demise of SFRY

The literature that embarks on the Sisyphean task to rationalize the violent dissolution of the Yugoslav federation[46] is voluminous. There are several rival camps offering competing theories. *The essentialist or primordial perspective* stresses the importance of the "Balkan temperament" and the "ancient hatreds" which were unleashed by the collapse of the communist regime (Silber and Little 1991, Vodopivec 1992, Kaplan 1993, Mearsheimer and Pape 1993, Gligorov 1995). An alternative school of thought *points at the international forces* as the central causes (Cvii 1993, Higgins 1993, Nuttal 1994, Pavlowitch 1994, Rief 1994).[47] Some scholars see the culprit in

---

45 See Sections 3.2.2.2 and 3.3.1.
46 Yugoslavia came into existence after the First World War in 1918 under the name of Kingdom of Serbs, Croats, and Slovenes, by the merger of the provisional State of Slovenes, Croats, and Serbs (formed from territories of the former Austro-Hungarian Empire) with the formerly independent Kingdom of Serbia and Kingdom of Montenegro. Serbian royal House of Karađorđević was the Yugoslav royal dynasty. The country gained international recognition on July 13, 1922, at the Conference of Ambassadors in Paris. It was renamed Kingdom of Yugoslavia on October 3, 1929. After the Second World War, the monarchy was abolished. Yugoslavia was renamed two more times: to the Federal People's Republic of Yugoslavia in 1946 (when a communist government was established), and to the SFRY in 1963.
47 This approach echoes a "tradition" in the literature discussing the history and politics of the Balkans in general. Although the accounts in this particular tradition differ significantly, they are inclined to place the blame for Balkan wars,

the processes of economic liberalization and global integration, which in their view undermined the institutions of the Yugoslav federal state (Woodward 1995). On their turn, *the instrumentalists* emphasize the role of political entrepreneurs such as Slobodan Milošević and Franjo Tuđman who exploited the ethnic cleavages and instigated ethnic hatred *in order to* mobilize supporters in their quest for power (Bookman 1994, Denitch 1994, Bose 1995, Zimmerman 1995). There are numerous objections to all of these approaches that cast a serious shadow on their heuristic value.[48] I shall not discuss them further. Instead I shall examine *the institutionalist analysis* in Crawford and Lipschutz's *The Myth of Ethnic Conflict*,[49] which in my opinion offers a deeper insight.

Institutionalists highlight the very nature of the principle of ethnofederalism, around which Yugoslavia's political system was built (which bears similarities to Czechoslovakia and the Soviet Union). Ethnofederalism, in general, is *characterized by structures of accountability and opportunities for resource control that prompt officials at both central (federal) and local levels to privilege specific ethnic constituencies. As the federal system of Yugoslavia weakened and the local officials relied more and more on the support of their ethnic constituencies rather*

---

in general, on the attempts of the great powers to carve up the states on the peninsula for their own advantage.

48 For example, contrary to the claims of *the primordialists*, during the decade before the start of the Yugoslav wars, the marriages between the different ethnic groups were on the rise (Woodward 1995: 36). The 1981 census also indicated a substantial increase of the number of people who identified themselves as "Yugoslav" instead of "Serb," "Croat," "Muslim," etc. (Crawford and Lipschutz 1998: 201). Germany's diplomatic recognition of Croatia certainly hastened the dissolution of the Yugoslav federation, as asserts the approach that blames *the international forces*, but this theory is unable to explain why the war began six months earlier. The argument based upon *the negative role of the global financial players* is contradicted by the fact that the International Monetary Fund's policies in the 1980s were actually designed to strengthen the federal institutions (Crawford and Lipschutz 1998: 203). The political messages of *the ethnic entrepreneurs* are undoubtedly an important factor; however, the theory that paints them as the main "perpetrators" does not investigate into why they successfully played the ethnic card in Serbia, Bosnia, Kosovo, Macedonia, and elsewhere but failed in other countries with ethnically mixed population.

49 See Crawford and Lipschutz (1998).

than the central government, the logic of identity politics strengthened. The creation of ethnic nationalist parties and the interethnic political rivalry was rooted in the institutional legacies. The effects of bandwagoning in Serbia, Croatia, and Bosnia, on the eve of the violent ethnic conflicts, drastically reduced the chances of nonnationalist alternative parties (Crawford and Lipschutz 1998: 205-7).

The analysis must also take into account the traumatic heritage of the Second World War during which Croatian and Bosnian Muslim elites allied with the Nazis against the Serbs.[50] President Josip Broz Tito (1892-1980) believed that the federal polity, established as a system of six ethnic republics (Bosnia and Herzegovina, Croatia, Macedonia, Montenegro, Serbia, and Slovenia), and enshrined in the Constitution of the SFRY promulgated on January 31, 1946, would provide better guarantees for the national equality than the previous unitary state[51] (Christman 1970: 56). However, unlike the United States, the Federal Republic of Germany and, especially, the Soviet Union, the federal system in Yugoslavia was noncentralized[52] and the constituent units exercised a large degree of authority. The 1946 Constitution stipulated that all mineral wealth, power resources, means of communication, and foreign trade are under the control of the federal government. However, the latter could take decisions on a very limited number of issues without the approval of the constituent units (Koštunica 1988: 78-92).

La raison d'être of the institutions of ethnofederalism was *to transform the politically charged ethnic identities into much safer cultural identities.* The Constitution essentially differentiated between *two types of national groupings* that were in hierarchical relations (Peši 1996: 10). On the one hand, Serbs, Slovenes, Croats, Macedonians, and Montenegrins were territorially organized in republics in

---

50 After the defeat of Germany in 1945, Croatia surrendered and Serbia took revenge by "killing thousands of Croat and Muslim prisoners" (Crawford and Lipschutz 1998: 213).
51 See as well Auty (1970: 226).
52 Tito opted for noncentralized federalism because of the divisions created by the Second World War.

which they had the position of "constituent nations." The census conducted in 1971 recognized Muslims as a separate nation and in 1974 it was declared (following the national principle) that Serbs, Croats, and Muslims are the constituent nations of the republic of Bosnia and Herzegovina. On the other hand, there was, however, a significant number of "others" (Jews, Czechs, Romanians, Russians, Bulgarians, Romani, Vlachs, Albanians, and Hungarians) who were less represented in the political institutions. Nonetheless, after the legislative amendments in 1974, Kosovo (with a majority of Albanian population) and Vojvodina (with a Hungarian majority) gained increasing autonomy and enjoyed equal representation at the federal level with the six constituent nations.

The principle of federalism was implemented in two distinct ways (or at two different levels). The Federal Assembly consisted of a Federal Council (for which citizens voted as Yugoslavs) and a Chamber of Nationalities (in which citizens were represented as nations and nationalities). The objective of this system was to achieve a balance between the interests of all peoples of Yugoslavia. Tito realized that *if even one of the constituent nations was favored by the masters of the political game, the hegemon could jeopardize the whole system.*[53] The constituent nations, in principle, had equal say. Since they were far from being homogenous,[54] the territorial ethnofederalism was cemented with ethnic quotas for the allocation of resources. The appointments to public office followed "a formula for the proportional representation, or sometimes of the equal representation," of individuals by constituent nation/nationality (Crawford and Lipschutz 1998: 210). The reforms created socioeconomic divisions *that transcended ethnic cleavages and were potentially cross-cutting*. This essentially meant that the various ethnic groups who belonged to the same socioeconomic class had more in common with each other than with their ethnic compatriots; thus ideological

---

53   Serbia, given its larger population and history of independent state, was the "usual suspect" of hidden hegemonistic ambitions. Therefore, it is sometimes said that the federal system implemented the credo "Weak Serbia, strong Yugoslavia" (Peši 1996).
54   Most territorial units had mixed populations.

consensus and division *could potentially overcome* regional and cultural differences (ibid.: 216).

The integration policies initially relied on Marxist ideology and oppression. The public debates on ethnic issues were stifled and prosecuted.[55] The demands of the ethnic groups had to be voiced in economic and social terms in order to be accepted as legitimate by the institutions.[56] Although these restrictive measures were largely abandoned in the 1960s, the expression of nationalism continued to be illegal as was, for example, the incitement to discrimination on the grounds of religion, race, and ethnicity. Two political institutions—the League of Communists of Yugoslavia and the Yugoslav National Army—as well as the allocative policies that privileged partisans from all national groups who fought against fascism had important roles in the integration processes. These helped to build new types of solidarity (mainly on the grounds of the Marxist ideology which corroborated the belief that one day all ethnic groups will become a single Yugoslav nation) *and were, to a certain extent, successful* in their attempt to mitigate the painful ethnic cleavages. In fact, there was an abundance of evidence, which suggested that the economic cleavages, mainly between the urban and rural population,[57] were *more important* than the ethnic ones. In addition to that, the regional divisions became even deeply rooted than socioeconomic and ideological cleavages (Crawford and Lipschutz 1998: 220-2).

The entities in the Yugoslav federation were not equally developed economically. The two main objectives of the economic planners were to maintain a high rate of growth in conjunction with a reduction of the intraregional economic disparities. For these reasons, each five-year plan demanded the equalization of conditions

---

55 It was perceived that the political differences must be among class and not ethnic lines.
56 See Todorova (1992: 135-55).
57 Similar to the most communist countries behind the Iron Curtain, the allocation of resources by federal government in Yugoslavia *favored the industrial development over the rural sector*. Thus the peasants were driven off the land and into the factories.

in the regions. As a result of these policies, *the republics fought bitterly over their share of the investment funds distributed by the federal government*. Slovenia and Croatia were the richest and the most efficient and they demanded that resources be allocated by efficiency criteria. Serbia, Bosnia, Macedonia, and Montenegro were poorer. They fought for funds as development subsidies, because all funds were administered from a central General Investment Fund and the industrial development was regulated by the central government:

> Divisions among the republics over investment took the form of centre-region controversies. The poorer republics were dependent on the centre for development funds, and the richer republics wanted autonomy from the centre to free them from subsidies and regulation. In addition […] partisan elites pressed for regional credit allocations based on political criteria rewarding partisan loyalty and punishing those who had opposed the partisans in the war. (Ibid.: 218)

In a nutshell, the policies of central economic planning and distribution of resources created discontent among all entities of the federation.[58] The policies had two important consequences: first, the disputes that they instigated fueled constitutional debates which in turn exacerbated the conflicts between the regions as the attempts for their resolution weakened the administrative center of Yugoslavia; second, they led to the development of regional and republican loyalties that were stronger than the loyalty to the federation (Crawford and Lipschutz 1998: 220–1). The entrenchment of ethnofederalism, which politicized cultural identity, consolidated the power of the local elites and *thus made cultural divisions even deeper*. The legislative changes in 1953, 1963 (when a new constitution was

---

58 For example, the economic planners gave priority to the industries contributing to national growth. These were predominantly located in Croatia and Slovenia which had the most competitive enterprises in Yugoslavia. The five-year plans mandated that the row materials for these enterprises be *underpriced* in order to keep them competitive. Most of the materials came from Serbia, Montenegro, Bosnia, and Macedonia. At the same time, the wealthier regions disputed the huge income transfers required for the development of the poorer republics. People who were critical of these policies in Croatia and Slovenia stated that Montenegro and Serbia received disproportionate investment credits, because of the strong patronage networks of partisans in these regions (Crawford and Lipschutz 1998: 219–20).

drafted), and 1967, which were designed to appease the rivalries between the republics and to combat the deepening economic problems, favored the decentralization as a solution. *Ironically, the result was further economic decline.* The central government grew weaker and the disintegration of the market "into eight mercantilist and protectionist regional fiefdoms" hindered efficiency and growth[59] (Rusinow 1985: 140-2). The strengthening of the Chamber of Nationalities, "at the expense" of the federal chamber which was downgraded, bolstered ethnic and regional political power and embittered ethnic tensions. Because representation in the Chamber of Nationalities was based on the principles of equality and proportionality, each of the six republics, *regardless of the size of their population*, had 20 delegates. This meant, essentially, that Serbs, who had about 40% of the total population of the federation, had only 14% of the votes in the Chamber — the same as the Slovenes, who represented merely 8.5%. This formula of representation benefitted the smaller and richer republics in order to compensate them for the disproportional burden in the regional development policy that they bore. However, the policy backfired because it channeled resentments and privileges "away from territorially defined republics and directed them toward specific ethnic groups"; thus, "Serbs began to resent Croats, not just Croatia" (Crawford and Lipschutz 1998: 225).

The devolution reached a climax in the constitution adopted in 1974, which virtually transformed Yugoslavia into *confederation*. The authority retained by the center was further restricted and confined mainly to the fields of foreign policy, defense, and the protection of national rights.[60] The principle of proportional representation in federal appointments was abandoned in favor of complete

---

59   The economic reform in 1965 removed the central government from the position of provider of investment funds to the republics; instead a system of banks at the level of the republics was created. These banks became autonomous enterprises under the control of the republican governments. The federal government turned to the republics also most of its prerogatives to raise taxes.

60   The decisions in the above-mentioned fields were further limited because they required the consensus of the entities of the de facto confederation.

equality between the constituent entities[61] *regardless of the population size*. In short, the smaller subjects of the federation were highly overrepresented, while the larger ones were acutely underrepresented. *The legacy of ethnofederalism thus had three main consequences*: the demise of the authority of the center which effectively put an end to the federal protection of the rights of minorities and provided incentives for the local politicians to exploit ethnic resentments; it prevented the formation of coalitions across ideological lines that could help to consolidate the dissolving federation; and it also blocked the possibility of coalitions across regional lines (Crawford and Lipschutz 1998: 238–39). The gates were opened wide for ethnic violence to enter the political scene.

1.3 The Bulgarian ethnic models

We can distinguish between four models of ethnic relations,[62] consolidated through the legislation, which existed in Bulgaria after its liberation in 1878 from the Ottoman yoke.[63] The chief mark of the government policies toward minorities until 1989 was their *highly contradictory character*. One of the invaluable lessons from the analysis of the collapse of the Yugoslav federation is that, in general, *the conflict potential of ethnic identity can be unlocked and storm out of control when it becomes a criterion that determines access to (power) resources, i.e.,*

---

61 As we already saw, with the newly adopted constitution, Kosovo and Vojvodina became autonomous provinces in 1974. Essentially, the Albanians in Kosovo received the same political status as the constituent national groups at the federal level. The six republics and the two provinces were equally represented in both chambers of the Federal Assembly.

62 Below I use this term and the term "ethnic model" interchangeably.

63 Following the Russo-Turkish War (1877–78), the Treaty of Berlin (July 13, 1878) created the Principality of Bulgaria as a de facto independent vassal state of the Ottoman Empire as well as the autonomous unit (*vilayet*) of Eastern Rumelia (the ethnic Bulgarians were 70% of the population). The Treaty also recognized the independence of the principalities of Romania, Serbia, and Montenegro. In 1885, the Principality of Bulgaria unified with Eastern Rumelia, officially under a personal union. Bulgaria continued to be de jure an Ottoman province until 1908 when declared independence.

when identity is politicized. Such politicization was present in all three models before 1989. The first of them, "the archetype," operated until 1944. Although some scholars claim that it was designed "to ensure the rights and freedoms of all ethnic groups and confessions" (Aresnova and Kertikov 2002), the reality was different.

As it is apparent from Table 1, the two largest minorities in the country since 1878 have always been the Turks and the Roma. As a whole the minorities *did not have* their own, significant presence in the political process until 1944, perhaps, even until 1989. Indeed, in the Constituent Assembly (February 10, 1878–April 18, 1879) – the first Bulgarian Parliament after 1878, there were 16 representatives of ethnic/religious minorities (12 Turks, 2 Greeks, 1 Jew, and 1 Bulgarian Protestant), or 6.9% of all members of the Assembly (Todorov 2010: 270). Nonetheless, this in fact was a confirmation of "the unwritten rule" that minorities might participate in politics but only *as members of Bulgarian parties* (Nazurska 1999: 19–22). After the term of the Constituent Assembly ended, the situation changed. There were no more Jewish or Greek members of the parliament.

Table 1. Main ethnic groups in Bulgaria since 1878

Year	Bulgarians	%	Turks	%	Roma	%
2011*	5,664,624	84.8	588,318	8.8	325,343	4.9
2001	6,655,210	83.9	746,664	9.4	370,908	4.7
1992	7,271,185	85.7	800,052	9.4	313,396	3.7
1975	7,930,024	90.9	730,728	8.4	**	**
1946	5,903,580	84.0	675,500	9.6	170,011	2.4
1926	4,557,706	83.2	577,552	10.5	138,844	2.5
1900	2,888,219	77.1	531,240	14.2	89,549	2.4

Source: Miris (2001) and NSI (2011).
Note: *The data for 2011 are from the population census conducted in 2011 (see NSI 2011). The problem with these data is that they are *not calculated on the basis of 100% of the population* (the figures only reflect those who responded to the question regarding their ethnicity; 683,590 did not respond to this question). Therefore, it is hard to make comparisons with previous years.
**The asterisks in the table signify "no available data."

The (Bulgarian) parties preferred "to work" with the "more compact" minorities of Turks and Pomaks, who were cautious and reluctant to express demands; this "formula" was continuously implemented until 1944 (Todorov 2010: 270). The Roma were almost completely excluded from the political process. For the most part (until 1934) the attitude of the authorities toward the Turks was tolerant. However the latter remained isolated politically. One of the reasons for that was their low literacy—only 6% of them were literate in 1910, 14.5% in 1934; among the Pomaks[64] the respective numbers were 3.8% in 1910 and 8.6% in 1934 (Daskalov 2005: 36–8). Until 1944, Bulgarian Turks retained their religious autonomy, including the related Sharia traditional judicial system. Following the defeat in the First World War, Bulgaria signed an agreement on minority rights (1919). After 1934, however, began the policies of assimilation in the Rhodope Mountains. As far as other, smaller minorities are concerned, the Jews and Armenians were well integrated, at least until the beginning of 1940s (Todorov 2010: 270), when as an ally of the Nazi Third Reich, the Bulgarian government passed anti-Semitic laws (the Law on Protection of the Nation, 1941; the Law for the One-Off Tax on Property of Persons of Jewish Origin, 1941). Only the timely intervention of the monarch himself, members of the parliament, the Bulgarian Patriarchate, and the society as a whole saved from deportation to the concentration camps 48,000 Bulgarian Jews (Makariev 1999: 240).

Three other ethnic models have been established after the Second World War. Two of them operated under the totalitarian regime (1949–1989). *The first one* (until 1956), the "Dimitrov–Chervenkov" model, was characterized by the protectionist policy of cultural emancipation of ethnic communities through specifically designed for their (social) benefits. *The second model* (1956–1989) brought *an abrupt change* in the direction of "ethnic homogenization"[65] (Kalinova and Baeva 2001). Still, some of the government

---

64   The Pomaks are Bulgarian-speaking Muslims, indigenous to Southern Bulgaria, Northern Greece, Turkey, Albania, Republic of Macedonia, and Kosovo.
65   The model followed the famous slogan of Todor Zhivkov: "one ethnicity, one culture, customs, religion and traditions." Some scholars explain this dramatic

measures had positive character, such as the rise of educational status of minorities, the formation of (minority) elites through special quotas in party-state apparatus, creating jobs, providing housing for the Turks and the Roma,[66] etc. In December 1984, the government abandoned the policy of peaceful integration and began to forcefully change the Turkish-Arab names of Turks to Bulgarian (the official term used for this policy was "Revival Process" or "Process of Rebirth"). The process was not dissimilar to some of the previous policies of other Balkan countries toward their own minorities during the twentieth century, including the SFRY.

The third, currently operating in Bulgaria ethnic model, has been established after the collapse of the communist regime in 1989. This model provides much more significant means and possibilities for the protection of rights and the expression of the interests of the minorities, especially in comparison to its "predecessors" which operated in the conditions of ideological monism and one-party dominance. The model is supported, although not without problems, by the Constitution (1991), the Framework Convention for Protection of National Minorities ratified by the BNA (1995), the Act on Confessions (2002), the Protection against Discrimination Act (PADA, 2003), as well as, in general, the policies of the executive. At the heart of the model is *the institutionalization of the ethnic cleavage*. This has been achieved mainly through the party of the ethnic minorities — the MRF, founded in 1990 — which has been represented in all Bulgarian parliaments after the democratic changes. The political support for the party comes predominantly from Bulgarian Turks (almost 90% of the electorate) followed by Roma and Pomaks.[67] The movement has a prominent role in the postcommunist political system and has taken part in three governments. The party is also well represented at municipal level.[68]

---

policy shift with the fear of the authorities of the propaganda of Turkey at the time, see Kalinova and Baeva (2001).

66 There were also periodicals and stage plays in theaters in Turkish language, etc.
67 See Karasimeonov (2010: 240). For an in-depth analysis of MRF, see Section 2.2.
68 In 2001–2005, the MRF obtained ministerial seats as a coalition partner of the NMSP (Bulgarian — Национално Движение Симеон Втори). The MRF was

There are several reasons why the politicization of ethnic identity during the totalitarian regime did not escalate to armed conflict or brought the collapse of government. First and foremost, unlike the entities of SFRY, the ethnic minorities in Bulgaria never enjoyed a territorial autonomy and thus avoided the potentially tormenting relationship with the administrative center which comes "bundled" with it, nor they had the history of independent (ethnically based) polities. Second, as opposed to the dying moments of SFRY, the Bulgarian totalitarian machine was, even during the final years of its existence and operation, powerful enough to suppress and keep within safe limits the fire of interethnic tensions, as well as to impose its public policies. Third, in general, the tolerant, political culture of the dominant ethnic group (Bulgarians) was a natural barrier to the political perversions and excesses of government. The Revival Process contributed to the delegitimization of the regime. Although the process embittered and deepened the ethnic cleavage, the actions of the establishment, who inspired the repressions, were not condoned by the majority of Bulgarians. Fourth, the very nature of the Orthodox Church (free of religious zeal or militantism) contributes to the relatively tolerant political culture of Bulgarian people. In general, the orthodox Christianity is characterized by deeply rooted passivity and contemplation. Perhaps these traits were further strengthened by mediaeval Hesychasm, which occupies an important place in Orthodox culture and spirituality. At the same time, the Islam which Bulgarian Turks profess has never been radical. Fifth, not without significance is the fact that a substantial part of the elite of the ethnic groups in this period was "created" and/or "recruited" by the state. Thus the ethnic tensions could be kept "under the hood."

The question of mechanisms of politicization of ethnic identity *is not sufficiently developed in the study edited by Crawford and Lipschutz (1998). In my view, depending on the subjects and objects of politicization, its intentional or rather inadvertent (unpremeditated) character, we can*

---

also part of the government of Mr. Sergei Stanishev during 2005–2009 and was later represented in the government led by Mr. Plamen Oresharski. See Section 2.1.

distinguish between several mechanisms serving this purpose. The first of them, as demonstrated above, is actually transforming ethnic identity "into an entry ticket" used to obtain political rights and economic resources. The subject of this politicization is the dominant ethnic group through the means of state institutions, including the repressive apparatus, which are controlled by it, while the objects are the subordinate ethnicities (examples from Bulgaria are the infamous attempts to assimilate Bulgarian Muslims in the 1930s, 1960s, and 1970s, as well as the Revival Process, 1984–1989). Second, the political mobilization, which tries to manipulate identity, can be directed to members of the own ethnic group. The mechanism often operates on the basis of invoked "existential" and "inevitable" "dilemma" — "it is either we or them." In this fashion, "work" the slogans of Bulgarian PRR parties Ataka and National Front for the Salvation of Bulgaria (NFSB), which call for immediate action against the threat of "Osmanization" and "Turkish assimilation" of Bulgaria.[69] The principal goal of this mechanism is to "awaken" or "activate" the ethnic group to which the political messages are targeted, by making it "aware" of its identity. Such messages, which are based on striking fears (of assimilation or even extermination — ethnocide, etc.), can also be directed toward the members of the ethnicity by its leaders. Ethnic minorities themselves (or their individual representatives) may decide or be forced by circumstances to politicize their identity in order to increase and optimize, if we use Ralf Dahrendorf's dictum, their "life chances" (Dahrendorf 2007). The process can be aimed at inclusion into the dominant ethnic

---

[69] See, for example, the statements of Volen Siderov, the leader of Ataka, broadcasted by the Bulgarian National Television during the presidential elections in 2011, see "Volen Siderov on Bulgaria becoming a 'Gypsy State'" (2013). A similar discourse has been used by Bulgarian politicians before the political changes in 1989. For example, Todor Zhivkov, the secretary general of the Communist party, defended the "necessity" of the so-called Big excursion — the forced migration of Bulgarian Turks in the summer of 1989, claiming that "if we do not reduce by 200,000–300,000 this population, in fifteen years Bulgaria will seize to exist. It will be like Cyprus or something like that," see "The 'Big excursion' and the collapse of assimilation" (2013).

group (as was the objective of many of the founders of the organization "Rodina," operating in the Rhodope Mountains during 1937–1947, who were in fact Bulgarian Muslims); or it can be led by duty to return to the "true fatherland" (as was during the emigration of thousands of Bulgarian Muslims to Turkey); it can further be an expression of political mobilization for the protection of the minority (e.g., the MRF rejects the claims that it is an ethnic party; in the same vein were the political messages and activities of Kamen Burov—the mayor of a village of Jyltusha, located in the eastern Rhodope Mountains, and the Democratic Labour Party,[70] which he established in 1992). Third, the subject of politicization can be organizations, which are external to the country, while its objects are ethnicities that live in it. In this category belong the actions of Islamic missionaries among Bulgarian Muslims.

Fourth, the mechanism of, what I shall call, "involuntary politicization" must be studied separately. The measures of positive discrimination of state institutions to vulnerable ethnic groups, and the actions of nongovernmental organizations (NGOs) in defense of these ethnicities *often further enhance the negative stereotypes in the dominant ethnic group toward minorities. Thus, ironically, these measures politicize ethnic identity.* For example, the need for desegregation in education and housing, which has been one of the chief causes of Bulgarian and foreign, international human rights organizations[71] and activists promoting the rights of Roma, in general, is met by the cold shoulder of the dominant ethnicity, and (probably) further mobilizes public opinion against political minorities. Seventy-one percent of other ethnic groups believe that the segregated Roma neighborhoods (ghettos) should remain, while 57.6% of respondents reckon that "it will be better if Roma children do not attend the same school as Bulgarians" (Mantarova and Zaharieva 2007: 131–2). This taxonomy of mechanisms of politicization of eth-

---

70 This party claimed to represent the Pomak minority.
71 The segregated education and housing has been criticized in several important verdicts of the European Court of Human Rights. See Part 3.

nicity is by no means exhaustive. Different versions of these mechanisms operate in political practice and, almost always, work simultaneously.

1.4 Contemporary challenges to ethnic relations

The first challenge is the demographic crisis. The population growth in Bulgaria is negative (−0.83% for 2014) and is the fifth lowest in the world. Only Syria, Cook Islands, Moldova, and Saint Pierre and Miquelon have lower population growth (CIA 2014). The death rate for 2014 is 14.3, the sixth highest in the world (ibid.). In 1990–2005 between 937,000 and 1,200,000 left Bulgaria due to the acute economic crisis.[72] According to the 2011 census, the population of Bulgaria is 7,364,570 people. Bulgarians are the largest ethnic group and comprise 84.8% of the population. Turkish and Roma minorities comprise 8.8% and 4.9%, respectively[73]; some 40 smaller minorities comprise 0.7%, and 0.8% do not self-identify with an ethnic group (NSI 2011). However these data should be taken with a grain of salt because they are not calculated on the basis of 100% of the population. According to the *CIA World Factbook for 2014*, the population of Bulgaria is actually *significantly smaller* or 6,924,716 people (July 2014 estimate).[74] The demographic crisis, combined with the fact that the Roma are subject to a number of measures of positive discrimination, while distinguished by criminal activity that exceeds many times that of the other groups, fuels the extremely negative ethnic stereotypes toward this ethnic group (Mantarova and Zaharieva 2007).

Therefore, a second challenge, intertwined with that outlined above, is the raise of discrimination on ethnic grounds, particularly against Roma (see Figure 1). According to a representative survey conducted in 2011 as part of the project "EU INCLUSIVE — data

---

72 See "Will EU Entry Shrink Bulgaria's Population Even More?" (2006).
73 See Table 1.
74 See CIA (2014).

transfer and exchange of best practices between Romania, Bulgaria, Spain and Italy relating to the inclusion of the Roma population," nearly 46% of Roma believe that nowadays discrimination against their community has increased significantly in the last 10 years (see Figure 1). The share of those who report no change is 24% (Petkova 2013). Research conducted by the "Open Society" Institute, which analyzed the Roma Inclusion (Metodieva et al. 2012) demonstrated that, in fact, a relatively small part of the members of this ethnic community live on state benefits. The data are contrary to the popular opinion that Roma do not work because they live on the money for child allowances. Only 4.3% of the representatives of this ethnic minority receive maternity benefits and child allowances for children up to one year, and 9.6% receive support for socially disadvantaged (see Table 2).

Figure 1. Discrimination against Roma
Source: Petkova (2013).

Today, compared to 10 years ago, the Roma are:

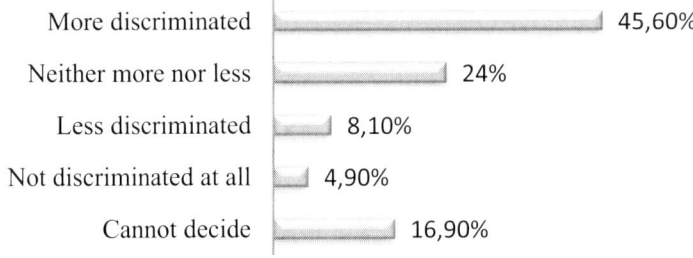

Table 2. Main sources of income for Roma households
Source: Metodieva et al. (2012: 46).

Wages or salaries	32.3%
Income from casual work	18.2%
Pension based on working experience and/or age	10.6%
Pension for disability or sickness	9.1%
Child allowance, for children up to the age of 18, if in school	6.0%
Monthly allowance for poor households	4.5%
Money transfers from people working abroad	3.7%
Profit from own business	3.1%
Monthly allowance for pregnancy, birth, child up to one year	2.8%
Unemployment benefits	2.5%
Monthly allowance for raising a child up to one year	1.5%
Social pension for old age	0.6%
Other social benefits	1.5%
Other pension	1.4%
Other income	2.3%

Third, various studies, based on the famous scale of Emory S. Bogardus, demonstrate *the increase* of social, interethnic distances that are an indicator of tolerance of a given society (Mantarova and Zaharieva 2007, Pamporov 2008, Pamporov 2016). As far as the two most significant minorities are concerned, these distances remain the largest vis-à-vis the Roma. Usually the respondents who "agree" that Turks should live in Bulgaria are in the range of 80–89%, regarding Pomaks—81–87%, and Roma—in the range of 66–76%. In 2007, 56.1% of Bulgarians "agreed" with Pomaks living in the country, while, regarding the Turks and the Roma, these figures were respectively 54.7% and 44.4% (Pamporov 2008: 107). It appears that the "new minorities"—Arabs, Vietnamese, and Chinese, who are often "invisible" to the state administration and the media—"are much more rejected by the Bulgarians and the population of the country as a whole" (ibid.: 109). As far as the other Balkan peoples are concerned, the social distances are largest in regard to Albanians. Other scholars provide more optimistic data (e.g., Nedelcheva 2011). While some distances indeed are increasing (there is, e.g., a greater confinement in the personal space, which makes it even more difficult to accept persons who have a different ethnicity), others are diminishing (Nedelcheva 2011). In 2009, for example, 37.8% of Bulgarians believe that the Turks are a threat to national security of Bulgaria, while in 1992 this percent was higher—51.1%. The share of Bulgarians and Turks, who perceive Roma as criminals, is decreasing (ibid.: 88–9). In 2009, in comparison to 1992, a smaller percentage of Turks (66.9% vs. 42.4%) and Roma (68.6% vs. 61.4%) believe that Bulgarians are a privileged ethnic group. There are signs, according to Nedelcheva, of an on-going crisis and destruction of national identity, but I think that this does not necessarily mean that Bulgarians "embrace European values" or that "their biographies are globalizing," as this scholar claims (Nedelcheva 2011: 90–6).

A study of "Gallup International" — *At the End of the Decade of Roma Inclusion: Symptoms of Permanent Exclusion*, which was conducted between June 26–July 2, 2015 — confirms that the social distances between Roma and the other large ethnic groups are increasing (Gallup 2015)[75] in spite of state's integration policies. Attitudes toward Roma do not differ significantly in between social groups. In fact, people "who are in a favorable life situation" *are even more alienated against this ethnicity*. In the public eye, politicians are to blame "for problems" with Roma communities (Gallup 2015). The survey was conducted in the immediate aftermath of the ethnic tension in Garmen and Orlandovtsi, which might have had an impact on results; however, according to the analysis, the data are unlikely to be significantly different "in a more relaxed atmosphere" (ibid.). *In general, the attitude toward Roma is not noticeably affected by the level of education*. For example, university graduates are no more tolerant than those with secondary education. A specific case is the group of respondents with primary or lower education where the negative

---

75   The survey is representative of the adult population of the country and covers 1,011 adult Bulgarians through direct interview. The maximum standard statistical deviation at 50% shares is ±3%. The methodology is comparable to all regular monthly surveys conducted by "Gallup International" in Bulgaria since 1992. See Gallup (2015).

attitudes also prevail, but not to the extent mentioned above. The reason is that many Roma fall in this educational group. Negative attitudes seem even more significant in the larger settlements where the Roma communities are isolated in ghettoes and slums. The latter create "a sense of privilege before the law," which is an additional factor for the negative attitudes. More negative attitudes toward Roma are expressed in the private sphere/family life. For example, only 9% answered positively to the question whether they would marry Roma, while 85% gave a negative answer. Only 4% of ethnic Bulgarians and 6% of Turks state that they would marry a representative of the Roma minority (ibid.). In Part 2,[76] I explore the way in which the increasing social distances affect the perspectives in front of the populist radical parties in Bulgaria.

Fourth, the radical antiestablishment attitudes and nationalism are further amplified by the repercussions of the civil war in Syria. Since 2013 we have witnessed an unprecedented growth of refugees who seek asylum in Bulgaria. In October 2013, the vast majority of Bulgarians (83%) expressed concern that the Syria refugee crisis is coupled with hidden security risks (Alpha Research 2013). Around this position is consolidated a majority encompassing all sociodemographic groups. Only 17% see no serious reason for concern (ibid.). A study published in January 2014, however, shows that the public is calming down regarding the refugee crisis (Gallup 2014a). Fifty-two percent believe that Bulgaria should help Syrian refugees; 28% think that the country should not accept them and expel those who have already entered. Strikingly, the PRR party Ataka, on the one hand, and political formations, which claim that they are representatives of Roma like DROM (Movement for an Equal Public Model), on the other, *share a similar, negative stand toward the refugees*. The refugee wave, which has been widely covered by the media, has been used by a number of political formations (e.g., by IMRO and the newly formed Nationalist Party of Bulgaria) in their xenophobic propaganda. The fears that a new,

---

76   See Section 2.3.4.

bigger "refugee wave" might sweep over Bulgaria are likely to draw even more water into the "mills" of ethnic entrepreneurs.

The fifth challenge is a complex one. The national security of any polity that is guided by the principle of popular sovereignty is dependent on the homeostasis of democratic political system. In theory, the *differentia specifica* of this system is shaped by three interlinked components. The first is the existence of active civil society, which by definition must be unrestricted by state interference (the latter could often be masked under the role of "benevolent" stewardship). The second is the presence of effective political intermediary institutions — political parties, movements, interest groups, media, etc. The main task of the intermediaries is to aggregate and express the interests arising in the civil society, which then receive the chance to be presented at the level of parliament, and central and local government. The third component consists of the institutions of the state, which are to be guided by the fundamental constitutional principles of liberal democracy (separation of powers, rule of law, popular sovereignty, freedom of speech, etc.). *These interrelated components define the character of a democratic political system and are not only its greatest strength but also its paramount weakness.* If only one of them deviates of its purpose or loses its legitimacy due to political malignancies like corruption and nepotism, the whole delicate mechanism becomes in danger. For example, the obstruction of the channels of political participation entails the sclerosis of the democratic political system. The symptoms for the latter are, for instance, the raise of political tensions, the increase of pressure from protests, and acts of civil disobedience.

The analysis reveals *problems in all three components* outlined above. These issues reflect on ethnic tensions and conflicts, crippling the possibilities for their peaceful transformation. The defects in the modus operandi of Bulgarian political system, most of which could be traced back to the dark history of the Bulgarian transition to a market economy and democracy, pose *the most significant challenge* to the ethnic model. As far as civil society is concerned, it should be pointed out that despite the active involvement of various NGOs that chivalrously take up the cause of ethnic minorities they are often not recognized as legitimate representatives of their interests. The capacity of these organizations to influence state institutions and polices remains very limited, while their weak contacts and representation at European level contribute further to their marginalization. The media, which should serve as a compass to civil society, continue to suffer from *severe censorship* in Bulgaria. The country was ranked 109 in the 2017 World Press Freedom Index.[77] The Press in Bulgaria is the least free of all EU countries (Reporters Without Borders 2017).[78] The significance of the other components (the party and the judicial system, as well as the integration policies of the Bulgarian state) for the ethnic relations will be analyzed in the following sections of this work. Here I would only make two important conclusions from the analysis of the SFRY which are directly related to the state of the components.

Although Bulgaria is a unitary state under the Constitution of 1991, the contemporary *model of ethnic relations which was established in the 1990s bears similarities* to some of the characteristic features of the ethnofederalism in the wretched Yugoslavia. Both political systems utilize the institutionalization of the ethnic cleavages as *a safe valve* through which the tensions between the ethnic groups could be peacefully channelized and defused. However, *institutionalization, as we already established, is not without significant drawbacks. First,* it politicizes ethnic identity and thus, ironically, vindicates the actions of ethnic entrepreneurs. *The mere existence* of the parties of ethnic minorities in Bulgaria, such as MRF, has become a justification for the existence of political formations such as Ataka and NFSB.[79] The support for these parties, as well as the "nationalist" vote, in general, *is boosted further* by the allegations of corruption against some of the leaders and functionaries of the MRF. The latter suffers from opaque decision-making procedures and limited intraparty

---

[77] See Reporters Without Borders (2017).
[78] The Press is freer not only in the other EU states but also in countries such as Surinam (20), Samoa (21), Namibia (24), Belize (41), Burkina Faso (42), ibid.
[79] Of course the opposite is also true. The hate speech of populist right parities like Ataka and NFSB "helps" to mobilize the minorities.

democracy (Karasimeonov 2010, Cholakov 2014b).[80] It has to be emphasized that these negative traits are not limited to the MRF. Many of the political parties in the country are marked by them, although to a different extent.[81] There are also the ominous signs of, if we use the well-known concept of Peter Mair, the cartelization of the political system (Katz and Mair 1995, Mair 1998). This leads to *the second issue*. As the analysis of SFRY has demonstrated, the politicized ethnicity, in itself, could become dangerous *only* when the institutions that are meant to channelize the ethnic conflicts are eroded and their legitimacy disputed. Unlike the federal institutions of Yugoslavia that initially were strong but were undermined by decentralization and devolution, the postcommunist political institutions in Bulgaria *remain weak, underdeveloped, and fragile*. They are plagued by sluggish bureaucratic procedures. The justice system,[82] including the defense of the right of the minorities, is inefficient and prone to political influences (Cholakov 2014a).[83]

1.5 Strength of state institutions and ethnic conflicts

There is another problem in the paradigm of conflict analysis proposed by Beverly Crawford and her colleagues[84] in *The Myth of Ethnic Conflict*, which is more imperious than the explanation of the precise mechanisms of politicization. As mentioned, that study postulates that *the strength of state institutions in the management and control over ethnic conflicts can offset their illegitimacy*. The term "strength of institutions" requires further examination. Following the classic definition of Max Weber, political scientists and sociologists often

---

80   See Section 2.2 dedicated to the MRF.
81   The party system in the Bulgaria has been in constant crisis during the last 15 years. It is not coincidental that, upon entering the political contest, most of the newly formed political formations prefer to name or describe themselves as "popular movement," "citizens' initiative," etc.
82   In theory, judicial institutions must be impartial and "politically blind." This principle conceals the fact that they are also political. See Section 3.2.1.
83   See Part 3.
84   See Crawford and Lipschutz (1998).

understand state as a "human community which exercises monopoly over the legitimate use of physical force [violence] within a certain territory" (Weber 2003: 310–11). The essence of "stateness," according to this approach, is the *enforcement* (Fukuyama 2004a: 21). However, as Fukuyama points out, it is necessary to distinguish between the "strength" of state institutions and the "scope" of state functions (ibid.: 21–2). This distinction, which will help to better understand how a state deals with interethnic tensions, is lacking in the classic analyses in *The Myth of Ethnic Conflict*. The "*strength*" or the "capacity"[85] of institutions is a testament to their quality and describes the ability:

> to enact statutes and to frame and execute policies; to administer the public business with relative efficiency; to control graft, corruption, and bribery; to maintain high levels of transparency and accountability in governmental institutions; and most importantly, to *enforce* laws. (Fukuyama 2004a: 22)

There is no commonly accepted mechanism to measure institutional capacity. Furthermore, the process of making comparisons between political systems is greatly complicated by the fact that the performance of state's agencies can fluctuate significantly. A given country can simultaneously have, for example, efficient repressive apparatus and extremely cumbersome bureaucratic procedures.[86] The Worldwide Governance Indicators[87] (WGI) and the Corruption Perception Index (CPI) of Transparency International can be used as criteria to assess the strength of institutions and place them in a comparative, international perspective.[88] The "*scope*" of state functions refers to the extent of prerogatives or the catalogue of actions and goals that are taken on by the government (Fukuyama 2004a: 21). The *1997 World Development Report: The State in a Changing*

---

85   I use the terms "institutional strength" and "institutional capacity" interchangeably.
86   Fukuyama (2004a: 22).
87   Developed under a project funded by the World Bank.
88   Fukuyama (2004a: 23). The American political scientist proposes as well other criteria for measuring "strength," such as the International Country Risk Guide (ibid.: 23).

World, which Fukuyama uses as a basis of his analysis,[89] classifies government functions along a continuum,[90] and divides them into three groups: minimalist, intermediate, and activist (World Bank 1997: 27). Regarding "scope," Fukuyama postulates that it is best to array states "according to the most ambitious functions which they seek to perform, even if they fail at or do not care much about the more basic ones" (Fukuyama 2004a: 22). The further to the right on the axis depicted in Figure 2 belong "the most ambitious" functions, the broader the scope, and vice versa. There is, however, an issue with this method to measure scope, which I shall address below.

Figure 2. The scope of state functions
Source: Fukuyama (2004a: 23).

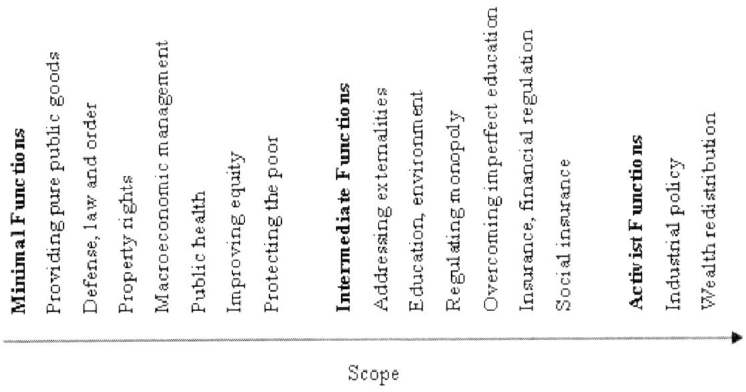

Minimal Functions
Providing pure public goods
Defense, law and order
Property rights
Macroeconomic management
Public health
Improving equity
Protecting the poor

Intermediate Functions
Addressing externalities
Education, environment
Regulating monopoly
Overcoming imperfect education
Insurance, financial regulation
Social insurance

Activist Functions
Industrial policy
Wealth redistribution

Scope

---

89 See Fukuyama (2004a: 22, 2004b).
90 At one end of the spectrum are positioned the activities that will not be undertaken at all without state intervention, while at the other end are those in which the state plays a leading role in coordinating markets or redistributing assets (World Bank 1997: 26).

Figure 3. Strength of state institutions and scope of state functions

Source: The figure builds on the discussion of these issues in Fukuyama (2004a: 23).

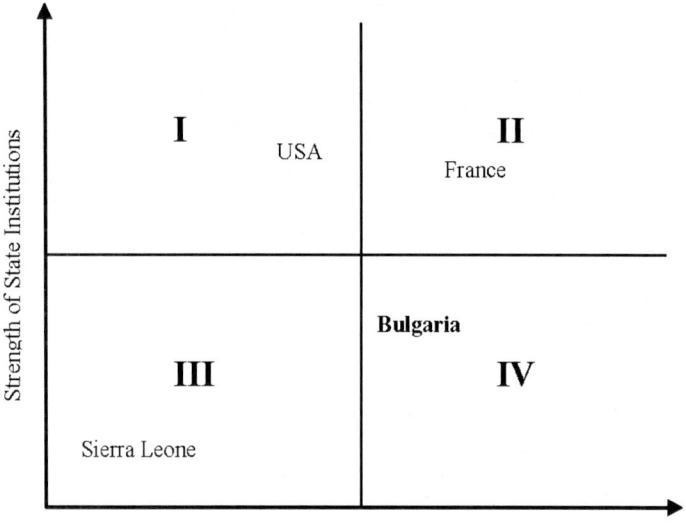

Scope of State Functions

The four quadrants of Figure 3, which is based on the famous analysis of Fukuyama (Fukuyama 2004a: 23), represent different combinations of "strength" and "scope." The purpose of the figure is to serve as a *general orientation without claiming statistical or other precision*. The American political scientist does not indicate the specific criteria that were used in order to position the countries in the appropriate quadrants.[91] Bulgaria is not part of the original analysis. In Figure 3, I have compared the Balkan state with three of the countries in the analysis of Fukuyama — the United States, France, and Sierra Leone.[92] *In order to do that, I reconstructed the figure through the*

---

91 As mentioned above, Fukuyama states that the data from the 1997 World Development Report can be used to measure scope, while WGIs, the CPI, and similar indexes can serve as reference points in order to determine the strength of institutions. However, he does not clarify which of these criteria and for which particular year(s) were used in order to place the states that he analyses in the four quadrants of Figure 3.

92 See Fukuyama (2004a: 23).

help of data describing the welfare regimes in the states in question (Fenger 2007) and the WGI for 2013. The study of welfare regimes essentially describes how the state performs regarding the most "ambitious functions" (if we use Fukuyama's term) such as social security and income redistribution. Therefore, it allows us to "gauge" and compare scope. This criterion is particularly appropriate, because, as we have already seen, the ethnic minorities in Bulgaria are perceived as heavily dependent on the social security policies of the state.

In his classic work on social policy *Three Worlds of Welfare Capitalism*, Esping-Andersen[93] distinguishes between three ideal types of welfare regimes[94]: liberal, conservative-corporatist, and social-democratic. This distinction is based on the degree of decommodification and the type of stratification, which they produce in given society[95] (Esping-Andersen 1993). *The liberal welfare states* are characterized by means-tested assistance and modest social-insurance plans. Benefits cater predominantly to a clientele of low-income state dependents. If we apply this analysis to Fukuyama's four quadrants (see Figure 3), we can conclude that, in comparison to the other two types, the states that favor this regime must *embrace the ideal of limited scope*. It is typical for countries like the United States, which are distinguished by parsimonious social security policies and a strong drive toward economic deregulation, based on the liberal faith in the "invisible hand" and, in general, animosity toward income redistribution. *The conservative-corporatist regimes* in France and Germany have moderate levels of decommodification.

---

[93] Esping-Andersen (1993). See as well the pioneering work on social policy of Titmus (1950).
[94] "A welfare regime can be defined as the combined, interdependent way in which welfare is produced and allocated between state, market and family." See Esping-Andersen (1993: 34–5).
[95] Decommodification "occurs, when a service is rendered as a matter of right, and when a person can maintain a livelihood without reliance on the market" (Esping-Andersen 1993: 21–2). Stratification refers to the intensity of redistribution and the level of universality of solidarity that is imposed by the welfare state.

The state provides income maintenance benefits related to occupational status. *The social-democratic regimes* in Sweden and Norway are characterized by high levels of decommodification and redistribution. The generous benefits do not depend on any individual contributions (Esping Andersen 1993, Arts and Gelissen 2002).

This classification triggered a heated discussion, a plethora of new typologies, and received both prize and criticisms. What is important, from our perspective, is that two of the countries in question — the United States and France — "fit" relatively well into these ideal welfare regime types, which allows us to measure and compare their scope. However, neither Bulgaria nor Sierra Leone is part of Esping-Andersen's classification. The Bulgarian case[96] has been described as a mixture between the social-democratic and conservative-corporatist regimes (Todorova 2008). The hierarchical cluster analysis of Fenger[97] which builds upon and expands the work of Esping-Andresen in order to classify the states in Central and Eastern Europe *demonstrates that Bulgaria is a part of a separate postcommunist European type (to which belong as well Croatia, Czech Republic, Hungary, Poland, and Slovakia).*[98] If we use the total government expenditures[99] as a leading indicator, this cluster in fact *must be positioned somewhat between the conservative and the liberal regimes.* It should be noted, however, that according to Fenger's analysis, the societies in the postcommunist European welfare regimes are more egalitarian than the conservative regimes.[100] *As to Bulgaria, this conclusion is apparently based on old data. The country's Gini index measuring the distribution of family income and inequality is higher (rank*

---

96 Here and below, I am writing about the contemporary social policies after the fall of communism in Bulgaria as well as in the other countries in Central and Eastern Europe.
97 For his methodology, see Fenger (2007: 16–20).
98 See Fenger (2007: 24).
99 On health, education, social protection, etc., see Fenger (1997: 23) (Table 2).
100 And, hence, much more egalitarian than the liberal regimes.

38, Gini index for 2007 – 45.3[101]*) than any other state in the EU (e.g., France has rank 114, and Gini index for 2011 – 30.9*[102]*) and higher than the United States (rank 41, Gini index for 2007 – 45).*[103] The negative trends regarding some of the other social situation variables (such as inflation, life expectancy, infant mortality, and unemployment), as well as the main political participation variable (level of trust in the institutions) which Fenger takes into account[104] in his analysis, pose significant challenges in front of operation of the welfare states of this type.

Regarding the institutional scope of Sierra Leone, the fourth country in our comparative analysis, it suffices to say that it is characterized by a *permanent emergency welfare regime in transition* (Cerami and Wagué 2013: 252–7). The latter is typical for the most of sub-Saharan Africa and has specific features, which make it very different from the welfare regimes that we examined above: a low impact of the state in welfare promotion due to limited budget capacity; political and bureaucratic clientelism in order to obtain access to benefits and services; high production of vertical and horizontal inequalities; vital importance of the family as well as the local and religious communities in social protection; strong reliance of the informal economy and informal networks in welfare production; welfare goals aiming at securing "basic services in provisions"; and survival-oriented skill production regime characterized by low human capital formation (Cerami 2013: 9–10). *In a nutshell, the scope of state institutions in Sierra Leone is extremely limited.*

---

101 The more nearly equal a country's income distribution, the lower its Gini index, e.g., a Scandinavian country with an index of 25. The more unequal is a country's income distribution, the higher is its Gini index, e.g., a sub-Saharan country with an index of 50. If income were distributed with perfect equality, the index would be zero; if income were distributed with perfect inequality, the index would be 100.

102 The EU as a whole has rank 117 and an estimated Gini index for 2012 – 30.6; see CIA (2015).

103 See CIA (2015).

104 Recent data regarding some of these variables have been provided above; for Fenger's data see Fenger (2007: 23).

Using the WGIs for 2013 (see Table 3 and Figure 4), I compared the strength of state institutions in Bulgaria to these in France, Sierra Leone, and United States, as well as in Brazil and Turkey. Although the last two countries are not represented in Figure 3, they are given as examples of quadrant two countries in Fukuyama's analysis[105] and it makes sense to see how Bulgaria stands in juxtaposition to them. The indicators fluctuate in the range between −2.5 and 2.5; higher numbers indicate better performance. On the grounds of the indicators for 2013 we can conclude that, as far as "political stability and absence of violence/terrorism" and "regulatory quality" are concerned, Bulgarian institutions are doing a relatively good job (see Table 3 and Figure 4). The country follows the lead of the United States and France; it is ahead of Brazil, Turkey, and Sierra Leone. However, regarding the indicator "voice and accountability" Bulgaria lags behind France, United States, and Brazil. Bulgaria also runs behind the United States, France, and Turkey in the domain of "government effectiveness." In addition to that, with respect to "control of corruption" and "rule of law" Bulgaria is *at the bottom of the chart*. The state capacity measured by these indicators is weaker only in Sierra Leone.

---

105 See Fukuyama (2004a: 23).

Table 3. Comparison between six states in 2013, based on WGI

Source: Kaufman et al. (2010) and World Bank (2015).

Indicator	Country	Governance score (from −2.5 to +2.5)
Voice and accountability	Brazil	0.37
	Bulgaria	0.32
	France	1.20
	Sierra Leone	−0.39
	Turkey	−0.26
	United States	1.08
Political stability and absence of violence/terrorism	Brazil	−0.28
	Bulgaria	0.18
	France	0.42
	Sierra Leone	−0.15
	Turkey	−1.19
	United States	0.61
Government effectiveness	Brazil	−0.08
	Bulgaria	0.15
	France	1.47
	Sierra Leone	−1.14
	Turkey	0.37
	United States	1.50
Regulatory quality	Brazil	0.07
	Bulgaria	0.52
	France	1.15
	Sierra Leone	−0.69
	Turkey	0.42
	United States	1.26
Rule of law	Brazil	−0.12
	Bulgaria	−0.14
	France	1.40
	Sierra Leone	−0.88
	Turkey	0.08
	United States	1.54
Control of corruption	Brazil	−0.12
	Bulgaria	−0.29
	France	1.30
	Sierra Leone	−0.90
	Turkey	0.11
	United States	1.28

Table 4. Control of corruption in six states in 1996, 2003, 2008, 2013

Source: Kaufman et al. (2010) and World Bank (2015).

Country	Year	Governance score (from −2.5 to +2.5)
Brazil	1996	−0.07
	2003	0.10
	2008	−0.02
	2013	−0.12
Bulgaria	1996	−0.78
	2003	−0.07
	2008	−0.30
	2013	−0.29
France	1996	1.26
	2003	1.34
	2008	1.38
	2013	1.30
Sierra Leone	1996	−0.77
	2003	−0.91
	2008	−0.96
	2013	−0.90
Turkey	1996	−0.23
	2003	−0.23
	2008	0.08
	2013	0.11
United States	1996	1.57
	2003	1.77
	2008	1.41
	2013	1.28

ETHNIC ENTREPRENEURS UNMASKED 69

Figure 4. Comparison between six states in 2013, based on WGI (Graph View)

Source: Kaufman et al. (2010) and World Bank (2015).

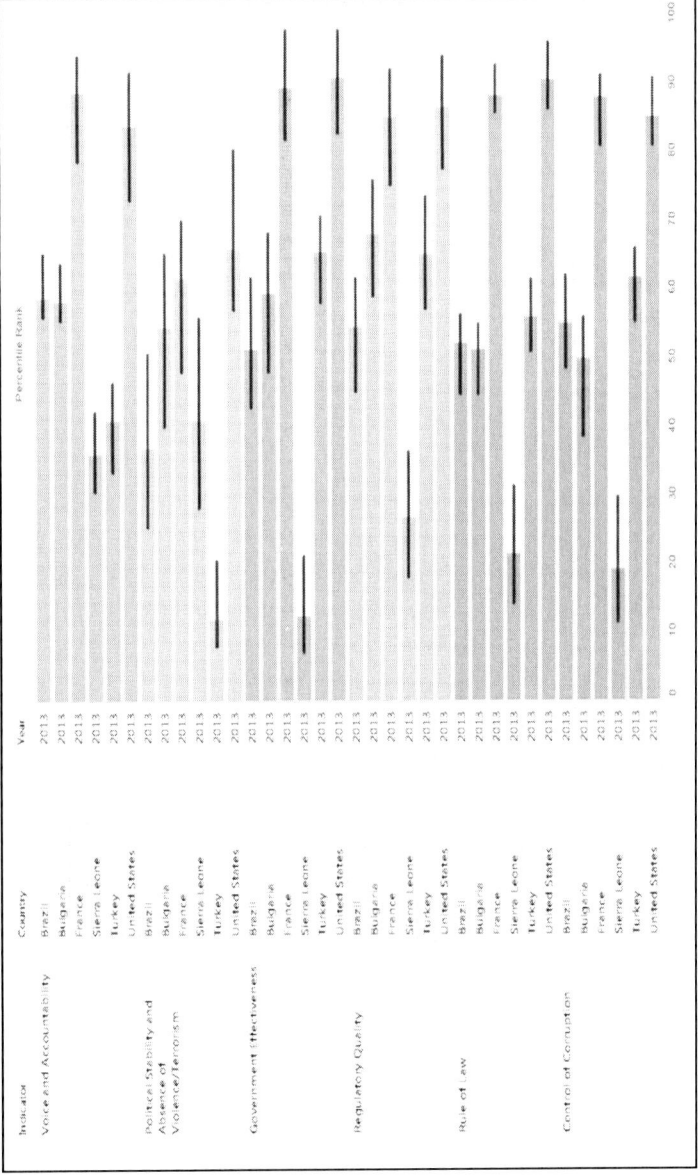

Table 4 allows us to monitor how the "control of corruption" in the six states in question changed between 1996, 2003, 2008, and 2013. *The analysis shows that the state capacity regarding this indicator actually worsened in Bulgaria between 2003 when it was −0.07 and 2013 when it was −0.29.* In comparison, this indicator points to a positive development in Turkey, where corruption was in fact reduced between 2003 (−0.23) and 2013 (0.11). The data from Transparency International's CPI for 2014 and 2015 provide a further, deeper insight into this problem. A country or territory's score in the CPI indicates the perceived level of public sector corruption on a scale of 0 (highly corrupt) to 100 (very clean). In 2014, Bulgaria had the same score (43) as Greece, Italy, and Romania (Transparency International 2015).[106] These are the EU member states that are most affected by corruption (in comparison the cleanest EU countries are Denmark, which has a score of 92, and Finland — 89). Bulgaria's score for 2015 is 41; it is lower than 2014 (Transparency International 2016). According to the CPI, our neighbors to the north and south have achieved better results. Romania and Greece share the 58th place in the ranking of Transparency International with a score of 43, while Bulgaria appears to be firmly anchored to the bottom in the EU according to this criterion and occupies the unenviable 69th position in the ranking (ibid.). Long before Bulgaria are not only other European countries but also countries like Bhutan (with a rank of 27), Rwanda (44), and Namibia (45).[107] The systematic manifestation of political corruption in Bulgaria has led to constant allegations of state capture against several governments of the country, the cabinet of Plamen Oresharski (2013–14), in particular.[108]

From the viewpoint of political and economic neoliberalism, the first quadrant in Figure 3 is the most favorable position. It is characterized by strong institutions and limited scope (Fukuyama 2004a). Another is the logic of the "more leftist" (in comparison)

---

106 There is a slight improvement in relation to 2013 when the country had a score of 41; the only other EU state that had a lower score was Greece — 40. See Transparency International (2015).
107 See Transparency International (2016).
108 See Section 2.1.2.

thinking which claims that the optimal positioning is somewhere in the second quadrant, where thrive countries such as France. They also have robust institutional capacity, but, as we saw, sport wider functions. On the basis of the analysis of scope and capacity, I have positioned Bulgaria in the fourth quadrant of Figure 3. This "location" is a result of the history of the transition to democracy in Bulgaria which bares similarities to the route that other countries, which belonged to the former Communist bloc, took. The transition proved that institutional capacity and scope *are interconnected*. Following the liberal imperatives of the "Washington Consensus," the countries that used to be behind the Iron Curtain strived after its demolition to minimize the scope of state functions through accelerated privatization. In many of them—including Bulgaria—however, the reduction of scope was entrusted to weak institutions. Privatization requires high state capacity. The plundering of public resources by the oligarchs in Russia, for example, greatly contributed to the delegitimization of the postcommunist Russian state (Fukuyama 2004a: 28). This was also the fate of Bulgaria.

Capacity is the more important condition for economic prosperity than the scope of state functions (ibid.: 28). Of course the role of the former must not be exaggerated or seen as a *panacea* for all governance problems. The totalitarian polities usually have the strongest institutions. Both scope and certain aspects of capacity were reduced in Bulgaria after the democratic transformation in comparison to the regime that ceased to exist in 1989. The reduction of scope was a conscious choice and stemmed from economic liberalization. As far as institutional strength is concerned, the hyperefficiency of the totalitarian machine came at the expense of neglect for the main principles of democratic constitutionalism and human rights. Democratic governments should not aspire to the tyrannical perfectionism of the totalitarian state. The reduced scope of the latter was a victory for individual freedom—a welcome positive change. Unfortunately, symptomatic for the weakened capacity of Bulgarian state continues to be the disregard of the principle of rule of law, manifested in untouchable figures of the "gray economy," nepotism (which affects not only the local government but also the higher echelons of the state administration), metastases of corruption, and the ominous signs that point to the existence of institutional racism.[109]

How do the insights from analysis of "strength" and "scope" relate to ethnic conflicts in Bulgaria? First, the claim that the ethnic model today depends primarily on the legitimacy of institutions, while in the totalitarian period (1945-1989) it relied on the strength of the state, is inaccurate. In both cases the institutional capacity, in the strict sense of the word — understood as the ability to maintain public order and enforce laws, is of paramount importance. Of course, the coercive power of the totalitarian apparatus was illegitimate in the eyes of the oppressed. *In procedural plan, the legitimacy of the contemporary model and the authority of the institutions stem from society's consensus regarding the necessity of principles of liberal democracy.* These principles are the fundament of Bulgarian Constitution from 1991, and, in particular, the antidiscrimination legislation. The latter, although not without problems, allows and encourages the inclusion of minorities and is a means to resolve ethnic conflicts. The existence of this progressive legislative framework *will become meaningless if the state "abdicates" from its role to implement and enforce laws, to punish criminals, and to exercise prevention.*

Second, as a "quadrant four country," Bulgaria is challenged by the tension created by weak institutional capacity and wide scope of state functions. Simply put, this means that the state has undertaken too many tasks *although it does not possess enough capacity to implement them*. This explains, for example, why the measures for positive discrimination, the beneficiaries of which are the Roma communities, are met with resignation by many ethnic Bulgarians. The "anemia" of state institutions hinders economic development. The continuing low confidence in the political system (in June 2015, only 10% of the interviewed gave a positive evaluation of the work of the parliament[110]) and the recession (a few facts: the unemployment reached 13.8% in the first quarter of 2013; the average monthly salary remains one of the lowest in the EU — approximately EUR

---

109 See Part 3.
110 See Alpha Research (2015a).

478[111] in December 2015; more than a fifth of the labor force are employed on a minimum wage of €1 per hour[112]) are favorable incubation environment for intensification of ethnic entrepreneurs who label minorities as "parasites" dependent on state welfare. The weakness of government institutions and the inefficiency of political intermediaries (political parties) place a *stigma on the Bulgarian ethnic model*. As we shall see in the next sections of this work, the ethnic entrepreneurs point to the generic connections of this model to the diseases of the political system. Given that even the optimistic forecasts do not envisage a significant, positive change in the economic situation in the short term, the tardy implementation of the emergency reforms in the political system, in particular in the judiciary, carries a high risk of further increase of interethnic tensions.

---

111 See NSI (2015).
112 Eurostat (2012).

2. The Role of Political Parties

The analysis of the function of political parties in channeling, resolution, or instigation of ethnic conflicts must account for their surroundings and natural "habitat." In other words, it cannot be surgically severed from the place of these institutions in the political system and processes.[113] Here I examine the aspects of political behavior, interaction, and rivalries between main political forces in Bulgaria in the last 27 years, which are a manifestation of inter-ethnic relations and/or attempt to influence them. The MRF deserves special attention. Since its establishment in 1990, the MRF has acquired and continues to hold a unique monopoly in the political system. It is the leading,[114] in terms of the marginality of its competitors, political force that claims to represent the demands and interests of minority ethnic communities. Due to the overwhelming support it receives from the latter and the idiosyncrasies of the party leadership, the MRF continues to be a magnet for incessant attacks by the PRR. To avoid (or disprove) the thesis that it relies on (the ethnic) encapsulation of its supporters, the MRF has long declared its ambition to protect the rights and legitimate interests of all Bulgarian citizens. Self-described as a flexible centrist formation, in different periods of its history, which encompasses almost three decades, the movement shifted between "collaborations" with center-right and center-left parties several times and (often) played contradictory roles. Last but not least, it is important to see, through the means of concrete examples, the specific interconnection between, on the one hand, the status of Roma — the most marginalized of the large ethnic minorities, and politics and crime, on the other.

In the view of the above, this part of the work embarks on several tasks. First, in order to describe the place which the ethnic

---

[113] For the role of political institutions in the political process, see Karasimeonov (1997, 2000) and Rhodes et al. (2008).
[114] Although recently, in 2017, DOST started to successfully challenge this hegemony, in particular, regarding the Turkish votes from "abroad."

model has in Bulgarian politics, I examine the genesis and transformation of the postcommunist party systems and the interacting participants. Next, I explore the electoral support, ideology, and decision-making procedures in the main ethnic party in the country — the MRF. The following chapter is dedicated to the PRR, the "sworn enemy" of the ethnic formations. Then, in the last chapter in this part, I tackle the problem of "Roma crime." The latter has been constantly in the focus of the "crusade" led by parties like Ataka, NFSB, and IMRO. The case studies provide an in-depth view of the way ethnicity and politics are intertwined in Bulgaria. They capture some of the key strategies and tactics employed by political actors.

2.1 The contemporary party systems in Bulgaria

2.1.1 Bipolarity (1990–2001)

There are two party systems that have emerged in Bulgaria after the beginning of the democratic changes. *The first one is the bipolar model; the second is characterized by polycentrism, populism, and nativism.* The totalitarian regime in Bulgaria (1946–1989) has been characterized by ideological monism and façade pluralism in which organizations such as the Bulgarian Agrarian People's Union[115] (BAPU) and the Fatherland Front[116] were instrumental. The façade masked the dominance of the Communist Party. As already stated, the policies toward ethnic minorities were extremely inconsistent (Todorov 2010: 273-75, Baeva 2011: 78-9). The "dismantling" of *l'ancien régime* proceeded through *three distinct stages* (Karasimeonov 2010: 30-40). During the *first stage* (November 10, 1989–January 13, 1991) began an urgent replacement of the members of the apparatus who were still faithful to Todor Zhivkov. The main organization of the anticommunist opposition — the United Democratic Forces (UDF) was

---

115 Bulgarian — Български земеделски народен съюз, БЗНС.
116 Bulgarian — Отечествен фронт, ОФ.

established on December 7, 1989, de facto in violation of the Constitution of 1971. *The contemporary ethnic model* was born on December 29, 1989, when a plenum of the Communist Party (which on April 3, 1990, was renamed to Bulgarian Socialist Party) embraced the principle of ethnic pluralism.[117] On January 4, 1990, was created the "representative" of the ethnic minorities—the MRF.

The meetings of the Round Table (January 3–May 15, 1990) have been a key element of *the second stage* (January 18–June 10, 1990). Regardless of contradictory opinions on it, the forum helped to legitimize and raise the prestige of the opposition and, above all, made possible the peaceful transition to democracy (Engström 2009, 2014). The legal restrictions on pluralism, which were enshrined in Art. 1, Paragraph 2 of the Constitution of 1971,[118] were abrogated; the primary party organizations were dismantled; all political activity in institutions such as the army, police, security services, courts, and prosecution was prohibited. After heated discussions, protests, and rallies (mainly against the unwillingness of the BSP to consistently implement the changes), a consensus was reached on the necessity to conform to fundamental liberal principles—political pluralism, personal freedom, popular sovereignty, rule of law, and separation of powers. During *the third stage* (May 1990–July 12, 1991), these principles were embodied in the work of the Grand National Assembly and, above all, the Constitution of July 13, 1991. The elections for Grand National Assembly, which included for the first time representatives of the MRF, launched the formation of legitimate, democratic institutions.

The existence of ethnic pluralism is *impossible without the precondition of political pluralism*. The national project that united most of the political elite at the beginning of transition from communism

---

117 Regarding the model, see Krasteva (1998, 1999), Kertikov (2003), Dronzina (2004), Mitev (2005), Pamporov (2008), Todorov (2005, 2010), Mizov (2010), Mirchev (2011), and Cholakov (2013a, 2013b, 2013c).

118 This infamous article proclaimed and defended "the leadership" of the Communist Party and de facto severely limited any opportunities for emergence or existence of other parties and organizations.

to democracy had three pillars or imperatives: to build a functioning democratic political system and market economy; to integrate the country with the West,[119] while embracing its values (by becoming, for example, a member of the European Community (EC)/EU and North Atlantic Treaty Organization (NATO)); and, last but certainly not least, to maintain the ethnic peace. These pillars have been christened "the sacred cows" of transition while the opposition to or the encroachments on them have been dubbed as sui generis "taboos" (Raichev and Stoichev 2008, Smilov 2008, Karasimeonov 2010). The imperatives determined the nature of politics in *the first* (1989-2001) and the beginning of *the second party systems* (until 2005) that consecutively operated in Bulgaria.

In its election "debut" — the Seventh Grand National Assembly elections — the MRF received 23 members of parliament (MPs) and thus became the third political force.[120] The election outcomes showed the serious bid of the movement to participate in Bulgarian politics on par with the bigger players. However, the attitudes of ethnic Bulgarians to the Turkish minority were, and remain, contradictory. The consequences of the "Revival Process" (1984-89) were still palpable. An immediate result from the "Process" was the significant growth of the politicization of Bulgarian Turks. Many of them changed their stance toward the state. The Bulgarian society became divided on the scope and nature of individual and collective rights that were to be granted to minorities (Todorov 2010: 278). On the one hand, in November 1990, the authorities recognized the right of Turks to restore their names. The right to study their mother tongue in public schools was also guaranteed in the newly adopted Constitution. On the other hand, the restoration of names was met with disapproval from parts of Bulgarian society. The negative reactions catalyzed the emergence of nationalist organizations such

---

119 Here, again, I use this term in the sense of Samuel Huntington — as the "Western civilization," its values, and achievements, see Huntington (2011).
120 After BSP and UDF which received, respectively, 211 and 144 seats in the Grand National Assembly, which consisted of 400 MPs.

as the Nationwide Committee for the Protection of National Interests,[121] the Rhodope Union "Patriotism," and the Patriotic Labor Party.

A number of politicians from the Socialist Party pointed out that the registration of MRF, in its essence, an ethnic party, was a direct breach of the Political Parties Act (Art. 3) and the Constitution (Art. 11, Para. 4; Art. 13, Para. 4). On October 8, 1991, ninety-three MPs made a referral to the Constitutional Court regarding this issue. The judgment from April 21, 1992, dismissed the request MRF to be declared unconstitutional. However, the judgment was upheld in the Court by the very narrow majority of only one vote. The movement was registered as a political party in 1994. It has to be noted that in the main representative of the anticommunist opposition, the UDF, unlike the BSP, dominated a positive attitude toward MRF during this period. The anticommunism, which the two formations held as their creed, made them, at first glance, natural allies. The movement joined the demands of the staunch anticommunists in UDF and its representatives in the Grand National Assembly who refused to put their signatures under the new Constitution.

The elections for the 36th National Assembly (October 13, 1991) confirmed the status of MRF as the third largest force in the political system (it obtained 24 seats). The decision of the Constitutional Court helped to legitimize the movement. The election results showed that it managed to increase its electorate in relative and absolute terms—from 6.02% to 7.55%. The elections were won "by a small margin but forever" (according to the popular dictum by UDF's MP Aleksandar Yordanov) by the UDF, while the socialists (in coalition with nine parties) remained second. The minimal difference between the two political giants (34.36% for the UDF against 33.14% against BSP and its coalition partners) created favorable conditions for the MRF. The latter was able to take the advantageous role of a "counterweight" in the political process, which had a substantial impact on the composition of the executive. It is

---

121 NCPNI, Bulgarian—ОКЗНИ.

important as well to highlight the failure of the ambitions of a number of political forces[122] to occupy the political center in this period.

The elections outlined the shape of the emerging postcommunist party system. This *highly confrontational bipolar model* included a third key player (MRF), which, *a prima vista*, sided with the anticommunist right. The system was characterized by instability and fluidity. In 1991 the movement supported the UDF in its pledge to ban the socialist party. UDF's leader at the time — Zhelyu Zhelev, who won the race for the presidency of Bulgaria in January 1992 — received the decisive support of MRF's voters in the election. MRF's MPs helped to overcome a motion of no confidence initiated by the left on July 24, 1992. However, in conditions of declining support in society, to which contributed the "friendly fire" by President Zhelev and the negative campaign in the media (especially in the newspaper *Trud*) against the cabinet, several months later, on October 28, 1992, the first government of the UDF with Prime Minister Filip Dimitrov fell from power, losing a vote of confidence, when MRF withdrew its support. The new cabinet of Lyuben Berov,[123] composed with the help of the mandate of the MRF, governed the country until the early parliamentary elections on December 18, 1994.

The predominantly ethnic-based party support and the trauma of "Revival Process" notwithstanding, the leaders of MRF have managed to a large extent to refute the fears that the movement will have separatist ambitions. Striving to play down the ethnic character of the party, they invested in building an image of centrist liberal formation which "hospitably" opens its ranks and lists for members of the dominant ethnic group (i.e., the Bulgarians). This process was related to the intention of the movement to distance itself from the UDF. In March 1993, the MRF along with

---

122 Some of the "contenders" such as the UDF Center (Bulgarian — СДС Център), in which the main parties were Bulgarian Social Democratic Party (BSDP) (БСДП), BAPU-United (БЗНС Единен), and BAPU "Nikola Petkov" (БЗНС "Никола Петков"), were very close to overcome the electoral threshold of 4%.
123 The support of the MRF for this government led to the "cooling" of the partnership between MRF and UDF.

Bulgarian Social Democratic Party (BSDP), Alternative Socialist Party (ASP), the Green Party, and other formations initiated the establishment of a council for cooperation of the parties and movements from the political center. Therefore, the MRF has already begun "joint action" with center-left parties in this period.

Following the elections for the 37th National Assembly (December 18, 1994), the MRF was again represented in the parliament, but lost about 80,000 votes (mainly due to the emigration of part of the supporters of the movement to Turkey).[124] The number of its seats in the legislature was reduced from 24 to 15. Thus the MRF could no longer perform its strategic "role of counterweight" in politics. It entered into the coalition of the right United Democratic Forces (ODS),[125] which was formed in August 1996. However, the MRF did not adopt the conditions proposed by the ODS for a new election agreement and left the coalition in February 1997. The ODS was victorious on the early elections that took place on April 17, 1997.[126] The MRF was part of the coalition Union for National Salvation (UNS),[127] which received 7.6% of the votes and 19 seats in the National Assembly. In November 1997, UNS left the "reformist majority" and joined the opposition to the ODS government led by the Prime Minister Ivan Kostov.

The attempts of ODS to break the monopoly of MRF on the votes of Bulgarian Turks after 1998 inspired the creation of a new

---

124 The movement became the fourth largest party in the National Assembly after BSP, UDF, and People's Union (Bulgarian Agrarian People's Union and the Democratic Party).

125 Bulgarian—ОДС, Обединени Демократични Сили. Here and below, I use the abbreviation ODS (instead of UDF) in order to avoid disambiguation with UDF (СДС). ODS was directed against the ruling BSP and, at this initial stage, consisted of UDF, MRF, and People's Union.

126 UDF obtained 52.26% of the votes cast (137 seats) and became the largest political formation in the parliament. The BSP, which was experiencing a deep internal crisis and a sharp drop in confidence of voters, received its worst result since 1989—22.07% (58 seats).

127 Bulgarian—ОНС, Обединение за национално спасение. The UNS included as well the party of Democratic Center, led by Ventsislav Dimitrov; the Green Party, the party "New Choice" of Dimitar Ludjev; and the Federation "Tsardom of Bulgaria" of Hristo Kourtev.

political force, loyal to UDF. These attempts led to a rift between the leaderships of MRF and UDF (ODS) and deepened the confrontation between them. It should be emphasized that the vast majority of MPs in the parliamentary group of the UNS were from the MRF. They dominated and determined to a great extent the political behavior of the group. Therefore, after the parliamentary elections in 1997 the political situation changed. Bulgarian party system partially lost its bipolar character because of the emergence of new political entities, primarily UNS and BEL,[128] which gravitated toward the center.

2.1.2 Polycentrism, populism, and nativism (2001 until present)

The transition between the two party systems that existed successively after 1989 did not happen overnight. It was neither harsh and brutal nor sudden. Gradual changes, which often remained undetected, transformed the political landscape. In the late 1990s, the mass ideological parties — the BSP and UDF — began to evolve into catch-all players. With their messages they tried to appeal to all layers of Bulgarian society. The process was intensified by the NMSP,[129] which managed to blur the perceptions of "left" and "right" in Bulgarian politics. The parliamentary elections on June 17, 2001, were the first since 1989, which took place after the regular, four-year term of the National Assembly. The unexpected "entrance" of the NMSP, hastily formed by Simeon Sakskoburggotski, marked the end of the first postcommunist party system.

There are several factors that have contributed to the electoral triumph of NMSP and the destruction of the bipolar model[130]: first, the disappointment and loss of legitimacy of the BSP and UDF, demonstrated by the fact that about half of the voters did not participate in the elections; second, the unpopularity of the reforms undertaken by the ODS was aggravated by signals that corruption and clientelism were deeply planted in public administration; third, the

---

128 The Bulgarian European Left (Bulgarian — БЕЛ, Българска Евролевица) was a social democratic political party established in 1997.
129 Bulgarian — НДСВ.
130 For the end of the bipolar model, see as well Avramov et al. (2009).

personality of Simeon Sakskoburggotski, in whom many saw a politician-messiah (a "tsar" in exile), who was untainted by "the sins of the transition"; fourth, the program and the messages of NMSP that not only emphasized the need of dialogue and consensus (in contrast to the political model which was driven by fierce conflicts) but also cleverly combined liberal and populist proposals for social reforms, which were aimed at all social groups (promises for faster economic growth, social justice, eradication of corruption, integration into the EU, and NATO). In the elections for the 38th National Assembly, NMSP obtained more seats (120) than the UDF (51) and BSP (48) combined. The MRF along with the Liberal Union Euroroma received 7.4% of the votes.[131] The vanquishing "platform" of NMSP quickly stimulated the growth of parties-copycats which were eager to follow in its footsteps. Their *trademark* was the refusal of clear program orientation. Since the beginning of the new millennium, political competition has become less and less about ideas and more about the personal qualities of politicians who willingly submerge into various operatic populist roles like that of the "steadfast indicter" of the corrupt elite (Smilov 2008: 39).

Since no party had obtained an absolute majority in the legislature, *the MRF was able once again to place its hand on the "steering wheel."* For the first time in its political biography, as a coalition partner of the NMSP, the MRF had two ministers in the executive branch. This fact reveals another important feature of the second party system in Bulgaria in existence since 2001 — *the change of the formula of governance from one party to coalition cabinets*. The functionaries of NMSP, for the most part, lacked sufficient political experience. The nature of this untypical for Bulgaria electoral formation,[132] which did not possess sturdy party structures (or those were in its embryonic form in 2001–2002), inevitably strengthened the influence of the other parliamentary-represented parties that backed up the government. The cabinet obtained the open support

---

131 Altogether, the coalition, which was fourth in the race, obtained 21 mandates.
132 The movement was transformed into a party in June 2002.

of the MRF and the tacit of the BSP.[133] The tendency to cartelization of the party system which emerged at the time continues to this day (Smilov 2008). Instead of real competition, parties often prefer to act on the basis of "arrangements" that allow them to share the "benefits" or rather the "spoils" of governance.[134]

The partnership between the NMSP and MRF was also significant in the domain of foreign policy. After an unsuccessful attempt to join the European People's Party (EPP),[135] NMSP turned to the Liberal International. The political project of Simeon Sakskoburggotski was accepted in the European Liberal Democrat and Reform Party[136] *with the support of the MRF which was already a member of this formation*. The NMSP embraced liberalism as the party's ideology and recognized MRF as its leading political partner. The MRF was conducive to the international legitimization of NMSP, remained a major political factor that ensured the parliamentary majority behind the government, and actively participated in the executive. The partnership between the two formations, despite a number of conflicts, was maintained during the four-year term of the cabinet. It became an alternative to the bipolar model.

The MRF has been on the political stage since 1990, but its participation in the cabinet "Sakskoburggotski" *helped for its final integration within the political system*. The party received opportunities to expand its presence in the public administration. It also gained access to additional power resources for the realization of the interests of its political elite and electorate. Through these new positions MRF managed to increase its influence in the local government. For

---

133 Two ministers in government were associated with BSP—Kostadin Paskalev (Deputy Prime Minister and Minister of Regional Development) and Dimitar Kalchev (Minister of Public Administration).
134 As noted by Smilov, the complete formula of the political cartel in 2008 was "8: 5: 3: 0.5: 0.1: 0.01." The parties not included in the ruling coalition (as DSB, UDF, Ataka, etc.) also received part of the profits from the governance and had their albeit tiny quotas in resource allocation, see Smilov (2008: 39).
135 The UDF effectively blocked the candidature of NMSP for membership in the EPP.
136 The Group of the European Liberal Democrat and Reform Party was a liberal political group in the European Parliament between 1994 and 2004.

example, the movement showed an impressive result in the local elections in 2003. It received 13.6% of the votes cast, had 695 elected councilors, and won numerous mayors in ethnically mixed areas, including Kardzhali. In terms of personnel policy, MRF has continued its efforts to expand its influence beyond the Turkish population. Ethnic Bulgarians are welcomed as party members. They are offered positions at all levels of the party machine as well as in the public administration. In terms of MRF's coalition policy, it should be pointed out that it was the initiator of the failed initiative to create a liberal alliance with NMSP and the New Time in order to allow these three formations to campaign and participate together in the 2005 elections.

The parliamentary elections, which took place on June 25, 2005, confirm the standpoint that the Bulgarian political and party system was undergoing a process of profound transformation. The latter had several dimensions (Karasimeonov 2010: 147–150). First, there was a clear trend toward fragmentation rather than domination of a hegemonic party. Second, the crisis of legitimacy of the system as a whole and of the individual parties was continuing and getting even deeper. About 45% of the voters did not participate in the elections; 8% of the poll were in support to Ataka—a formation with antiparty rhetoric, which pledged to change the political status quo; another 8% were "scattered" because they went to parties that failed to pass the 4% electoral threshold (a fact that indicated the existence of significant opportunities ahead of the newcomers who would attempt to mobilize the protest vote). Third, a PRR party entered, for the first time in recent history, the BNA. Ataka, led by Volen Siderov, mobilized the "losers" of the transition—the one who were or felt marginalized, and sharply criticized corruption and nepotism among the political elite.[137] Fourth, the changes in the party system affected the entire political spectrum. The elections exacerbated the conflicts between the remains of the disunited and weakened Bulgarian right (DSB, UDF, UFD,[138] etc.). Its anemia

---

137 For the idiosyncrasies of Bulgarian PRR, see Section 2.3.
138 DSB—ДСБ, Демократи за силна България, UFD—ССД, Съюз на свободните демократи.

opened a significant "free" niche for the emergence of new political actors in the right side of the political spectrum (e.g., GERB arose on this basis in 2006) and, to some extent, contributed to the preservation of NMSP. Although the electoral support for the party led by Mr. Sakskoburggotski was greatly reduced, the outcome of the election still guaranteed a place of the formation in the new "Triple coalition."[139] The BSP, which embraced the ideas of social democracy, returned to power after eight long years of isolation and dominated the left.

Three key features distinguish Ataka from other political formations, which, at the time, attempted to win the protest and nationalistic vote. Breaking the unwritten taboos, first, Ataka started an "offensive" against the relative ethnic peace, established in the country, through aggressive messages that targeted minority ethnic communities such as those of the Turks and Roma. Second, the party fiercely opposed the geopolitical orientation of Bulgaria to the EU and NATO. Last, but not least, the party led by Mr. Siderov was a pioneer in the exploitation of the new for the Bulgarian politics, but manifested in many European countries, political cleavage Europeanism/Euroskeptic nationalism. The birth of this "fault line" is hardly surprising. Later other political "actors" tried to reap dividends from its operation.

Of greatest importance, in view of this analysis, are the changes in the MRF, which in 2005 achieved its highest election result since it was established in 1990. The reasons for this are several: first, the mobilization of ethnic votes, including the immigrants in Turkey; second, the strategic inclusion of Bulgarians in the electoral lists of the party; third, the low voter turnout, which generally works in favor of political parties that can rely heavily on the loyalty of the electorate. The anti-Turkish statements of Ataka and, perhaps the criticisms of the leadership of the MRF by DSB and IMRO,[140] also contributed for the mobilization of the supporters of the MRF. *Although the movement was a coalition partner that actively*

---

139 The name "Triple coalition" was coined by the media and it stuck.
140 IMRO – BMPO.

participated in the office of Mr. Sakskoburggotski (2001–2005) and later within the "Stanishev" cabinet (2005–2009), in view of the public opinion at the time, it was burdened with only some of the negatives from the operation of these governments. The acute assessments made by Bulgaria's international partners, such as these which were published in the "Annual Reports of the European Commission," accelerated the discredit of the "Triple coalition." Furthermore, the ethnic entrepreneurs who did not hesitate to play the "anti-Turkish card" were facilitated by the numerous signals in the media that some of MRF's top officials were involved in corruption scandals.[141] Nevertheless, the result of the MRF in the parliamentary elections in 2009 was, in fact, higher than in 2005, and reached a new peak (see Figure 5). The movement received 38 mandates, or four more than 2005. Therefore, "miraculously," the criticisms against MRF have affected the party *much less* in comparison to the devastating impact which they had on BSP and NMSP. In any case, the campaign against the ethnic party *was unable to halt its strong performance in the elections.*

Figure 5. Votes for the MRF in the elections for BNA, 1991–2014

Source: Own work, based on data from CEC, www.cik.bg.

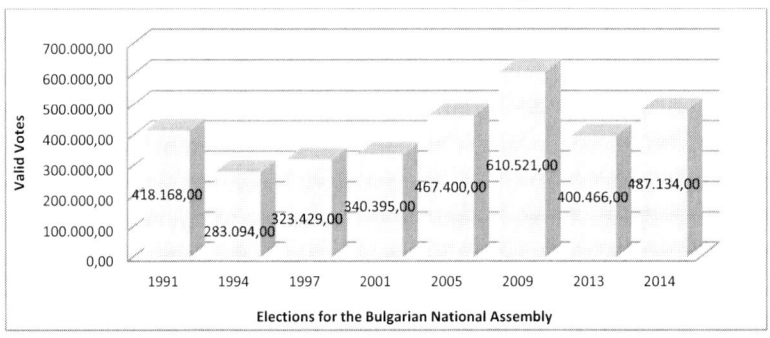

Corruption and clientelism in Bulgaria, which have inflicted heavy damages on the intermediary institutions — the political parties — have caused their inability to effectively express the interests that

---

141 See "Dogan: 'we have a circle of companies' 2005"; "Ahmed Dogan: 'I allocate funding in the state' 2009."

originate in civil society. The hope that this vicious model could be dismantled propelled GERB to power. The party received 39.71% of the votes cast (115 seats) in the general elections in 2009. The nationalist rhetoric was a prominent feature in the messages of the right-wing parties in the 41st National Assembly. Both GERB and OLJ[142] (a party, that initially supported the cabinet, then went into opposition) relied on the use of moderate nationalism and populism in the race. The leaders of these parties, as well as of the Blue Coalition, subjected to sharp criticism the cabinet of Sergei Stanishev and, in particular, the actions of Ahmed Dogan. Unlike GERB, DSB, UDF, and OLJ which, more or less, dispute and challenge mainly the "political management" of the MRF, the PRR, represented by Ataka, has repeatedly insisted on the necessity "to ban the Turkish Party." Purposefully or not, the PRR has boosted ethnic tensions and conflicts. The latter has rapidly increased in recent years. The events in front of the mosque Banya Bashi in Sofia and in the village of Katunitsa (the region of Plovdiv) in 2011 clearly show this. The murder of 19-year-old ethnic Bulgarian Angel Petrov in Katunitsa, deliberately run over by a van driven by a Bulgarian Roma man, unleashed the biggest anti-Roma demonstrations in the history of Bulgaria after 1989.[143]

The results of parliamentary elections in 2009 *demonstrate the collapse of political center*. The NMSP played the role of center-right party and the MRF of center-left formation. The idea of building a liberal alliance between the two was not realized into practice. At first glance, the BSP and MRF were the "logical opposition" of the new "Borisov" cabinet. In fact, there were symptoms that indicated that the processes of cartelization of political system had continued. For example, allegedly Delyan Peevski, an MP from the MRF and former member of the NMSP, as well as a deputy minister of state policy for disasters and accidents during Mr. Stanishev's office have provided a media "comfort" for the cabinet of Boyko Borisov.

---

142 OLJ (Order, Legality, and Justice) — РЗС (Ред, законност и справедливост) — is a Bulgarian political party led by Mr. Yane Yanev.
143 See Section 3.3.3.

Subsequently, newspapers, which are believed to be under the control of Mr. Peevski, began an "offensive" against the government of GERB (Roth 2013).

Initially, the protests, which began at the end of January 2013, voiced predominantly social demands (mainly directed against the energy distribution companies and monopolies in general). However, these were quickly transformed into acts of civil disobedience against the government.[144] The cabinet resigned on February 19 after violent clashes between protesters and police, and the public suicides of several Bulgarians that shocked the whole society. Those, who took their own lives, like the alpinist and photographer Plamen Goranov, named Varna's Jan Palach,[145] declared that they strongly oppose the policies of government and the local authorities (Spasov 2013). Many of the deceased were living in desperate, poor conditions. In a nutshell, GERB was under the fierce scrutiny of both left and right. The critics of the government pointed to the controversial appointments and personnel policy of the ruling party, as well as to the "attempts to interfere in the judicial system" (BHC 2013). According to Evgenii Dainov, the "regime" of GERB is not political in the sense of Aristotle; in fact, this regime entirely abandoned the principles of the civilized polity (Dainov 2013: 24). The Office of Borisov is based "on pure demonstration of force" and thus bares striking similarities to the "rule of barbarians" (ibid.: 24). During the term of Stanishev there have been signs of the "Putinization" of the political system, i.e., the government severely "deformed" the operation of democratic institutions and mechanisms but, nonetheless, preserved them (ibid.). "The rule of GERB," however, launched an attack at these very institutions; it tried to destroy them by replacing them with interpersonal agreements and shady schemes (Dainov 2013: 26).

The month before the early parliamentary elections was saturated with political scandals. The elections were held on May 12,

---

144 „The protests start to turn into a civil disobedience" (2013).
145 See Dainov (2013) and Spasov (2013).

2013, at a record low for the country turnout — 51.33% (Central Commission on Elections 2013). GERB remained the leading political force; however, its electoral support was seriously reduced (the party lost 20 seats compared with the 2009 elections). At the same time, the left enjoyed an electoral upsurge (the number of BSP's MPs increased more than twice — from 40 to 84). The MRF got one seat less. The elections, as a whole, showed the rise of nationalist formations. Ataka had two more mandates, in comparison to the way it was represented in the 41st National Assembly, and the NFSB led by Valeri Simeonov received 3.70% (131,169 votes). It was the party that came closest to pass the electoral threshold and was ahead of MBC,[146] UDF, DSB, and OLJ. The new government with Prime Minister Mr. Plamen Oresharski was elected by the parliament on May 29, 2013, with the mandate of Coalition for Bulgaria (in which the main party was the BSP). The government received the official support not only of the MRF but also, de facto, of Ataka. *The nationalist formation was criticized for becoming a pillar of a cabinet, in which was represented its main political opponent (the MRF).* That, of course, did not mean that there were no conflicts between the governing formations. Following the proposal of the Prime Minister Oresharski, on June 14, 2013, the parliament elected the media mogul Delyan Peevski as head of the State Agency for National Security.[147] Almost immediately in Sofia and elsewhere thousands went into the streets to protest against the appointment. In some cities like Plovdiv and Blagoevgrad, the protests were also against the governors of the regions, who were appointed with the support of MRF.[148]

In November 2013, BSP and MRF conducted their first "historic" joint rally in Sofia. The aim was to demonstrate their support for the cabinet and the solidarity between the ruling partners amid

---

[146] Movement Bulgaria of the Citizens (ДБГ — Движение България на Гражданите) led by the former EU Commissioner Meglena Kuneva.
[147] Bulgarian — ДАНС.
[148] Regarding the protests see, e.g., Smilov and Vaysova (2013).

student protests and "record" low trust in the institutions.[149] Overall, 2013 was a political success for MRF. The movement was once again part of the executive. Despite the fact that Delyan Peevski was an MP from the ranks of MRF and amid new reports, describing cases of corruption of top party functionaries (this time provoked by the ongoing investigation against Mr. Hristo Bisserov for money laundering[150]), *the main negatives of the operation of the cabinet were accumulated by BSP and Ataka* (Alpha Research 2014). Study of Gallup International, carried out between January 31 and February 10, 2014, did show that the level of political support for MRF remained stable—6.7% had stated that they would vote for the party in the elections for European Parliament (EP) in May. The revival of the movement ABR,[151] a political project of the former President Parvanov, further afflicted "electoral damages" on BSP (Alpha Research 2014). ABR also managed to attract part of the nationalist vote. In the struggle for it was also involved the movement of Nikolay Barekov—"Bulgaria without censorship." Ultimately, the troubled government of Mr. Oresharski resigned on July 2014.

In order to explain the erosion of political support for BSP, we have to mention that, first, in its capacity of a successor of the former communist party, this political formation has been and still is heavily dependent on the votes of those Bulgarians who tend to assess positively the period of socialism. However, BSP has gradually lost its "majority share" over the nostalgia to this past (Popivanov 2015: 187). GERB, BSP's main rightist opponent, draws successfully a chunk of its legitimacy from the (positive) memories of this era. Second, the political behavior of BSP undermined its image of a party of moderate nationalism and Russophilia. On the one hand, the long-term partnership with MRF disillusioned and drove back the nationalistic supporters of the socialists. On the other, although

---

149 In October 2013, less than 20% supported the government; see Alpha Research (2013).
150 Who was at the time Vice-Chair of the Bulgarian National Assembly and of the MRF. On December 21, 2016, Bisserov was acquitted by the Final Court of Appeal.
151 Alternative for Bulgarian Revival (АБВ).

BSP had to team up with Ataka in the 42nd National Assembly, the socialists were forced by domestic and international criticisms to distance themselves away from the party of Volen Siderov (Popivanov 2015: 187–88). It is, in fact, Ataka who opposed the decision of the Triple coalition led by BSP to allow American military bases on Bulgarian territory (a decision that angered Bulgarian Russophiles); it was Ataka who advocated Russia's annexation of Crimea, while the government of Plamen Oresharski took a critical stand on President Putin's policies toward Ukraine (Popivanov 2015: 188).

Most of the parties and coalitions in the 43rd National Assembly, composed after the snap elections in October 2014, have juggled and toyed, albeit in varying degrees, with nationalist rhetoric and slogans. This fact is not the result of chance. In recent years, nationalism is among the most profitable "products" sold in the political market. Radical variants of nationalism are traditional pillar and source of support for the PRR (Ignazi 2003, Mudde 2007). *Overall, this stage of the development of the Bulgarian political system is characterized by a deepening of the crisis of legitimacy of the ethnic model and especially of the role of the MRF.* For these reasons, at least publicly, the movement declared that it will not participate in the government and will, instead, "sit on the bench" after the early elections in October 2014. It would appear that "the categorical imperative" for the right today in Bulgaria reads "all without the MRF." The Prime Minister Borisov did not accept the "gratuitous" parliamentary support of the movement and the PRR, whose representative in the office was NFSB, denounced all "ethnic parties." Despite these "declarations," however, the ethnic party's MPs occasionally voted together with the representatives of BSP and of GERB.

2.2 MRF — electoral support and ideology

Most of the parties that have appeared and "performed" on the Bulgarian political scene during the past 27 years share two main features. First, they place a lot of emphasis on political labels and less on substance (Karasimeonov 2010). Many of them arise on "empty space" and largely define themselves ideologically. Usually, the attempts and aspirations of the new parties to "draw" their pedigree of political entities that existed before the totalitarian period have fable grounds. Second, they are often leadership parties and can be defined, to use anachronistically the apt expression of Max Weber, as "purely personal followings" (Weber 1994: 335). The establishment of party organization usually begins and proceeds in a downward fashion, i.e., from the top of the party pyramid. *This "building technique" almost automatically leads to weak links with civil society and limited internal party democracy, and respectively, to the worsening of the "iron law" of Robert Michels.*[152] *To a large extent, these characteristics outline the essence of main political parties — antagonists in ethnic conflicts since 1989.*

According to Ahmed Dogan, the MRF is the successor of the illegal Turkish National Liberation Movement in Bulgaria (TNLMB[153]), established in Varna in July 1985 (Gocheva 1991). TNLMB was led by Nedzhemetin Haq and Medi Doganov (Ahmed Dogan). The latter, who at that time was an agent of State Security, was the ideologist of the organization. He managed to carry through the concept of nonviolent resistance or "fight without weapons" against the Revival Process, as stated in the program of TNLMB (Gocheva 1991: 20). In 1987, he was arrested along with the alleged organizers of the terrorist act at the Bunovo station (March 9, 1985) and thrown in a cell on death row.

The dissident groups that emerged in the context of Perestroika (such as the Independent Society for Human Rights, the Independent trade union "Podkrepa," "Committee 273," the Club for

---

152 See Michels (2001).
153 Bulgarian — Турско национално-освободително движение в България (ТНОДБ).

Support of Glasnost and Perestroika, and "Ecoglastnost") also opposed the Revival Process. In the second half of 1988, many Turks and Pomaks joined the Independent Society for the Protection of Human Rights. On November 13, 1988, was founded the Democratic League for the Protection of Human Rights in Bulgaria chaired by Mustafa Ömer. The organizations mentioned above were instrumental in the events of May 19–27, 1989 (which consisted of hunger strikes, marches, demonstrations, and rallies in support of Bulgarian Turks). At that time, in northeastern Bulgaria, was the culmination of the struggle of Turkish population in Bulgaria for democracy and human rights. Various documents (e.g., Angelov 2010) cast doubt on the exact role of Ahmed Dogan in these events, which considerably undermined the public support for the communist regime and delegitimized it. After the political changes in 1989, Dogan was the founder of MRF and its chairperson, since its inception, for 24 years (1990–2013). *This mere fact, along with, as we shall see, the party's constitution clearly shows its highly hierarchical, leadership character.*

On January 19, 2013, at the eighth National Conference of MRF in Sofia, hours after 25-year-old Oktai Enimehmedov attempted to shoot him in the head with a gas pistol, Dogan gave up the leadership and offered the Chair to his deputy Lyutvi Mestan. However, after these events, Dogan remained honorary chairman of the party. In December 2015 in an address to senior functionaries of MRF, he sharply criticized the policy led by his successor Mestan and particularly his comments on the incident with the Russian Sukhoi Su-24M attack aircraft.[154] In his remarks, Mestan defended the actions of the Turkish army in the incident. He, unlike Dogan, who was never well received in Turkey had and continued to maintain close ties with the regime of Recep Tayyip Erdogan. As an immediate result of Dogan's speech, Mestan was promptly removed and ostracized from the MRF. Subsequently, he headed a new political pro-

---

154 The Russian plane was shot down by a Turkish Air Force F-16 fighter on November 26, 2016.

ject—the DOST party. On April 24, 2016, Mustafa Karadaya, a confidant of Mr. Dogan, was unanimously elected as chairman of MRF by the IX National Conference of the Party. Nonetheless, *the real authority in the movement remains undisputed*, to this very day, in the hands of its founder—Ahmed Dogan. It is also important to mention that the speech of Dogan in December 2015 was received favorably by the Russian Institute of Strategic Studies, a top research center in Russia, the director of which is appointed by the Russian president (Podchasov 2016). The influence of Russia on the MRF, which is based primarily on economic interests, has been pointed out many times.[155]

The MRF, in its essence, is a political party that mobilizes the support primarily of Bulgarian Turks. Many Pomaks and Roma also vote for the formation (see Table 5). According to the 2009 data, 89.7% of the electorate of the MRF consists of Turks, 5.1% are Roma, 0.9% are Bulgarians, and 4.3% are classified as "others." The MRF participated jointly with Euroroma in the parliamentary elections in 2001—one of the most significant attempts to express the interests of the Roma ethnic group in the country to date. *It is important to note, therefore, that the MRF does not have a monopoly over the support of Roma voters.* In fact, for example in the 2017 snap election, the Roma votes were divided almost equally in-between GERB, BSP, and MRF. This "division of labor" is typical for the general elections in the country (see Table 5, which paints a similar picture but for 2009).

---

[155] For example by Ognyan Minchev, see Minchev (2016).

Table 5. Ethnic profile of the political parties in the Bulgarian National Assembly in 2009

Source: Karasimeonov (2010).

Political parties	Ethnicity	%
Ataka	Bulgarian	97.6
	Turk	0
	Roma	1.6
	Other	0.8
BSP	Bulgarian	92.8
	Turk	2.5
	Roma	4.3
	Other	0.4
DSB	Bulgarian	100
	Turk	0
	Roma	0
	Other	0
GERB	Bulgarian	94.7
	Turk	1.3
	Roma	3.1
	Other	0.9
MRF	Bulgarian	0.9
	Turk	89.7
	Roma	5.1
	Other	4.3
NMSP (НДСВ)	Bulgarian	96.4
	Turk	0
	Roma	3.6
	Other	0
OLJ (РЗС)	Bulgarian	93.8
	Turk	1.2
	Roma	3.5
	Other	1.5
UDF	Bulgarian	100
	Turk	0
	Roma	0
	Other	0

MRF's electorate is concentrated mainly in southwestern and northeastern Bulgaria. Especially strong is the influence of the party in Kardzhali, Razgrad, Targovishte, Silistra, Shumen, and Blagoevgrad. The movement is a regional party—over 60% of its voters live in 30 municipalities of Kardzhali and Razgrad districts

(Todorov 2010: 280). The majority of voters belong to the poor. Only 1.7% have higher education. About 70% of Turks live in villages. The employment structure is dominated by construction (30%), production and marketing (25%), and agriculture (20%).

Significant parts of Romani identify themselves as ethnic Turks. In the southeastern part of the country alone live about 200,000 Roma (Denton et al. 2003: 6). *Despite the existence of many parties that claim to represent their interests, the vote of this ethnicity remains scattered. Unlike the Turks, Roma have insignificant (practically negligible) representation in the branches of central and local government, as well as in the administration* (Engström 2014). *In my view, the main reasons for this are rooted in* the diversity of Roma ethnicity and lack of good communication between the main groups (the more important are Kalderash, Yerlii, Rudari, and Demirdzhii[156]); the widespread illiteracy (which leads to economic, social, and political marginalization); the fact that many Roma politicians prefer to take on the role of "brokers," which aim to take under control Roma votes in order to exchange them with the big (BSP and GERB) or smaller players for political and economic resources.

The ethnic essence of the MRF is among the most serious causes of criticism against the movement. According to Antony Todorov, if by "ethnic party" we mean one that attracts the majority of the votes of a particular ethnic group, until 2000 in Bulgaria there is none (Todorov 2010: 277). Two surveys from 1996 and 1999 show that Bulgarian Turks vote mostly for MRF—between a third and half of them have declared their support for the movement. This is not the

---

[156] Kalderash (sometimes referred to by the exonym Serbian Gypsies) are Eastern Orthodox and the Rudari (or Ludari) who speak a dialect of Romanian are known as Vlah Gypsies. They are further subdivided into three groups by their traditional craft: the Ursari or Mechkari ("bear trainers"), the Lingurari or Kopanari ("carpenters," the name perhaps originates from the wooden bowls with which they are associated), and the Lautari ("musicians"). The Demirdzhii are also known as "Asparuh Bulgarians" (Asparuh or Asparukh, Isperih, Ispor was the ruler of Bulgars in the second half of the seventh century and was credited with the establishment of the First Bulgarian Empire in 680/681); they self-identify as the descendants of blacksmiths for Khan Asparuh's army. Some of them deny any connection with the Romani ethnicity and most do not speak Romani.

majority of this ethnicity during this period. Furthermore, among the Pomaks and Roma, the support for MRF is not very pronounced (ibid.: 277). *In my opinion, the definition proposed by Todorov is problematic because it, to a great extent, masks the true nature of the MRF. If the vast majority of voters supporting a political entity belongs to certain ethnic minority group(s), this entity is obviously considered by them (whether all or a large part of the group) as "an instrument" for expression and protection of their interests.* However, we must emphasize that the popular thesis of "disciplined" or "obedient" electorate of MRF is, indeed, exaggerated. The dynamics of the vote for the MRF is significant. At least half of the voters of the movement in 2005 have not supported it in the local elections in 2003. The number of those who have voted consistently for MRF since the beginning of the transition to democracy does not exceed 240,000; the share of those who backed up the movement only once and then withdrew their support is equal or even larger (Todorov 2010: 281). *Nonetheless, the conclusion that the party relies heavily on "voters-tourists" from neighboring Turkey has been justified.* According to expert estimates,[157] their share in the elections in 2001 and 2005 was about 18% of the electorate of the MRF.

While it continues to "bet" mainly on the ethnic card, as stated, the MRF seeks to establish itself as a nationwide liberal-democratic party that occupies the political center and is ready to cooperate with other left and center-right formations. The program of the movement, adopted in 1996, stipulates that the MRF is a universal political organization protecting the rights and freedoms of all Bulgarian citizens. Documents such as the program declarations adopted on the sixth (2006), seventh (2009), and eighth (2013) national conferences of the MRF highlight the role of the party as the "pillar" of the Bulgarian ethnic model, as well as "of the values of the EU and NATO" (MRF 2009). According to the declaration adopted at the sixth national conference of the party, at the heart of Bulgarian ethnic model lies the "balance between, on the one side, the principles of integration of minorities in all spheres of social,

---

157 Ibid., Todorov (2010).

economic and cultural life of the country with, on the other side, the principles of preservation and development of their ethno-religious identity" (MRF 2006: 1). In the Program Declaration of 2009, the MRF expresses its "strong disagreement with the growing trend of replacing this model with a policy of ethnic and religious intolerance, which is incompatible with the value systems of the EU and NATO."[158] The document states that there are political forces that seek to destroy the Bulgarian ethnic model and that they lead "a campaign against MRF." The program defines as the most vivid tribune of this "campaign" "the company of parties whose electoral weight is shrinking."[159]

On the one hand, the analysis of the strategic priorities in the election programs of MRF in 1990–2009 confirms party's commitment to the values of multiculturalism (Lyubenov 2011). On the other hand, in comparison with other political formations in that period, the support for welfare state and the measures related to its expansion have most prominence in the programs of MRF (ibid.: 155). In 2005, the movement offered its "leftmost" political program to date (Lyubenov 2011). This was an attempt to meet the expectations of voters who belong to the poorer strata. MRF's electoral profile explains the great attention paid by the party to agricultural policies aimed at encouraging and supporting farmers. The necessity for establishment of a functioning welfare state, which is highlighted in the programs, brings MRF and BSP closer together. I believe that the similarity between the two parties in this respect shows that the sporadic partnership between them *cannot be explained merely as a result of cynical and pragmatic political calculations. Apparently there are deeper reasons arising from the social status and attitudes of their constituents.*

MRF is a membership party with a strong and highly centralized organizational structure. The movement's statute provides the leader with impressive powers, by allowing him to determine the personnel policy and

---

[158] See MRF (2009).

[159] Here, the authors of the program are apparently hinting at conservative parties like DSB and PRR formations such as Ataka who have criticized MRF many times.

course of the party (MRF 2017). The leader is the chairperson of the Central Council and the Central Operative Bureau (Art. 11, pt. 4); approves candidates for deputies and municipal mayors (Art. 11, pt. 3); and provides the structure and composition of the Central Operative Bureau—a permanent body of the Central Council, which chooses them (Art. 12, pt. 3).[160] MRF's leader is chairperson of the parliamentary group (Art. 21, pt. 3).[161] The strict internal party discipline is also maintained *on the basis of the conditions for expelling members of MRF*, which are outlined in great detail. The way of formulating these conditions, to some extent, allows their *arbitrary interpretation*: "violation of party secret," "exceeded powers," "defamation of the party in the media," "the creation of conditions for dissent and factionalism," etc. (Art. 6, para. 4 pt. 2 and 3).[162] In all likelihood, the influence of the main party "architect" — Ahmed Dogan—on the organization of MRF and the strong position of the leader cannot be understated. *The powers of the chairperson allow him to keep under control the internal opposition.*

The ethnic vote for the MRF opens the gates for the application of atypical means for mobilization of the electorate of the party. When there are (economic) difficulties, including dissatisfaction with the policy of the MRF, the leaders can appeal to fundamental values and fears of the Turkish community, as that of encroachment on their ethnic identity, religion, and customs. Data from a representative survey of the Alpha Research agency conducted with voters of MRF in August 2008 confirm this thesis: 41.4% believe that "high levels of corruption exist among MPs, ministers, and other representatives of MRF in power"; for 24% Ahmed Dogan "has very large estates and it is not known how he acquired them" (only 27.6% disagree and 48.4% "neither agree nor disagree") and for 43% the greatest danger for Bulgaria are the corrupted officials in the government (Alpha Research 2008). However, 27% vote for MRF because it "takes care

---

160 See MRF (2017).
161 See MRF (2017).
162 Ibid.

for our better living," another 23% — "because it protects our religion and customs" (ibid.). *These are the main reasons underpinning the vote in support of the party.*

Figure 6. Fears of the MRF voters: Which of the following in the government represents the greatest danger for Bulgaria at this moment (2008)?

Source: Alpha Research (2008)

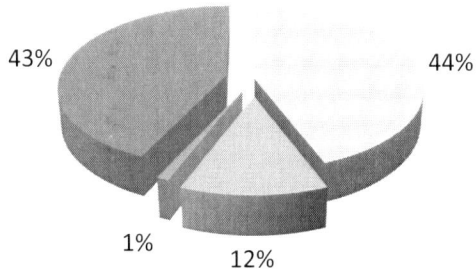

The raise to power of parties which will encroach on our religion
There will be no parties in the government which can protect people like me
Unanswered
That there are corrupted officials in the government

At the same time, in 2008, 44% of those who voted for the MRF state that the greatest danger for Bulgaria is the "raise of power to parties which will encroach on our religion," and for 12% — "that there will be no parties in the government which can protect people like me" (Figure 6). For about 68%, Ataka is a party that is an "enemy of MRF" (Alpha Research 2008). Most likely, the political messages of Ataka and the fears that they generate among Bulgarian Turks promote the mobilization of the electorate of the MRF. *In other words, MRF's voters are prepared to ignore the doubts that they may have in their leaders because they believe that the party, in a comparative perspective, could best protect their identity and (economic) interests.* Importantly, unlike the more critical attitude to the upper echelons of the party, 51.5% believe that MRF's local activists (the ones operating "in our region") are "trying to help people" (Alpha Research 2008). The pulse of a relatively closed community, as that of Bulgarian Turks, is determined by religion, traditions, and customs. *At the core of political action continues to stand paternalism and hierarchy, not the incentive of individuals. The policies are seen primarily as a means for preserving the community and its status. The MRF draws strength from conserving and reproducing these traditional social relationships.*

The MRF is a leader in some of the most effective and, at the same time, illegal methods, used by the political parties in Bulgaria, which aim to influence the outcome of elections (Stoychev 2016: 50). This conclusion is demonstrated by a survey examining the results from the parliamentary elections in 2014 (ibid.: 40). In general, the most common method employed by the political formations is to give money to voters in exchange for their support (81.5% of the cases of such practices). Other "strategies," employed by political brokers, are to offer essential commodities (16.4%), cash bonuses, promotions, advances, etc. (10.4%). It is not uncommon for local leaders to threaten members of the constituency (9.4%)[163] in order to secure or obtain their vote. The study *indicates that the MRF is the party most likely to offer money to constituents, followed by GERB, BWC,*[164] *and BSP (ibid.: 51). The practices of controlled voting are often directed by organized criminal networks — for them this is a profitable business; it suffices for the interested politicians simply "to place an order."*

The sociodemographic analysis of the controlled voting indicates that while ethnicity seems to be irrelevant vis-à-vis the amount offered by GERB, the respondents of the survey claim that, in average, BSP offers 10 leva more to ethnic Bulgarians. Ethnicity plays even bigger role for the political brokers of the MRF, which gave to Bulgarians 25 leva, to Turks twice as much, and to Roma — 40 leva (Stoychev 2016: 54). However, once we take into account the other smaller, but certainly not insignificant, players during the election in 2014, parties such as BWC, ABR,[165] and the Reformist Block, it appears that Roma voters are the ones who are the most

---

163 Ibid.: 50.
164 Bulgaria without censorship.
165 Alternative for Bulgarian Revival.

"courted" and well paid by the political organizations (ibid.: 54). Therefore, this ethnic group is the main target of brokers.

Nonetheless, the closer inspection reveals that the ordinary Roma often *do not receive money or anything else* for their "favors." It is not uncommon for moneylenders and employers to coerce Roma[166] to cast their vote for a particular political party (Stoychev 2016: 16). *This confirms the hypothesis that the institutions often not only fail to defend but actively work against the interests of minorities. At the very heart of ethnopolitics often lays the vicious interconnection between political, economic elites, and the organized crime.* Apart from the disputable role of the MRF in the political system, the ethnic entrepreneurs, who claim to protect the rights of ethnic Bulgarians, often point to "the issue of Roma crimes." This problem is widely publicized by the PRR parties.

2.3 The Bulgarian PRR

The rise of the PRR is a pan-European phenomenon. The eighth consecutive election for the EP held between May 22 and 25, 2014, was a triumph for the French Front National (FN) and the United Kingdom Independence Party (UKIP). The deepening migrant crisis and the unprecedented amount of terrorist attacks, becoming more frequent and ferocious in recent years, create a fertile ground for right-wing populists, euroskeptics, and ethnic entrepreneurs. For example, as the results of local elections[167] in France in 2015 demonstrated, the party of Marine Le Pen was able to capitalize on fears caused by the terror in Paris. The dread of the "invisible enemy" is boosting the popularity of Hungarian Prime Minister Viktor Orbán's Fidesz party as well as Frauke Petry's Alternative für Deutschland. The shocking outcome of the UK referendum held in June 2016, in which the pro-Brexit "Leave camp" won, was a personal victory for UKIP's leader Nigel Farage.

---

166 If they refuse to "oblige," the Roma and their whole families are persecuted ruthlessly.
167 Carried out on November 13, 2015.

The performance of Bulgarian PRR in the last European elections, the early parliamentary elections in 2014, the local elections in 2015, and in the presidential contest in 2016 cannot be described in simple terms or receive an unequivocal assessment. On the one hand, the support for Ataka marks a decline, on the other we observe the strengthening of formations such as NFSB (see Figure 7). The fragmentation of the votes for this party family masks the real weight of its ideas in the political system. Since 2016, there are unifying processes in the camp of the Bulgarian PRR. The candidates of the coalition United Patriots (Ataka, IMRO, and NFSB) — Krasimir Karakachanov and Yavor Notev — remained third in the first round of the presidential elections in 2016. This result, after a decade of discord and electoral draught, marked a new peak for the support for these parties. It was a *déjà vu*, a reminder of the votes that the leader of Ataka Volen Siderov managed to mobilize in his favor at the 2006 race for the presidency, during the "golden year" of Bulgarian PRR.

Figure 7. Votes for the main PRR parties.
Votes for Ataka — parliamentary (2005, 2009, 2013, 2014), presidential (2006, 2011), and European elections (2007, 2009, 2014); votes for NFSB — presidential (2011), parliamentary (2013, 2014 — part of the PF), and European elections (2014); votes for the United Patriots — presidential elections (2016)
Source: Original work based on data from CEC (Central Electoral Committee, Bulgarian — Централна Избирателна Комисия (ЦИК)), www.cik.bg

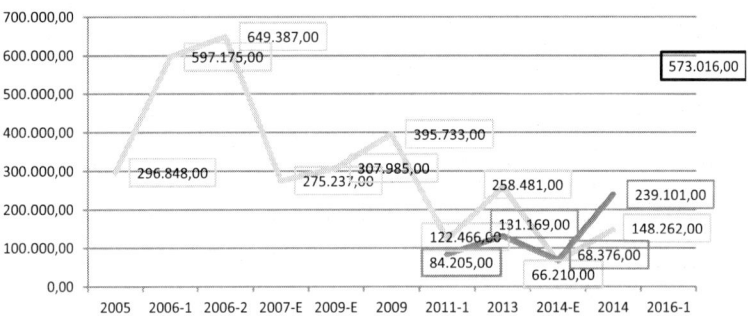

In this chapter, I examine the general characteristics and the main stages in the genesis and development of PRR in Bulgaria since

1989. Its pedigree is traced in the first and the second party systems. I explore the messages of the leading members of this party family in Bulgaria. I suggest several possible mechanisms that lie at the heart of the expansion of PRR.

2.3.1 Representatives

There is a discouraging terminological chaos in the scientific literature regarding our subject (Mudde 2007: 12). A plethora of notions are used to describe it: "extreme right," "far right," "radical right," "radical right populism," "xenophobic populism," "neofascism," etc. It is not uncommon for the scientists to use some of these terms interchangeably or as synonyms, therefore ignoring the fact that they have a rather different connotative and denotative meaning, and require further definitions.[168] The studies of Bulgarian scholars are also not immune to this problem. The paper "Extreme right in Bulgaria"[169] stands out as one of the exceptions. The author Antony Todorov distinguishes between five ideological features or *differenciae specificae* of this party family: "extreme forms of cultural conservatism" (patriarchalism, condemnation of homosexuality and other "deviations," etc.); organic conservative understanding of society"; xenophobia combined with "strong nationalism" and "often racism"; "particular devotion to order imposed by the firm hand" of the leader-patriarch; and a specific populism employing a strong "anticapitalist rhetoric."[170] For the purpose of consistency, I adhere to the term "populist radical right parties," which was coined by Cas Mudde, one of the leading experts in the field. The notion describes political parties whose ideological core combines three distinctive elements: authoritarianism, populism, and nativism (Mudde 2007: 26).

The political parties that match this profile or fit this description are Ataka (2005), Patriotic Front (PF) (2014) whose main components are NFSB, established by Valery Simeonov in 2011, and

---

168 Mudde (2007: 12).
169 See Todorov (2012).
170 Ibid.: 2.

IMRO, led by Krasimir Karakachanov. Some scholars include in this party family the OLJ of Yane Yanev (Avramov 2015). Here belong splinters from Ataka such as PROUD[171] (People for Real, Open and United Democracy, led by Slavi Binev), the National Democratic Party (Kapka Georgieva), as well as several other organizations created long before them: BNU,[172] Bulgarian National Radical Party (BNRP), Union of Bulgarian National Legions (UBNL), Bulgarian Christian Democratic Party of Father George Gelemenov, and "Guard" led by Bojan Rasate. We have to add the formations around the newspaper *Monitor*, the union "Guard," the circle "New Dawn," organizations such as "Bulgarian Horde," "Hearth," the Student National Society "Greater Bulgaria," the Bulgarian National Socialist Front, as well as the various "Tangrist" organizations[173] such as the society "Dulo" and "Warriors of Tangra".

Some of these parties, primarily Ataka, are often depicted or defined in the mass media as "extreme left."[174] The problem with the positioning of Ataka on the political scale left/right axis is discussed in scientific literature.[175] The prevailing opinion is that this is a "far-right" or "radical right" party.[176] In fact, the profound difference between the two poles of the political scale lay in their stances toward *inequality*, not toward the economy (Bobbio 1994). While the right is guided by the belief that it is "natural," the left perceives it as an artificial product, a human convention, or an artifact. Thus the primary purpose of political institutions (according to the left) is to be an instrument, which shall be used in order to reduce if not to eradicate completely social inequalities. Once we

---

171 Bulgarian—ГОРД.
172 A political coalition between three Bulgarian parties established in 2005. Not to be confused with the BNU "Kubrat," a radical right formation in Bulgaria that existed between 1922 and 1944.
173 They describe themselves as followers of Bulgarian pagan god Tangra.
174 Similar view, but toward the NFSB is upheld by the sociologist Yuliy Pavlov; see Pavlov (2014).
175 See, e.g., Zhecheva (2007).
176 See Mudde (2007), Lyubeonov (2011: 168–70), Todorov (2012: 2, 6–7), and Avramov (2015).

apply this criterion to distinguish ideologies and programs, it becomes apparent why the support that many of the representatives of the PRR are willing to give for a chauvinist welfare state does not make them stand closer to their opponents in the left (Cf. Mudde 2007: 27). For the PRR the welfare state is exclusive. This means that the goods or the byproducts of this state (unemployment benefits, old-age pensions, healthcare services, etc.) must be awarded only to those who "fall" in party-sanctioned definition of the nation. The latter excludes a priori the "slackers" who, to use the words of the leader of IMRO Karakachanov, "spend their whole day in the ghetto drinking beer and listening to chalga."[177] Differences of "origin or faith cannot be placed above nationality. Whoever does this *separates himself*[178] from the Bulgarian nation and state, and, therefore, can make no claims to them" (Twenty Items of the Agenda of Ataka Party 2009).

As the history of the formations reveals, their political nature is full of contradictions. The ideology of the party family combines messages from the arsenals of the extreme right and of the extreme left. On the one hand, the contemporary European PRR is a successor, or at least is influenced by the first catch-all parties such as the far-right National Socialist German Workers Party (Ignazi 2003, Todorov 2012). Some representatives of the PRR in Bulgaria are proud with their "kinship ties" to organizations that existed in Bulgaria before 1944, such as the National Accord, the Democratic Union, and the Bulgarian National Legions.[179] On the other hand, the decision of the Communist Party in December 1989 to restore the names of Bulgarian Muslims, which were forcibly changed during the "Revival Process," created a strong opposition in the party itself.[180]

---

177 "Quote of the Day: 'if somebody spends his whole day in the ghetto drinking beer …'" 2017.
178 The italics in the quote are mine.
179 The BDF (Bulgarian Democratic Forum), for example, is seen as the successor of the latter. BDF was part of the coalition of 16 parties under ODS.
180 Todorov (2012: 6).

2.3.2 Origins, ideology, development

Bulgaria has witnessed the rise of both models of radical right-wing formations: elitist and mass political parties. The Peoples' Accord (1921–1923) is one of the archetypes of this party family in the country. An elitist organization, the Accord, united opponents of the Agrarian Union and the communists. In its ranks were prominent bankers,[181] industrialists, entrepreneurs, academics, senior officers, and others. The Peoples' Accord proclaimed that its main objective is the "protection of national interests" (Todorov 2012). Although different from the fascist organizations in Bulgaria at that time (such as the Bulgarian sections of Italian PNF – Partito Nazionale Fascista) among its members there were unconcealed sympathies for the ideas of Benito Mussolini (ibid.). The Military Alliance had a significant impact on the Peoples' Accord. The Alliance was built on strict discipline, characteristic of conspiracy organizations, and the oath of allegiance to the Monarch – Tsar Boris III. The elitist image of the Peoples' Accord was enhanced even more in 1922, when the members of the BNU "Kubrat" joined its ranks.

With the coup-d'état on June 9, 1923, the Peoples' Accord has become the political formation ruling the country. After the Accord joined forces with the UNPP [182] (led by Atanas Burov, Ivan Evstratiev Geshov, Mihail Madjarov, Teodor Teodorov, etc.), it grew into a political party. On this basis was built the Democratic Alliance (which also included members of the Democratic Party). In the 1930s, this organization was left by the Peoples' Social Movement of Aleksandar Tsankov, which was inspired by the ideas of Fascism and National Socialism. Although elitist in its genesis, the party acquired a mass character and was banned in 1934. The fate of the UBNL, which was founded in 1935 (it appeared in the political scene as UYNL[183] in 1932), is similar. Its leaders were General

---

181 The business Association for Economic Development had a key role.
182 United National Progressive Party (Bulgarian – ОНПП, Обединена национално прогресивна партия).
183 Union of Youth National Legions.

Hristo Lukov, General Nicolay Jekov, and Iliya Minev, who continued the party tradition after November 10, 1989. Typical for UBNL are anticommunism, the rejection of liberalism, freemasonry, and pacifism. The Legions also expressed sympathy to a model of one-party dictatorship and insisted on the importance of maintaining close links with the Third Reich (Miller 1975, Daskalov 2005, Poppetrov 2009). With the end of the Second World War, all organizations that allegedly gravitated toward the ideas of Fascism and National Socialism were prohibited.

There are several theories explaining the genesis of the PRR parties in Bulgaria after 1989 (Karasimeonov 2010, Lyubenov 2011, Todorov 2012: 51). The leading one suggests that they emerged as a result of the cleavages during the transition to democracy.[184] The representatives of the party family in question were born in the shadows of the political giants. The first of these cleavages is, of course, the ethnic one. As we already saw, the involvement of the MRF in the political life of the country caused uproar in some circles of the left. At this time, in the 1990s, the National Committee for Protection of Peoples' Interests (NCPPI[185]), as well as other similar formations like the Patriotic Labor Party, "Era 3," Political club "Thrace," and the Union of Thracian Bulgarians[186] gravitated around the BSP. In the right side of the political spectrum rose the Bulgarian Democratic Forum (BDF), which was member of the coalition of 16 parties ODS and claimed to be an heir of the Bulgarian National Legions. Outside ODS, while orbiting around it remained the Bulgarian Nationalist Radical Party (led by Ivan Georgiev) and the Christian Democratic Party (led by Father Ivan Gelemenov). These formations depended on BSP and UDF/ODS, which tried to steer their behavior. These satellites remained on the periphery of the titanic clash between the two political giants. With the cooling down of the cleavage between communism and anticommunism,

---

184 See Todorov (2012).
185 Bulgarian—ОКЗНИ, Общонароден комитет за защита на Националните интереси.
186 Bulgarian—Отечествената партия на труда, "Ера 3," Политическият клуб "Тракия," Съюзът на тракийските българи.

these smaller formations started to become more active in the political arena. Privatization created a new cleavage—a rift between the impoverished, the losers of the transition to a market economy, and the ones who benefited from it. Political populism, which became the main weapon of the Coalition Ataka, established in 2005, thrived on the basis of this cleavage (Todorov 2012).

Although I do not underestimate or reject the thesis about the role of political cleavages in the origins of the PRR, *I believe that their beginnings and their evolution are also closely linked to the nature and stages of development of the contemporary Bulgarian ethnic model. In my opinion, this concept has a better heuristic and analytical potential. It offers a better explanation of the influence of ethnic cleavage.*[187] Before I examine more closely this concept, I shall highlight some important specifics of the political messages and rhetoric of the PRR in Bulgaria.

Despite the differences between the representatives of the party family, their ideology has several common pillars. The first is the pathos against minorities (ethnic, religious, sexual, etc.). The PRR has assigned the latter the unenviable role of scapegoats. Representatives of Ataka, the social and political circles around "Monitor," the Warriors of Tangra, as well as other parties and organizations of similar ideology do not conceal their suspicions and, to put it mildly, "antipathies" toward Jews, Turks, Roma, Arabs, homosexuals, etc. These parties disseminate and "preach" theories of global conspiracy, "directed" by the International Monetary Fund, the Club of Rome, the Bilderberg group, etc. Volen Siderov, for example, has repeatedly stressed the threat of "Islamization of Bulgaria which is becoming a Gipsy State" (Siderov 2011). Activists of the PRR have been accused of vandalizing temples and monuments of religious and ethnic minorities. Second, central to the ideology of these parties is the thesis of the importance of unity of the nation, the necessity of strict social hierarchy, and an omnipotent state. The nation is a natural community. Every person has a particular place

---

[187] In this sense, my view does not contradict, but complements the one which emphasizes the role of cleavages in the genesis of PRR in Bulgaria.

"reserved" in it.[188] Therefore, each member of the BNU, for example, pledges allegiance to the homeland and intolerance to its enemies.

Last but not least, these parties stress the need for concrete actions against threats from foreign powers (Todorov 2012: 10–11). For instance, parties like Ataka interpret the concerns voiced by the EU Commission and other institutions over the safety of the Nuclear Power Plant (NPP) "Kozloduy" merely as an attempt to damage Bulgarian political and economic interests. For this reason, these parties strongly oppose the demands to shut down the only Bulgarian NPP.[189] *Some, but not all, members of the PRR family in Bulgaria are against the participation of Bulgarian troops in Iraq and Afghanistan, against NATO and the EU.* For example, while Ataka's leader Volen Siderov has expressed his approval of Russia's policies toward Ukraine and supports the annexation of Crimea, the chairman of NFSB Valery Simeonov has been critical of the regime of the President Vladimir Putin and has stated that Bulgaria must observe its commitments to NATO. In 2016, Simeonov stated that "he would prefer a united fleet[190] in the Black Sea against a possible Russian aggression instead of breaking the readmission agreement with Turkey."[191] His comment came in connection with the information that Bulgaria's southern neighbor will abandon the deal with the

---

188 See Siderov (2011). The influence of the ideas of Hitler, Mussolini, and Ataturk is obvious.
189 The NPP previously operated four older reactors of the VVER–440/230 design. However, under a 1993 agreement between the EC and the Bulgarian government, Units 1 and 2 were taken off-line at the beginning of 2004. Throughout the 1990s and early 2000s Units 3 and 4, originally licensed for operation until 2011 and 2013, respectively, underwent substantial safety improvements. As a matter of fact, the two units received positive reviews from the International Atomic Energy Agency after a rigorous inspection was conducted. Backed by these findings, the Bulgarian government had hoped to convince the EC to allow a postponement of the agreed pre-accession shutdown. Despite these efforts, Units 3 and 4 were taken out of operation in the final hours of 2006, immediately prior to the country's accession to the EU.
190 A joined fleet composed of Bulgarian, Turkish, and Romanian vessels.
191 "Valeri Simeonov prefers a sea battle with Russia over a wave of immigrants" (2016).

EU and will stop accepting back thousands of illegal immigrants who pass through its territory on the way to the continent. Although on other occasions the leader of NFSB has expressed his disapproval of Turkey's policies, in particular those toward the Muslims in Bulgaria, his position toward this state is more nuanced than this of Volen Siderov and Ataka. The latter is strongly against Turkey's accession to the EU.

These "ideas" of the PRR have been manifested in a number of publicity stunts and/or political actions that were widely covered by the mass media, such as the clash near the Banya Bashi Mosque between members and activists of the Ataka on the one hand, and Bulgarian Muslims, on the other (in May 2011); the nationwide manifestations caused by the events in Katunitsa (in September 2011); the tensions between Bulgarians and Roma in the village of Garmen and in front of the Roma ghetto in the metropolitan district "Orlandovtsi" (in June 2015); the so-called Lukov march held annually in February in Sofia since 2003, in memory of the leader of the BNL General Hristo Lukov[192]; and the systematic attacks against gay parades.

2.3.3 The PRR and the Bulgarian ethnic model

In what way the history of the PRR is intertwined with the dynamics of the Bulgarian ethnic model? The model, which I define as an institutionalization of the ethnic cleavage, should be analyzed in the light of the two postcommunist party systems: the bipolar (1989–2001) and the polycentric (2001 until present). If we take into consideration the processes in the political system, which I outlined above, we can differentiate *between three stages* in the development of the model. At the dawn of *the first stage (1990–2001)*, the MRF was involved in a "balancing act." It successfully occupied a key position on the political scene, monopolizing the advantageous role of "a counterweight," which was "working" (depending on the contexts and its interests) with the BSP or the UDF (ODS). This stage

---

192 Lukov, a Bulgarian lieutenant-general and a Minister of War, was assassinated on February 13, 1943, by communist partisans in Sofia.

coincides with the chronological boundaries of the first party system in which much of the political elite observed a "vow of silence" on the precarious topic of ethnic minorities. But, even then, the legitimacy of this model was challenged by the fledgling populist radical right/left formations.

The second stage (2001–2011) is marked by the direct participation of the MRF in the executive branch with high-ranking public officials—ministers. This "breakthrough" happened in the government of NMSP (2001–2005). The erosion of political giants BSP and UDF, the increasing social and economic inequalities, have fed the political populism and led to the upsurge of radical right and left. As explained above, the appeal of Ataka was primarily based in its messianism and "antiparty" rhetoric; its promises to purge the "corrupt political elite"; its political messages against minorities, demonstrating the "negative effects" of ethnic peace, etc. As we saw, the roots or the beginnings of Ataka and similar parties were in the formations orbiting *around* as well as organizations *within* BSP and UDF, which criticized the MRF and demanded that the ethnic party is banned. The absolute peak in the political support for Ataka was during the second round of presidential elections in 2006 (Figure 8). Then, the party nominee for the presidency—Volen Siderov—obtained approximately 24% of votes.

Figure 8. Votes for Ataka— , votes for NFSB—, and votes for MRF—■ in the parliamentary elections (2005, 2009, 2013, 2014)

Source: Original work based on data from CEC, www.cik.bg.

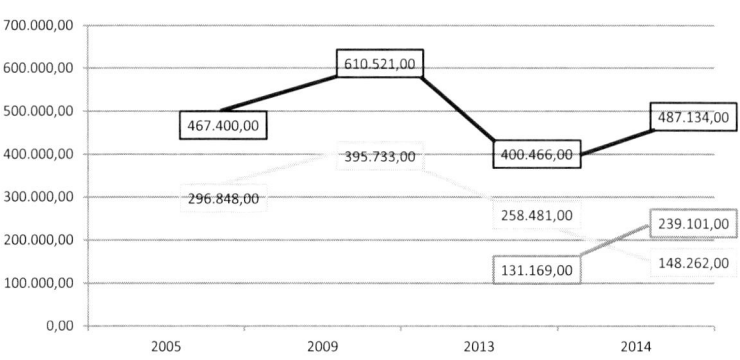

The PRR and ethnic parties are somewhat "dependent on" and "in need of" each other (see Figure 8, compared with the data in Figure 7). The highest result that Ataka was able to achieve in parliamentary elections was in 2009 when it received almost 99,000 votes more than in 2005; this very same election marked the peak for the support for the MRF (Figure 8). As already stated, the biggest fear,[193] which the electors of MRF have expressed, is of parties that threaten to endanger their religion and customs; the majority of MRF's voters have stated that Ataka is the enemy of the movement. *In a nutshell, the ideology and political messages of Ataka, as well as of other similar parties, more precisely the fears that they generate among Bulgarian Muslims, contribute to the mobilization of the electorate of the MRF. Nonetheless, another factor that may have boosted the political support for Ahmed Dogan's party could be, for example, the tactics of the movement to include more and more ethnic Bulgarians in its party lists. On their turn, the politicians of the PRR use MRF, DOST, and other ethnic formations as "scarecrows." Needless to say, these parties also capitalize on the fears and stereotypes that their constituents have.*

The analysis of the electoral support for the Ataka party shows that in the 2005 parliamentary elections, this formation won on three terrains: part of the voters disappointed by NMSP (НДСВ, the "royal" party, lost 1.2 million votes in 2005 compared to 2001), some of the voters of the small parties and part of the "abstentionists" in 2001, "which in turn, earlier were voters disappointed of the UDF's policies" (Todorov 2010: 420).[194] Possible reasons for the "migration" of NMSP supporters into the Ataka camp in 2005 are the unfulfilled generous social promises of Simeon Saxe-Coburg-Gotha, as well as the partnership of the "royal" party with the MRF. As for the leftist votes that Ataka attracted, these were probably electors who supported the BSP in the 1990s, but then abandoned its "ranks" (Todorov 2010: 420). These were not former BSP supporters from 2001–2005, but most likely from 1994 to 1995, who then had nationalist ideas (e.g., the circles around the NCPPI – ОКЗНИ) or

---

193 See Section 2.2.
194 For the profile of the voters of Ataka see as well Alpha Research (2009), Petrova (2009), Stoyanov (2009), and Todorov (2012).

some kind of neo-Stalinism and affection for the most strict application of law and order (Todorov 2010: 433).

The main electoral tide that the candidate of Ataka Siderov has utilized in the presidential elections in 2006 consists of voters of the NMSP from 2005 (between 160,000 and 180,000 votes), supporters of the UDF and DSB from 2005 (a total of about 160,000 in the second round), and, to a lesser extent, of BSP voters in 2005 (about 30,000 in the second round). We can speculate that the growth that Ataka registered in the parliamentary elections in 2009 was to some extent the result of the support of the former voters of the NMSP[195] as well as, but probably, to a smaller degree, former devotees of BSP. However, additional data are needed to verify this hypothesis as well as to better clarify the mutual influence between the MRF and the PRR. While it is not correct to compare the results of parliamentary and European elections, it is indicative that 5.8% of those who supported NMSP candidates and 4.2% of BSP voters in the European elections in 2007 preferred Ataka party in 2009. The transfer of votes to Volen Siderov's party came first of all from former NMSP and BSP followers (Alpha Research 2009). Meanwhile, in 2009 the BSP and especially Ataka lost votes mostly at the expense of GERB. Like the formation headed by Siderov, GERB has been very critical of the "Three-way coalition" and especially the MRF, but its political discourse is more moderate. In addition, Borisov's party obtained international legitimacy thanks to the support of the EPP (Todorov 2010: 434).

The third phase, which has started in 2011 and continues till present, is characterized by explosive escalation of the activities of ethnic entrepreneurs. The events in front of the Mosque Banya Bashi and, particularly those which occurred in Katunitsa in 2011 mark the beginning of the stage. Until 2016, the role of the PRR, generally speaking, fluctuated. This was due to *several facts*. First, the radical right was divided into a number of competing formations; many of

---

[195] Who were disappointed by the coalition of the "royal party" with the MRF (the NMSP lost nearly 600,000 voters compared to 2005).

them remained outside of parliament—a fact that concealed the potential cumulative effect of these ideas. Second, the charisma of Ataka started to fade out after the formation became a part of the status quo, which it previously denounced. The support that Ataka provided for the first cabinet of Boyko Borisov and, especially, for the unpopular government of Plamen Oresharski, which was based on a coalition between the BSP and MRF, led to severe erosion of the radical right party. The presidential elections in 2011 cemented this negative trend for Ataka. Its leader received a very low support in the race. Last but not least, the parties that confess the ideas of "moderate" conservatism, such as GERB and DSB, are a strong competitor to the populist radical parties in general. These "mainstream" formations are able to capture some of the messages and slogans of the PRR and to transform them into a more admissible or, rather, a more easily "digestible" form (i.e., more compatible with the principles of a democratic political system), in order to disarm their volatile potential. The end of 2016 saw the unification of the main PRR formations—Ataka, NSFB, and IMRO. The mutual interests of the United Patriots and the encouraging result which the coalition obtained in the 2016 presidential elections will perhaps be the glue that will hold them together.

2.3.4 A glimpse into the future of the PRR

Despite the trends outlined above, it should be emphasized that many features of the current political situation in Bulgaria and Europe are actually favorable for the PRR. A study conducted in November 10-18, 2015, just after the terrorist attacks in Paris, shows that according to 28% of the respondents there is a greater threat (in general) to Bulgaria than to the other EU countries (Alpha Research 2015b). The percent of people who see the international terrorism as a "leading international threat to the country" is increasing— 64% of respondents in 2016 versus 30% in 2006. The second biggest threat is posed by the influx of refugees; this is the opinion of 61% of the respondents in 2016 (Alpha Research 2016: 8). On the "domestic front," *seemingly, the likelihood of interethnic conflicts decreases*—in 2016 only 18% think that these conflicts are a threat to

Bulgaria, compared to 34% ten years ago (ibid.). In fact, some studies of social distances reveal that *there are no grounds for optimism*.[196]

In the *first* place, the people who identify themselves as Bulgarians are less willing to have Turkish, Arab, Roma, and Syrian neighbors (minorities that are often targets of PRR's politicians) in comparison with respondents as a whole (Figure 9). Second, the social distances between Bulgarians, on the one hand, and the two most significant minorities — the Turks and Roma, on the other, are increasing (Figure 10). In other words, Bulgarians are *becoming less tolerant* of these ethnic groups. This conclusion is confirmed by the findings of a study conducted in 2016, the results of which are compared with those of 2008 (Pamporov 2016). Even more unwanted than Roma is the Syrian minority. In comparison, the predominantly positive attitude in neighborhood communities toward minorities like Englishmen, Russians, and Armenians is further increasing (ibid.). Even more alarming is another social change. With regard to Roma, Turks, and Chinese, studies encompassing the 2008-2013 period show that the group of respondents aged 18-24 are the most tolerant. However, after 2013 there is "a sharp decline of this tolerance"; this age group now becomes "the most hateful toward the minorities" (Pamporov 2016). This negative transformation cannot be explained merely with the change of generations. The real smoking gun is in the hand of the government officials (ibid.).

---

196 For an analysis of social distances, see as well Section 1.4.

Figure 9. Social distances. "Would you agree that in your neighborhood live?"
(Answer: "Yes")
Source: Pamporov (2016).

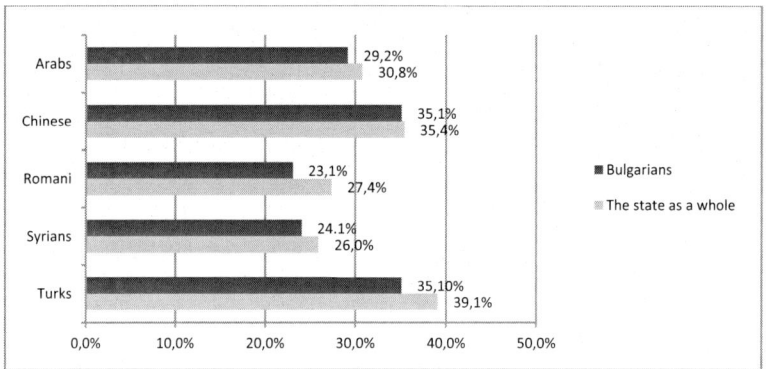

Figure 10. Social distances. "Would you agree that in your neighborhood live?"
(Answer: "Yes")
Source: Pamporov (2016).

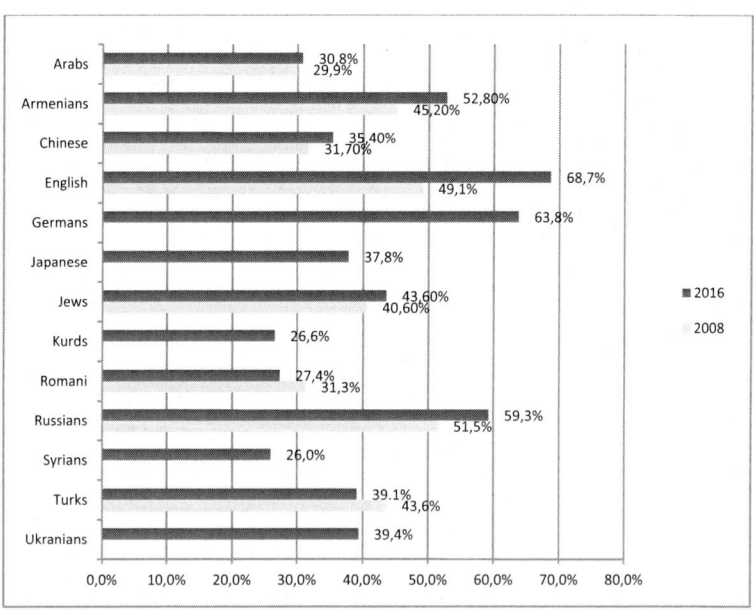

The increasing social distances, the unsuccessful Roma integration, the continuing flow of migrants and the looming threat of terrorism, the attempts at rehabilitation of the MRF and its return through the front door of Bulgarian politics,[197] *and the appearance of a new ethnic party in 2016 – DOST*[198] *(in coalition with PPFD*[199] *in the snap election in March 2017), all these events are a tailwind in the sails of the PRR. Nonetheless, a potential problem for the party family may emerge as a result of sharp inconsistencies between words and actions.* A month before the presidential election in November 2016, the BNA witnessed the formation of a new ad hoc majority, which included GERB, the PF, Ataka and, quite interestingly, DOST. The collaboration with the "sworn enemy" did not seem to put off the supporters of the "Patriots" in the election. Still, especially in the long run, the PRR parties will have a lot to lose if they become prisoners of opportunistic political bargains and arrangements (Cholakov 2016a). Furthermore, the opponents of the "Patriots" exploit the internal divisions in the camp of the PRR in order to encourage the potential deserters. Weeks before the snap elections in March 2017, Slavi Binev, one of the prominent MPs of the PF (and before that a MEP elected with the support of Ataka), left the party and became an MP candidate nominated by MRF; Evgeni Mihailov, a well-known politician during the Bulgarian transition to democracy, formerly a member of Ecoglasnost and UDF, joined the ranks of DOST. *The aim of the ethnic parties was to prove their vitality by showing that they are able to turn their unyielding adversaries into allies.*

The competition between the parties of the moderate conservatism (such as GERB, DSB, and UDF) and the PRR *does not mean that when there are mutual interests and benefits, the two "camps" cannot collaborate.* The partnership between IMRO and GERB is not a new

---

197 This is demonstrated, for example, by the role that the MRF played in key projects of the "Borisov 2" government, such as the infamous judicial reform.

198 A party that does not hide its close, amicable relations with the political regime of the Turkish President Recep Tayyip Erdogan.

199 PPFD, Peoples' Party Freedom and Dignity (Bulgarian—Народна партия свобода и достойнство, НПСД).

phenomenon.²⁰⁰ *But if politicians like Krasimir Karakachanov, Angel Dzhambazki, and Valeri Simeonov fail to clearly demonstrate their independence of "the parties of the status quo" (if we use their own lingo), the PF will follow the fate of Ataka and become an endangered political species.* According to the poll conducted by "Gallup International Balkan" in February 2016, the support for the PF (as a whole) is slightly higher than that for Ataka — 3.6% versus 3.3%.²⁰¹ Any wrong move on the part of the players in the nationalist niche will potentially have a devastating electoral price and throw them "outside the ring." As the elections in November 2016 and March 2017 demonstrated, the PRR parties appear to have learned the bitter lessons of the past and to realize that they can achieve much more *if they work together*. The strong performance in the race for the presidency stabilized the bonds between these formations even though the subsequent results in the general elections of 2017 were disappointing.²⁰² This collaboration, between PRR parties, has its roots in the past. Despite the conflicts that divided the representatives of the PRR, within certain political institutions they were able to work together. For example, in the Municipal Council of Sofia, IMRO and Ataka were united in the formation "Patriots for Sofia." *In conclusion, I expect a further increase of the market "shares" of PRR and its influence in the political system and process.*

---

200 For instance, Angel Dzhambazki, MEP and Vice President of IMRO from 2009, was elected municipal councilor in Sofia with the votes of GERB in 2007, following an agreement between the party of Boyko Borisov and IMRO.
201 See "Chart of the Day: The parties retain electoral support" (2016).
202 The three parties that form the coalition "United Patriots" (Ataka and the PF – NSBB and IMRO) received fewer votes in 2017 (318,513) than Ataka (148,262 votes), and PF (239,101) obtained separately in 2014.

2.4 Roma, crime and politics

This chapter tackles the issue of "Roma crimes." First, I examine trends and outline important problems in the collection of data regarding this issue. Then I explore several case studies. The latter demonstrate how and why the public attention is focused on the criminal activities of Roma. I also shed light on the way politicians are involved in this problem. As already stated, there are significant negative stereotypes among the Bulgarians toward the Roma, and the ethnic distances are increasing.[203] Romani, although they are a small percentage of the population, are the main recipients of social benefits, while their contribution to the state budget is negligible (Mantarova and Zaharieva 2007: 129). Among them the unemployment is high; however, they remain low educated and often refuse to accept low-paid labor (idem). According to Anna Mantarova, the Roma ethnic group's criminal activity surpasses several times that of other ethnicities.[204] In 1998, for example, it was 878 for the Bulgarians and 493 for the Turks per 100,000 Bulgarians, while for the Roma was 7.314 per 100,000 (ibid.: 129).

The term "Roma crimes" is widely used not only by the media but also in the scientific literature. *In my opinion, the problem with this term is that it seems to imply a connection between a particular ethnicity and criminal activities. Thus it can hardly be seen as a neutral notion or concept. Therefore, I as well as other colleagues, as a general rule, prefer to refrain from using it. Furthermore, it is important to point out that there is a lack of consensus among the experts in the field on whether there are reliable and credible data which will allow examining this phenomenon, particularly in comparative perspective, and especially in the new millennium.*[205]

The data, on which Figures 11–15 are based, encompass the period between 1995 and 1998. *As Figures 11–15 demonstrate, it appears that during the period in question and regarding violent crimes in*

---

203 See Sections 1.4 and 2.3.4.
204 Ibid., Mantarova and Zaharieva (2007: 129).
205 For further discussion of this point, see, e.g., Bezlov (2007a). For a general analysis of the interconnections between politics and organized crime in Bulgaria, see Bezlov (2007g), Bezlov and Gounev (2012a, 2012b, 2012c).

Bulgaria (thefts, robberies, premeditated murders, batteries, and rapes), the number of perpetrators of Roma origin exceeds many times those who belong to other ethnic groups.[206] There are two important clarifications that have to be made. First, the analysis concerns only the crimes against the person. Regarding the economic crimes (e.g., accounting fraud, corruption, and cyber crime), the breakdown by ethnicity is completely different. Due to the low educational status of the majority of Roma, the positions that might allow for major economic crimes are practically inaccessible to them (Mantarova 2002). Nonetheless, the violent crimes are the ones that provoke the greatest public outcry and are widely covered in the mass media. Therefore, not surprisingly, these crimes are used by ethnic entrepreneurs to instigate hatred against the Roma and to stigmatize the whole ethnicity. Second, the statistics used in the figures refers only to solved cases and known perpetrators of crimes.

Figure 11. Criminal activities among the main ethnic groups — thefts (solved cases)

(per 100,000 people belonging to the respective ethnic group)
Source: Mantarova (2002).

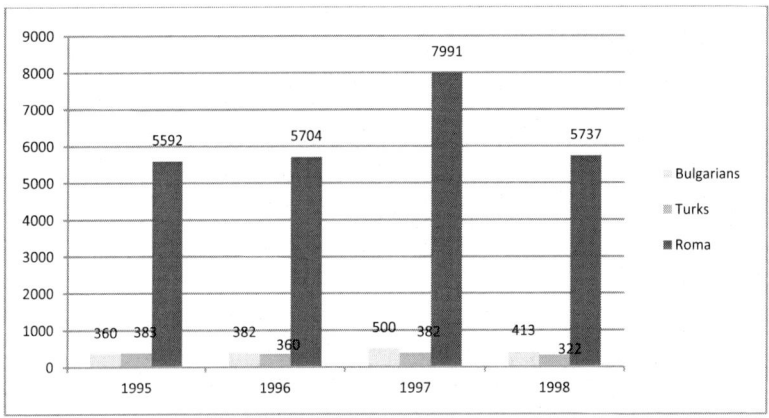

---

206 See Mantarova (2002). The data are from the annual bulletin of the council for criminological research at General Prosecutor of the Republic of Bulgaria.

Figure 12. Criminal activities among the main ethnic groups — robberies (solved cases)
(per 100,000 people belonging to the respective ethnic group)
Source: Mantarova (2002).

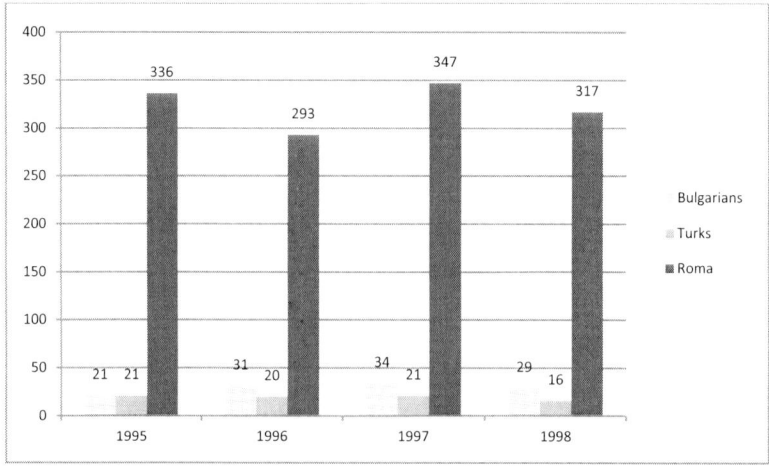

Figure 13. Criminal activities among the main ethnic groups — premeditated murders
(solved cases) (per 100,000 people belonging to the respective ethnic group)
Source: Mantarova (2002).

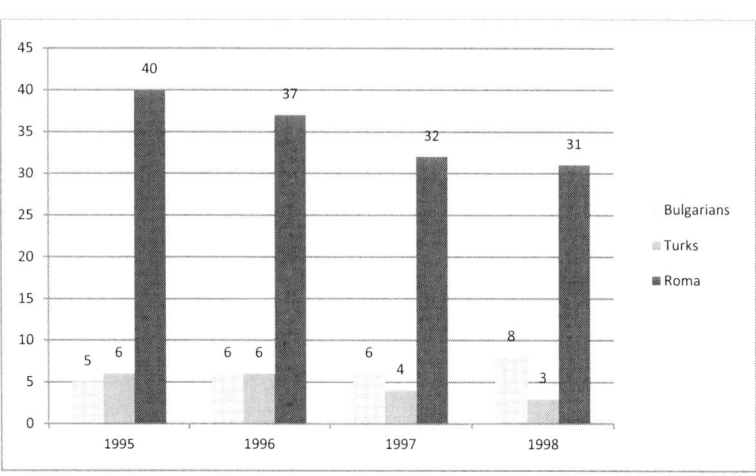

Figure 14. Criminal activities among the main ethnic groups — batteries (solved cases)
(per 100,000 people belonging to the respective ethnic group)
Source: Mantarova (2002)

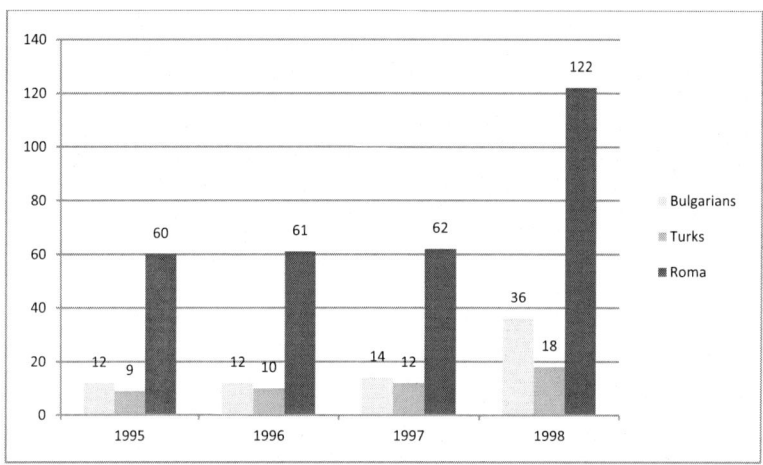

Figure 15. Criminal activities among the main ethnic groups — rapes (solved cases)
(per 100,000 people belonging to the respective ethnic group)
Source: Mantarova (2002).

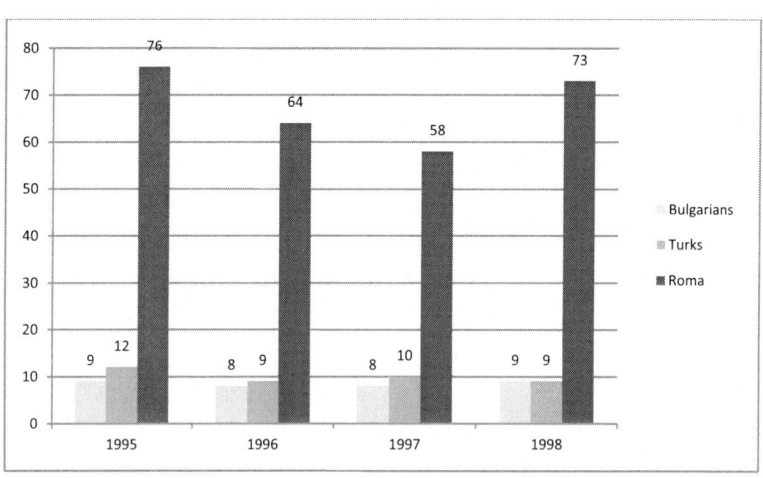

The bleak picture painted by these data is, however, not the whole story. The data related to the ethnicity of offenders, which are collected in the criminal justice system, are problematic (Bezlov 2007a). There are two main issues that hinder analysis of official information on crime and affect the police statistics. First, the introduction of major methodological changes in the collection, reporting, and recording of data on crime by the police in 1990–1997 makes it difficult to set side by side the statistical information for different years. This is the reason why, for example, the official statistics recorded a significant drop in the crime rates in 1998 vis-à-vis the previous 1997. Second, there are cases of manipulation of data by police officers (Bezlov 2007a).

The Personal Data Protection Act, in force since 2002, allows the collection of data on ethnicity, if the person gives his written consent (Art. 21).[207] Such permission, however, is not required in cases where the competent authorities are investigating a crime or administrative offense matter relating to national security. The Personal Data Protection Act allows ethnicity to be recorded for the purpose of the national statistics (Art. 20). Ethnicity is registered twice within the criminal process in Bulgaria. First, it is recorded by the police in its official contact with the suspect, and, second, when this person appears in court as a defendant. Suspects are not required to state their ethnicity and if someone refuses to name his identity, he is enrolled as "Bulgarian." *However, the main reason why it is difficult to analyze the ethnic data collected by law enforcement authorities is their inconsistency.* Some police departments simply do not collect data on the ethnicity of the suspects (Bezlov 2007 a). Another problem of rather technical nature is the fact that the available data on the ethnicity of suspects do not take into consideration recidivism in committing crimes. This means that the data of the same offender are registered again and again, in each subsequent offense for which the person is being investigated. Therefore, these data can be misleading because ethnic Roma and ethnic Bulgarians have dif-

---

207 See Personal Data Protection Act 2002.

ferent coefficient of recidivism (ibid.). *The problems with police statistics which I pointed out however cannot change or underplay the fact that a very significant number of Roma are involved in criminal activities.*[208] It is, nonetheless, imperative to take into consideration these issues when trying to outline or "discover" trends.

Although information on the ethnicity of suspects has been collected before 1990, the first publicized data on the ethnicity of crime perpetrators are from 1990 (see Table 6). The highly significant raise in the number of Roma suspects between 1990 and 1991 coincided with the considerable increase in unemployment among the representatives of the community. In some police departments, the registered increase of crime rate among the Roma is far above the national average, for example, in Botevgrad and Shumen, where the rise is, respectively, 15 and 12 times (Bezlov 2007b).

Since 1998, the proportion of registered police suspects of Roma ethnicity *has gradually diminished* (Bezlov 2007b). One, rather simplistic, explanation for this may point to the country's political and economic stabilization, but in fact the reasons are probably different. This decline can, perhaps, be attributed to the new statistical methods introduced by the Ministry of Interior between 1997 and 1998 as well as the decreasing number of cases in which the ethnicity of the suspect is registered (Bezlov 2007b). Nationwide, the number of Roma suspects during this period decreased from 39,367 to 22,923, while the change regarding the ethnic Bulgarians is much smaller—from 69,000 to 63,000. Since differences in the number of violations of the Bulgarians and Roma can hardly be explained by socioeconomic factors, the statistics on the declining number of Roma offenders are probably misleading.

The picture outlined by the above official data, especially for the period 1999–2004, tones down the widely publicized problem of "excessive" criminal activities of Roma. Since the perpetrators of 70% of all crimes are in the age range between 15 and 30 years old (regardless of ethnicity) and Roma account for 15% of this age

---

[208] This is conceded by Bezlov as well, see Bezlov (2007b).

group, the widespread idea that many Roma are engaged in criminal activity *in fact is greatly exaggerated* (Bezlov 2007b). According to these data, Roma are only 18.9% of suspects, which is slightly above the expected values for the group. However, the fact that the problem is not as "big" or "grave," as it is often stated *does not mean that it does not exist*. Even if we take into account changes in the statistical methods employed by the police in 1997 and the "sporadic" registration of the ethnicity of suspects, it can be concluded from the available data that the crime among the Roma *is disproportionately high*. The number of suspects per 100,000 persons of Bulgarian and Roma usually varies dramatically (Table 6); in 2004 this gap was between 2.7 and 4.7 times, depending on whether it is assumed that the total number of Roma is about 550,000 or if we use the officially accepted figure—370,000 (Bezlov 2007b).

Table 6. Crimes and Roma suspects
Source: Ministry of Interior (quoted in Bezlov 2007b).

Year	Crimes per 100,000 people	Roma suspects (% of the total)
1990	763	21.4
1991	1,949	32.2
1992	2,507	34.1
1993	2,485	31.9
1994	2,510	30.4
1995	2,336	27.9
1996	2,200	26.5
1997	2,728	27.5
1998	1,817	20.2
1999	1,623	18.6
2000	1,673	19.7
2001	1,778	19.4
2002	1,757	18.9
2003	1,662	18.8
2004	1,640	18.9

Although the police statistics is not reliable as a whole, there is no reason to think that the police will place too much importance on some types of crime committed by Roma and ignore other violations. The data indicate that the numbers of Romani perpetrators are higher regarding specific types of crime, like these against property and against person. The statistics of the Ministry of Interior indicates that the share of murders committed by suspects of Roma origin in 1993 was 35.83 per 100,000 (assuming that Roma are 500,000), while for Bulgarians it was 5.47 per 100,000 people (Bezlov 2007b). By 2003, the share of Bulgarians rose to 5.80, while Roma has dropped to 12.50. Here again it seems that the registration of ethnicity is a problem, since there are no other obvious reasons why the number of perpetrators of murder of Bulgarian origin has grown, while that of Roma has decreased three times. It appears however that cases of Roma's "collective violence" are on the raise — i.e., when groups of Roma are involved in a fight or a brawl, especially with ethnic Bulgarians (Bezlov 2007f). Such cases usually are receiving a lot of media coverage which focuses the public attention even further on the illegal activities of the ethnic group. *Roma's "criminality" diminishing or not, notwithstanding, as the protests that followed the events in Katunitsa demonstrated, the Bulgarian society is becoming less and less willing to put up with ethnic minority's brushes with the law. In my view, the problem is not that the PRR parties promote a zero tolerance policy toward criminals, but that these political formations are prepared to use the stain of "illegal activities" and place it as a stigma on the ethnic group as a whole.*

What are the reasons for the high crime rate among Roma? First, one has to take into consideration the cultural specifics, customs, and traditions. Many Roma are not aware, in general, of the differences between crimes and administrative offences. Police officers often state that some Roma subgroups[209] are, particularly, involved in petty crimes. They do not consider administrative offenses as something illegal. Roma often view and justify these offenses as a way of survival (Bezlov 2007c). Often times, the clan or the family to which a Roma belongs incites an illegal conduct from

---

209 Like the Kalderash, for example.

a very early age. The clan and/or the family often encourages, mediates, or directly organizes the participation of Roma in the informal economy. In addition to controlling the supply of illegal labor, Roma families are sometimes a basic unit in numerous criminal activities, including the organized crime (Bezlov 2007e). The family crime business is manifested in various forms, such as pickpocketing,[210] theft of farm animals, illegal logging, stealing of scrap metal, loan sharking, pimping, smuggling of goods (e.g., cigarettes) and antiques, and drug trafficking[211] (ibid.). The chaotic privatization and restitution intertwined with closure of thousands of factories, farms, military bases, etc., the abandonment not only of single buildings but often of whole villages—all these factors created numerous possibilities for crimes against property. Therefore, in the *second place*, there are objective political and economic conditions, which are favorable to crime. Roma took advantage of abandoned property and began collecting, in many cases stealing, everything of value in order to sell it: metals (like copper wire), building materials, etc.

According to different estimates the shadow economy is responsible for 27–35% of Bulgaria's GDP.[212] The functioning of many grey markets depends greatly on the availability of unskilled and cheap labor, and in many cases on criminal activities. This is seen most strongly in two niche markets—the collection of scrap metal[213] and timber (Bezlov 2007d). The work force that collects these materials is composed mainly of Roma. The firms that make profit from scrap or timber are typically not interested to check whether the materials that are brought to them are stolen or a result of illegal

---

210 The family plays a most significant role in the "apprenticeship" of children-pickpockets. As far as the custom of buying of brides is concerned, the price or the value of the bride to be may be highly dependent on her pickpocketing skills.
211 As for the distribution of drugs, the most appropriate example is the Roma neighborhood Stolipinovo. Initially the drug dealers there were able to meet the demand of the market in Plovdiv, but eventually Stolipinovo became a hub for the supply of narcotics to all of Southeast Bulgaria.
212 Bezlov (2007d).
213 These companies are predominantly owned by ethnic Bulgarians and Turks.

logging. *These companies operate under the benevolent eye of politicians and the police. The latter are often paid to turn their backs on crimes.* In some cases, the authorities arrest "the workers" but shortly after that let them walk free. The actual bosses and organizers are rarely prosecuted. There was an unsuccessful attempt to halt this illegal trade. In 2012, a new provision, imposing a ban on selling waste (including scrap), was incorporated in the Waste Management Act. However, in 2014 the Constitutional Court declared that this provision, which required that citizens simply collect and give for processing the waste, i.e., *without getting paid*, is unconstitutional. In reality, the provision worked *for* the firms, because if it was enacted, they would have received the waste for free.

The illegal actions of Roma have led to the increase of negative attitudes and stereotypes against the ethnic minority. Especially during the first decade after 1989, the police and the criminal justice system as a whole were subjected to countless reforms. Their workload and "productivity" decreased significantly[214] notwithstanding the rapid "jump" of the crime rate. Nonetheless, this negative trend was gradually reversed and in 2001 the number of convicted persons was six times more than in 1993 (Bezlov 2007c). Another important factor, which led to the reduction of Roma crime, is the more regular payment of social benefits and with the accession of Bulgaria to the EU in 2007 many Roma emigrated to try their luck in the richer Western European economies.

According to a very popular stereotype, widely propagandized by the nationalistic formations, the main sources of income of Roma, apart from the crimes, are the social benefits that they receive as well as the money that they get for selling their votes. In fact, once they receive their social benefits for the month, most Romani use the money in order to cover their debts, typically, in the local grocery store (Bezlov 2007c).[215] They can make the ends

---

214 The rock bottom was hit in 1993, when the number of sentences was three times less than in 1989 (Bezlov 2007c).
215 I have already discussed the legal sources of Roma income. See Table 2, Section 1.4.

meet for the next 10 days. During the last week of the month, however, they usually take new credits. Therefore, the ordinary Roma are often in the merciless hands of the local moneylenders who set unbearably high interest rates (100% and even more).[216] The organized crime and the political parties, which are shopping for Roma votes, typically use the loan sharks as an instrument in order to "motivate" or coerce the constituents that are in debt. The average Roma who sells his vote often does not get any money. Typically the profit goes in the pockets of political brokers and loan sharks who (may) agree to waive (a part) of their debts. *It is, thus, not surprising that political elites are not only not interested in working effectively for the integration of Roma, but are tempted to keep this ethnicity in a marginalized state — illiterate, poor, and unemployed, remaining outside the borders of society.*[217]

In many instances, the organized criminal activities in which Roma take part are under the protection of local political bosses. Furthermore, sometimes people who are related to criminals or themselves participate in illegal activities are directly involved in the political processes. The so-called Town of the pickpockets — Ignatievo — provides a telling example. The case was widely covered in the media (Dimitrova 2015). Subject to the raids of the pickpockets were primarily the major shopping malls in Varna. Journalistic investigations and reports indicate that the thieves were able to build expensive houses and enjoy luxurious lifestyle in Ignatievo. The value of the properties in question "clearly demonstrates" that

---

216 A moneylender in Sliven has been arrested after it was discovered that he took the debit cards of his debtors, on which the social payments were made. Another example reveling the might of loan sharks comes from Vidin, where the infamous Roma clan Zrunkovi killed one of their debtors; see Bezlov (2007c).

217 Politics aside, another widespread fraud in which the organized crime takes advantage of the illiteracy of Roma is by tricking them to sign documents which claim that they are the "owners" of shady companies. Such firms often do not pay taxes or are involved in other illegal activities. In 2005, it was revealed that the largest (individual) debtor of the state is a 26-year-old illiterate and unemployed Roma man from Ihtiman. Despite the fact that he lived in dare conditions in the ghetto "Iztok," his companies owed the Bulgarian state the whopping 15 million leva VAT (Mihalev 2005).

these cannot be paid with the (legal) income of their owners (Dimitrova 2015). According to the ongoing investigation conducted by the authorities (February 2016) some of the owners were able to hide income for a minimum of 200,000 leva while, at the same time, many of them were and still are registered as unemployed and receive social benefits. The husband and accomplice of a self-proclaimed Roma pickpocket was a candidate who stood at the local elections held in October 2015. He is a member of the political party Solidarity. The latter is little known in Bulgaria but apparently very influential in Ignatievo (Dimitrova 2015). Hristo Mladenov, the Chairman of Solidarity, is also the leader of the National Meshere.[218] The daughter-in-law of the candidate for mayor Georgi Botev is also a pickpocket (ibid.). In pickpockets' own words, the police "are not only aware but assist our crimes" (ibid.). For the time being neither the government nor the local authorities have taken significant measures in order to halt the alleged illegal activities perpetrated by some of the inhabitants of Ignatievo. These include not only pickpocketing but also telephone fraud, racketeering, loan sharking, and tax evasion (Dimitrova 2015).

The precise function and role of the informal Roma court—the Meshere—remain subject to debates and speculations in the media. Experts claim that the number of cases and community problems that the court is actually able to resolve is very insignificant while in reality, ironically, it most likely directs and coordinates a complex criminal network (Aleksandrova 2011). According to crime experts, there are rumors (which have never been confirmed) that the court has even ruled death sentences in the 1990s that have been executed (ibid.). The Roma "baron" Kiril Rashkov (aka "Tsar Kiro"), who was involved in the events in Katunitsa in 2011, has also been sentenced by this institution in 2007 (ibid.).

Rashkov's biography demonstrates the deep interconnection between the criminal underworld on the one hand, and the political

---

[218] "Meshere" is the name of the informal Roma tribunal in Bulgaria. See "The Roma Meshere elected its boss" (2013).

aspirations of Roma's nefarious "elite"[219] and the protections from the powers that be, which it usually has, on the other. Rashkov received seven sentences (or a total of 30 years prison time) before 1989; however, after the political changes he was swiftly pardoned and subsequently has received mainly administrative penalties (Georgieva 2011). After November 10, 1989, Kiril Rashkov registered an alcohol producing company named "Tsar Gogo." The production plant was raised near the village of Katunitsa. In 1993, he was arrested for producing fake alcohol. In a warehouse rented by him, the police found 126 tons alcohol and 140 boxes of fake brandy—200,000 bottles and 14 illegal machines for bottling alcohol ("Who is Kiril Rashkov" 2011). However, Rashkov was released on bail of 10,000 USD.[220] In 1998, Rashkov founded his own political party—"Free Bulgaria." The latter was able to obtain seats in the municipal councils in Stara Zagora and Pazardzhik. That same year, three subordinates of Rashkov were arrested and convicted for placing explosives in front of offices of the newspaper *Trud*. In 2001, Kiril Rashkov and his family bought over 100 acres of land in Katunitsa and built several cottages. Because of these illegally acquired properties, communal areas, and illegal constructions, he was in conflict with the then mayor of Katunitza—Sofia Hristeva. She organized a petition among her fellow villagers and informed authorities vis-à-vis Rashkov's illegal activities ("Who Is Kiril Rashkov" 2011). A bomb was thrown at her home in 2010. She points to Kiril Rashkov as the man who organized and/or instigated the crime. Only after the unprecedented public unrest which followed the tragic events in Katunitsa in 2011, Tsar Kiro was arrested and spent two years in prison.[221]

The illegal Roma housing in Sofia, Plovdiv, Varna, the region of Blagoevgrad, and many other locations is a pressing issue. Here I will not dwell on the legal side of the problem; this is accomplished in Part 3. Instead, I will show why the illegal housing is a

---

219 Of course, here I "speak" about the criminal bosses, and not the real elite of Roma—a very well-educated and integrated in society minority.
220 See "Who is Kiril Rashkov" (2011).
221 See "Who is Kiril Rashkov" (2011).

source of interethnic tensions. The story of the conflict in the village of Garmen is rather typical. In May 2015, a drunken brawl between Bulgarians and Roma threatened to escalate when several Bulgarians attempted to storm Roma neighborhood Kremikovtzi and attack its occupants.[222] Thanks to the timely intervention of the police, violence has been avoided. Many Bulgarians in the village perceive Roma as a major source of crime. According to Ivan Kremenliev, the leader of a protest against the illegal Roma houses in the area: "the problem is the Roma migrants from all parts of Bulgaria who come to live in the village because they steal crops and rob the homes of locals and have respect for nobody."[223] He further emphasized that the police and the judicial system "do nothing to protect the citizens from the crimes and punish the ones who are responsible" (ibid.). The focus of the discontent became the Roma neighborhood, or, to use the more precise term, the ghetto Kremikovtzi. About 120 illegal Roma houses are due to be demolished in Garmen. The process has already begun. Residents of the Roma neighborhood Kremikovtzi declared that they are ready to protest in front of the Council of Ministers' building if the destruction of their houses does not halt. In early September 2015, most of the windows of the municipality of Garmen were broken.[224] Mayor Minka Kapitanova requested from the Ministry of Interior to send guards, however that was refused ("Roma in Garmen prepare for national protest" 2015).

The nationalistic formations, i.e., IMRO, NFSB, Ataka, etc., proclaim that the illegal buildings in Garmen and elsewhere are a symbol of Roma standing above the law. They also point to the fact that many Roma systematically do not pay their utility bills. Yet the authorities often turn a blind eye to their violations. *In my opinion, the problem of illegal housing has clear political dimensions. Many politicians have personal interest in the preservation of the ghettos. The symbiosis between local "feudal lords" and Roma barons is perpetuated in the principle: "protections against political support."* Politicians from almost

---

222 Similar to this is the case in Orlandovtsi (Sofia) in June 2015.
223 "The protest ended peacefully in Garmen" (2015).
224 The perpetrators are still unknown.

all parties prefer to deal directly with Roma leaders who have placed under their control a number of votes. Thirty-five percent of the Roma state that they have been offered money or favors in exchange to their "support" in the local elections in October 2015.[225] As I already stated, buying and selling votes is a practice in the slums that is very hard to eradicate. It is not my intention to exonerate the citizens who are prepared to trade their vote. But it has to be reminded once again that political elites and the organized crime, who are interested in maintaining the marginalization of Roma, Turks, and Pomaks, leave little choice for the marginalized and impoverished.

The former mayor of Garmen, Ahmed Bashev,[226] who was a candidate supported by the MRF in the local elections in 2015, challenged the claims that the number of inhabitants of the ghetto has multiplied because of migration. According to him, most of Roma have lived in the ghetto since 1940s. In recent years, the residents of the ghetto have increased because the birth rate among Roma is high. According to Bashev, while he was the mayor, many Roma "won auctions and bought the land," on which their houses were subsequently built ("Ahmed Bashev: No Romani …" 2015). Thus, he emphatically rejected the accusations that the land was donated by the local authorities in exchange for the (political) support of Roma.[227] The current Mayor Kapitanova, previously a deputy of Bashev in the municipality, who was also supported by the MRF, claims that he instigates Roma and tries to provoke an ethnic conflict in the village.[228]

One of the most disturbing consequences of marginalization of Roma, as well as the isolation of other minorities in society, is that it creates a fertile soil for political and religious radicalism. In 2012, in the district court of Pazardzhik began the process against 13 imams, most of them Roma and Pomaks but some of Arab origin. According to

---

225 "'Alpha Research': Campaigning for local elections is becoming a direct marketing" (2015).
226 See "Ahmed Bashev: No Romani were settled in Garmen" (2015).
227 See "Ahmed Bashev: No Romani were settled in Garmen" (2015).
228 "Minka Kapitanova: Ahmed Bashev personally incited Roma in Garmen" (2015).

the prosecution they were connected to Al Waqf al-Islami, an organization accused of spreading what the indictment calls a "radical version" of Salafist Islam between 2008 and 2010 ("Trial of suspected Bulgarian 'hate preachers' begins" 2012). According to the prosecution, the organized criminal group operated in the municipalities of Blagoevgrad, Rudozem, Smolyan, Plovdiv, Velingrad, and Pazardzhik and disseminated "antidemocratic ideology" — opposition to the principles of democracy, separation of powers, liberalism, statehood and rule of law, fundamental human rights such as gender equality and religious freedom, "by preaching the ideology of the Salafi Islam and imposition of Sharia state."[229] Most of the accused, including organization's leader Said Mutlu, were educated in Saudi Arabia. In 2014, the Pazardzhik Regional Court sentenced the thirteen imams. One of them received effective sentence, two — suspended sentences, while 10 were fined (Bedrov 2014). Chief Mufti's Office has repeatedly said that it does not accept the charges against imams (ibid.). The Court of Appeal in Plovdiv extended the sentence of the imam of Pazardzhik Ahmed Musa Ahmed to two years in 2015. However the Court revoked the conditional sentences of the regional mufti of Pazardzhik Abdullah Salih and the imam of Sarnitsa — Said Mutlu. On both of them were imposed administrative penalties. Each was fined with, respectively, 3,000 and 4,000 BGN. The administrative sanctions imposed by the District Court in Pazardzhik on the other 10 defendants remain unchanged.[230] Antonina Zhelyazkova, expert in the field of ethnic conflicts, disputes the verdicts against the Pomak imams[231] but also shares the view, expressed here, *that the Roma ghettoes with their poor infrastructure, high unemployment, and crime rates are the ones most*

---

229 See "Trial of suspected Bulgarian 'hate preachers' begins" (2012).
230 See "Ahmed Musa Ahmed got two years in prison for preaching radical Islam" (2015).
231 She claims that the verdicts are mostly a result of the state security services' ambition to demonstrate their usefulness and to vindicate their generous funding. See "Is the Bulgarian 'division time' coming back?" (2012).

likely to become a breeding ground of radical Islam and the dangerous activities of its preachers.[232] *The dire conditions in the ghettoes create time bombs. In my view, in order not only to dismantle these "explosives" but to prevent their (further) appearance in the first place, the Bulgarian government must urgently improve on its integration strategies, policies, and measures. I address this issue in the next part of the book.*

The vow of silence on the subject of minorities, which the representatives of Bulgarian elite have sworn at the beginning of the transition to democracy, was a sacred rule governing the political theater during the first postcommunist party system. This rule was fundamental for ethnic relations. It had two dimensions. The first was the delegitimization of any attempt to reap political dividends by instigating hostility between ethnic communities; the second was to create space for the expression of their interests and their involvement in all phases of the political process. The latter aspect has enormous political implications. It cannot be assessed unambiguously. Several conclusions could be made on the grounds of the analysis. First, the institutionalization of ethnic cleavage forms the bedrock of the ethnic model. It enables the reduction or "cushioning" of emerging tensions between ethnic groups by means of political debate. Thus, the violent fratricidal wars that ravaged our western neighbors in the Balkans have been avoided. In this respect, the policy of MRF, at least initially, has contributed to the preservation of ethnic peace.

Second, as shown by the analysis, MRF has a highly centralized party leadership. Among significant part of movement's supporters, there are serious doubts about the way in which they are represented, as well as, diplomatically speaking, the respectability "of the management" of MRF. Although the defects of MRF are somewhat idiosyncratic (the ethnic specifics of the party support provides powerful management levers), they are inextricably linked with sclerosis in the party and the political system. The anemia and lack of efficiency of intermediary institutions, which on paper should represent the interests emerging in civil society, stem

---

232 "Is the Bulgarian 'division time' coming back?" (2012).

from the fact that these institutions, although to varying degrees, are affected by corruption, nepotism, and oligarchic tendencies. The crisis of the party system continues with fluctuating dynamics and intensity for more than two decades. Its symptoms are the melting of many ideological barriers between left and right; the decline in mobilizing force of party programs; the triumph of political (particularly socio-oriented) populism; the attempts to disguise the discredited processes of party construction through movements, "civil" initiatives, etc.; and the cartelization of political system.

Third, the study confirms the thesis that the political behavior of MRF, the PRR, and of every political institution for that matter can be understood only after thoroughly analyzing the interconnections with the other players in the political game. The significant influence of the MRF in both postcommunist party systems is not merely a function of the "flexibility" of its leadership program documents or its characteristic electoral support. The role of "balancer" which the party performed in the decade after 1989 was caused by tides and refluxes in the right, as well as the fluctuations and internal collisions in the left. The diminishing turnout, fatigue, or "frustration" of the voters are trends that plague the political system from the beginning of the new millennium until this day. Practically, they do not have negative effects on the MRF, and even strengthen its position. The MRF managed to "saddle" and "ride" both NMPS's populism and to "surf" on the leftist wave that we observe in recent years. I do not have reasons to believe that the new ethnic party—DOST, a fierce competitor of MRF—will do a better job as far as defending the rights of minorities is concerned. Furthermore, this organization operates under the influence of the autocratic political regime in Ankara.

Fourth, the extreme discontent among a substantial part of Bulgarians from the way the transition was conducted and its negative effects erupt in antisystem political actors who categorically reject "the rules" of political theater. For the supporters of Ataka, NFSB, and other formations, the MRF, a party represented in all parliaments since the beginning of the democratic changes, is among the most grotesque symbols of the status quo and its "genetic abnormalities." On the one hand, the existing "defects" in the functioning of the movement are a solid foundation for its demonization. On the other, the institutionalization of ethnic conflict (the fact that minorities are in power, receive posts, etc.) leads to the politicization of ethnic identity. Parties such as MRF, DOST, NMFD thus become the raison d'être of Bulgarian ethnic entrepreneurs. The converse is also true—the ethnic parties need the latter. The politicization of ethnic identity is not necessarily an alarming phenomenon. It can, however, easily become one when the institutions that must channel conflicts peacefully are discredited. The ethnic entrepreneurs successfully feed, parasitize on the ongoing economic crisis, the high emigration among Bulgarians, combined with low fertility and high mortality, and, lately, the peak in immigration.

Fifth, these conclusions give reason to expect deepening and further escalation of ethnic conflicts. It is important that reason and political pragmatism prevail. Bulgaria is a multiethnic country. The high-pitched cries urging to ban one or another ethnic party (especially when their existence is already a fait accompli) will inevitably deepen the rift between ethnic groups. They can lead to local reconstruction of the Bosnian "scenarios" or elements thereof. The short-sided political trickeries that aim to "repair" the model simply through "modification" of procedures (e.g., the amendment of electoral legislation in order to reduce the weight of the ethnic votes—which was a tactics employed against Mestan's DOST) essentially are a faint-hearted attempt to escape from the main challenge—the policymakers can restore voters' confidence in the democratic poglitical process only when they reform the institutions themselves.

3. Channeling Ethnic Conflicts

According to the liberal ideal, the political institutions of democracies should be able to capture and represent the interests, as well as to channel the conflicts that emerge in the civil society. This is their contribution to the peaceful coexistence of individuals and groups. The government, legislation, and judicial system are political institutions that have a salient role in the process. In the analysis that follows I explore their effectiveness in Bulgaria for prevention and resolution of the ethnic conflicts after the collapse of the former communist regime. First, in Section 3.1, I examine the policies of government. I am interested, in particular, in the main directions and challenges in front of the integration of Roma in Bulgaria. I ask whether the country nowadays involuntarily repeats some of the disastrous mistakes and shortcomings of the integration strategies applied in the SFRY,[233] thus failing to learn from the bitter lessons of history.

In my opinion, *the Roma constitute an ethnic underclass in the Bulgarian society*. The paramount argument in support of this thesis is the fact that they are subjected *to major social exclusion or the inability to participate in society's structures and institutions* (Tomova 2006).[234] As already mentioned, in spite of Roma political parties and organizations in existence, the representation of Roma in the parliament, the executive, and the local government is insufficient and ineffective (Tomova 2006: 541). Among the Roma population only 50.2% of the economically active persons are employed, that is 19.35% of all Roma aged 15 and more.[235] Because of this the state is losing approximately 700 million leva/pa (Bozukova 2011). The

---

233 See Section 1.2.
234 For other definition of social exclusion see, e.g., Room (1995), where it is characterized by dropping out of the main social spheres and, in particular, the employment sphere.
235 About 53.5% of all ethnic Bulgarians aged above 15 are economically active, compared to 45.4% of the Bulgarian Turks and only 38.8% of the Roma people. See NCCEII (2012).

segregation of Roma community has in fact increased between 1980, when 49% of the ethnicity lived in segregated neighborhoods and communities, and 2006, when this percentage has risen to more than 75% (Tomova 2006: 542). One of the worst consequences of segregation is the deterioration of the ability to prepare the younger generations for the formal economy and the major obstacles that the residents of segregated neighborhoods face in finding employment (ibid.: 542). The main questions that I attempt to answer are: what are the problems which plague the integration strategies and why they continue to be mostly a virtual, paper-made reality; what are the reasons for the continuing marginalization of Roma; why ghettoes and segregated education remain; why the employment strategies give little or no results; what are the risks that Roma exclusion raises; what are the necessary policy measures that must be applied in order to break this vicious cycle. I seek the answers to these pressing issues.

Section 3.2 is dedicated to the analysis of the legislation and judicial system. Under the Constitution from July 13, 1991, Bulgaria is a unitary state with continental legal system—the principle of *stare decisis* is not applied. The Constitution and the ratified international instruments are directly enforceable by the general courts. The judiciary is overseen by the Ministry of Justice. The Constitutional Court has exclusive authority to bindingly interpret the Constitution, while the Supreme Administrative Court (SAC) and Supreme Court of Cassation are the highest courts of appeal and oversee the application of the laws. The Supreme Judicial Council manages the system and appoints judges. Currently, there are around 100 ratified international instruments[236] as well as primary and secondary national legislation, which concern the discrimination on

---

236 Bulgaria is a signatory to the UN human rights instruments: International Covenant on Civil and Political Rights, 1966 (in effect for Bulgaria from 1970); International Covenant for Economic, Social, and Cultural Rights, 1966 (in effect for Bulgaria from 1970); International Convention on the Elimination of All Forms of Racial Discrimination, 1966 (in effect for Bulgaria from 1992); The Convention on the Elimination of All Forms of Discrimination against Women, 1979 (in effect for Bulgaria from 1982); Convention on the Rights of the Child, 1989

the basis of ethnicity in Bulgaria (Berov 2009).[237] The most important national acts are the Constitution (1991), the Law on Confessions (2002), and the PADA (2004). For practical reasons, I will limit the analysis to the latter instrument, which is the main antidiscrimination law, and the way it transposes the EC antidiscrimination legislation, in particular Directive 2000/43/EC and Directive 2000/78/EC. To this issue is dedicated Section 3.2.2. Before that, in Section 3.2.1, I set up a general framework for analysis of the judicial system in its interconnection with the political processes in society. Section 3.2.3 includes several case studies. Of the larger ethnic groups which traditionally live in Bulgaria, the Roma are most often a target of discrimination (Metodieva et al. 2012, Petkova 2013). I outline and analyze cases that concern this ethnic group. The case studies illuminate the ways in which the judicial system and the relevant legislation operate. They help to reveal and map the problematic issues.

3.1 The integration policies of Bulgarian governments after 1989

A representative survey conducted by Gallup at the end of the Decade of Roma Inclusion demonstrates that the respondents perceive

---

(in effect for Bulgaria from 1991), etc. The country also adheres to the EU political and legislative framework for the protection of human rights, of ensuring equal opportunities for all citizens and prevention of discrimination based on various grounds, including ethnicity, such as the Charter of Fundamental Rights of the European Union, Council Directive 2000/43/EC of 29 June 2000 implementing the principle of equal treatment between persons irrespective of racial or ethnic origin, Council Directive 2000/78/EC establishing a general framework for equal treatment in employment and occupation, etc. Of significance are also the European Convention on Human Rights (ECHR, formally the Convention for the Protection of Human Rights and Fundamental Freedoms, drafted in 1950 by the then newly formed Council of Europe) and the case law of the European Court of Human Rights, which the ECHR established. In 1999, the Bulgarian Parliament ratified the Framework Convention of the Council of Europe on Protection of National Minorities (1995).

237 The primary legislation is adopted by the parliament, and the secondary by the executive branch of the government.

that the integration policies toward Roma are flawed (see Figure 16). Thus 57% believe that "almost all money used by the programs to support Roma was stolen" (Gallup 2015). On the one hand, the majority of the respondents (55%) are convinced that the problems between the Roma and the Bulgarians are deliberately caused by the politicians (ibid.). On the other hand, the negative stereotypes against the Roma remain strong—62% think that the Roma cannot integrate even when the state makes efforts.

Figure 16. Social distances.
"Do you agree or disagree with each of the following statements?"

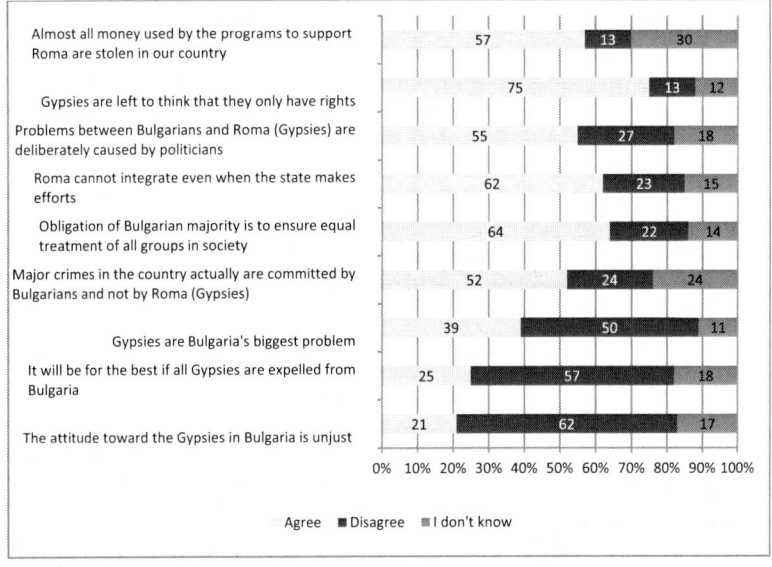

Source: Gallup (2015).
Note: In my view, the use of the term "Gypsies" in the statements demonstrates a lack of elementary political correctness on behalf of the researchers.

The lack of political will of the ruling parties and coalitions is often indicated as *the chief impediment* in front of integration of minorities in Bulgaria (OSI 2002, Rechel 2007, 2008). Politicians are reluctant to promote tangible and effective changes because racism (especially toward Roma) is widespread. Measures of positive discrimination are perceived as undeserved privileges by the majority of ethnic Bulgarians, who live in daring economic conditions (Mantarova and Zaharieva 2007). Instead of real changes, governments often create a "virtual reality" in order to appease the demands and pressure from EU institutions for reforms (Rechel 2008). Although I do agree with this conclusion, I believe that it is, rather, *one-dimensional*. Indeed, as stated above,[238] there is empirical evidence that shows an increase of ethnic distances, in particular between Bulgarians and Roma. Nonetheless, the widening of "the void" between the ethnic groups *is also caused by the political entrepreneurs who denounce the ethnic model as part and parcel of a façade democracy drafted by the architects of political transition in Bulgaria*. Other drawbacks from which the polices in question suffer are the incoherent legislation and the problems in its implementation; the absence of vision and direction for the policies, as well as effective monitoring mechanisms; the relatively limited amount of national funds (part of the state budget) and their inadequate distribution[239]; the small participation of the representatives of the minorities in the process of tailoring and implementation of programs (EC 2004, BHC 2012, BHC 2013, Cholakov 2014a). In order to further analyze these issues, I explore below one of the key domains in the integration policies, the role of the National Council for Cooperation on Ethnic and Integration Issues (NCCEII) and its predecessors NCEDI (National Council on Ethnic and Demographic Issues) and NCCEDI (National Council for Cooperation on Ethnic and Demographic Issues), established for the protection of minority rights. I shall also analyze some of the key policy documents such as the Framework Programs[240] for Integration of Roma.[241] The emphasis will be on the

---

238 See Sections 1.4 and 2.3.4.
239 The country relies mostly on foreign funds for the integration of minorities (e.g., the PHARE program).
240 *The Framework Program for Equal Integration of Roma in the Bulgarian Society*, 1999, followed by *The Framework Program for Integration of Roma in the Bulgarian Society, 2010–2020*.
241 See NCEDI (1999) and NCCEDI (2010).

policies toward the Roma — the third largest ethnic group[242] whose integration remains the most problematic.

During the 1990s many countries in Central and Eastern Europe established institutions that were (at least partially) concerned with the rights of minorities, mostly in order to satisfy the expectations of foreign NGOs and the EU. The majority of these institutions were marginalized politically because they did not have enough financial resources and political support (OSI 2002: 225). Since 1994, the National Councils in Bulgaria were organized within the structure of the Council of Ministers. The Interdepartmental Council on Demographic Issues established by the government of Lyuben Berov (1992–1994) was never summoned (Rechel 2008: 88). The National Council on Social and Demographic Issues was created in 1995 in order to contribute to the solution of the social problems of "pensioners, people with disabilities, women and ethnic groups" (Gazette 1995).[243] The NCEDI, which was set up in 1997, was intended as a platform for consultations, cooperation, and coordination between the government agencies and the NGOs with the aim to create and implement the national policies in the sphere of ethnic and demographic issues, as well as migration (Gazette 1997).[244]

The main shortcoming in the operation of NCEDI, as the EU institutions pointed out in their reports during 2000–2004, was that *it did not possess a real authority to direct or to implement any programs*

---

242 As I have already mentioned above, the population census conducted in 2011 shows that 325,343 people, i.e., 4.9% of the Bulgarian citizens, identified themselves as belonging to the Roma ethnos. Most likely the real number is higher. Because of the stigma on their ethnicity, Romani sometimes prefer to identify themselves, for example, as Turks or, simply, do not indicate their belonging to any ethnic group. See NSI (2011).

243 Its *Program to Solve the Problems of the Roma in Bulgaria* (adopted on January 30, 1997) was never implemented because the country was in the midst of severe political and economic crisis.

244 NCEDI was composed of ten deputy ministers, four directors of state bodies (The National Agency for Bulgarians Abroad, the State Agency for Refugees, the National Statistical Institute, and the Council on Religious Issues of the Council of Ministers), the Directorate on Religious Affairs of the Council of Ministers, as well as representatives of NGOs.

that concerned the minorities. In 2004, the Council of Ministers transformed NCEDI into NCCEDI, while its administration became Directorate on Ethnic and Demographic Issues (Gazette 2004). The status of the bodies was not affected much. The Monitoring Reports of the EU in 2005 and 2006 emphasized that NCCEDI *remained a consultative body that was bereft of executive powers* (Rachel 2008: 89).

The *Framework Program for Equal Integration of Roma in the Bulgarian Society* was adopted by the Council of Ministers in 1999. The program reflected not only the standpoint of the government but also the views of Roma organizations. However, the latter were taken into consideration only as a result of the pressure by the Council of Europe and the media (Rusinov 2001). Many alarming facts regarding the place of Roma in society were admitted in the program, for example[245]: that they were "not adequately represented in the political institutions" and occupied "the lowest rung of the social hierarchy"; that their status was "drastically lower than the average for Bulgaria—they are plagued by high unemployment, deplorable living conditions, poor health, high rate of illiteracy" (NCEDI 1999). The program envisaged a variety of measures for a period of 10 years in the spheres of: legislation (amendments to ensure better protection against discrimination, including the establishment of specialized state body for prevention); economic development (employment, social assistance, land settlement); health care; housing; education (e.g., desegregation of schools and the possibility to study Romani language as an optional subject); fostering of Roma culture; access to national media; and empowerment of Roma women.[246] The program was described at the time as "the most significant achievement of Roma in public life" (Rusinov 2001) and was prized by the EU institutions, including by the then president of the Commission Romano Prodi (OSI 2002: 116).

Unfortunately, until April 2003, the ambitious goals that were set in the program *remained mostly on paper*—a fact that was

---

[245] However, other facts, as the practices that testified to the existence of institutional racism in the police, were omitted (Rachel 2008: 90).
[246] For further details see NCEDI (1999).

acknowledged by the authorities (Kanev 2003: 10, Republic of Bulgaria 2003: 37). The unsatisfactory implementation ensued mainly from: the very limited legal competences of the NCEDI (the recommendations of the Council were not mandatory, therefore, for example, the respective ministries were not obligated to draft reports on the steps they took in order to achieve the objectives); the fact that the measures were relying heavily on foreign funding (mostly from the EU) while some of their goals were not compatible with the PHARE program.[247] Critics also underlined the lack of consultations with the civil society and the absence of political will for fulfilling the objectives (Angelova 2001, OSI 2002: 116). The Action Plan for implementation of the program was adopted *with a four-year delay* on October 6, 2003. The plan specified more precise measures, as well as a schedule and a budget for the process of implementation (NCEDI 2003). The Roma representatives *were largely ignored* in the debates during the elaboration of the plan (Rechel 2008: 92). Although the latter marked a relative progress it was not without flaws. The main issues were the discrepancies between the goals of the program and the plan (Rechel 2008: 92), the lack of funding for the desegregation of Roma schools, as well as the fact that "no adequate reforms were provided for the key spheres of education, healthcare and housing" (EC 2004: 25).

A new, more detailed action plan was adopted in June 2006 in the view of the forthcoming accession of Bulgaria to the EU in 2007 (NCCEDI 2006: 5). Important highlights, which addressed some of the criticisms above, were: the raised awareness of the fact that Roma organizations *had to be included in the decision-making process* (the authors of the plan admitted that a "plethora of projects failed because they had not been discussed with their beneficiaries," ibid.:

---

[247] The program is one of the three pre-accession instruments financed by the EU to assist the candidate countries of Central and Eastern Europe in their preparations. It was launched in 1989 as the *Poland and Hungary: Assistance for Restructuring their Economies (PHARE) Program*. PHARE (which means "lighthouse" in French) has expanded to currently cover ten countries. It assists eight of the ten 2004 accession Member States: the Czech Republic, Estonia, Hungary, Latvia, Lithuania, Poland, Slovakia, and Slovenia, as well as those countries that acceded in 2007 – Bulgaria and Romania.

9); the ambition *to improve coordination* between different policies and institutions that were committed to the integration of Roma (ibid.: 11–12); the necessity to strengthen the efficiency of the administration of NCCEDI (ibid.: 14–16); the more precise measures in the fields of education[248] (ibid.: 18–20), social services and protection (ibid.: 20–2), employment (ibid.: 22–3), health care and housing (ibid.: 25–9); and the elaboration of two types of indicators for evaluation of the results of the program (ibid.: 36–40).

No further action plans for the implementation of 1999 Framework Program were ever drafted. However, a year before, in 2005, was adopted a National Action Plan[249] for the pan-European Initiative "Decade of Roma Inclusion, 2005–2015" (NAP-DRI).[250] As far as the implementation of the measures depended on the state budget, these *were bound to become a hostage of the outcome of political battles for allocation of resources. Therefore it was not possible to make realistic long-term planning.* Essentially, without prior secured financing, this political document (NAP-DRI) was mainly *an expression of wishful thinking* (Grekova 2008: 124). Until at least 2008, there was no formal mechanism for monitoring. Apart from the reports of some of the high-ranking state officials, which were incomplete, the results of the NAP-DRI were not disseminated to the public (Grekova 2008: 127).

The *Framework Program for Integration of Roma in Bulgarian Society, 2010–2020* has been adopted in 2010. The 2005 NAP-DRI is

---

248 With respect to the desegregation of schools, in particular.
249 I shall not discuss the plan here because this has already been done painstakingly and in a great detail, e.g., in Grekova (2008).
250 The initiative was launched on February 2, 2005, in Sofia, Bulgaria, where prime ministers of the participating governments (of Bulgaria, Croatia, the Czech Republic, Hungary, Montenegro, Romania, Serbia, Slovakia, and the FYRM) signed the Decade Declaration, with the commitment to work toward eliminating discrimination and closing the unacceptable gaps between Roma and the rest of society. The founding international partner organizations included the World Bank, the Open Society Institute, the United Nations Development Program, the Council of Europe, the Organization for Security and Cooperation in Europe, and various Roma organizations. The Decade also had benefitted from the support of the EC, a member of the International Steering Committee.

used for the purpose of implementation and monitoring of this program (NCCEDI 2010: 3, 21). The latter is guided by the *10 Common Basic Principles of Roma Inclusion of the Council of Ministers of the EU* (2009)[251]: constructive, pragmatic, and nondiscriminatory policies; explicit but not exclusive targeting; intercultural approach; aiming for the mainstream; awareness of the gender dimension; transfer of evidence-based policies; use of EU instruments; involvement of regional and local authorities; involvement of civil society; and active participation of the Roma (NCCEDI 2010: 3). The program is drafted in conjunction with the political and legislative framework of the EU, as well as the *Framework Convention for the Protection of National Minorities* (1995) of the Council of Europe (ibid.: 4). According to the text of the program, its strategic goal is to create conditions for equal integration of Roma in society, economics, and politics by pursuing "equal opportunities and equal access to the rights, benefits, goods and services, participation in all public areas and improving the quality of life while respecting the principles of equality and non-discrimination" (ibid.: 5). The priority areas are similar to these that we already saw in previous documents: education, health care, housing, employment, nondiscrimination and equal opportunities, and culture.

I shall briefly examine here only the measures foreseen in education, because this field is, perhaps, the one that is the most crucial for the success of integration. *Education is the most important prerequisite for subsequent inclusion in the labor market, for improving the health status and the housing conditions of the Roma.*[252] The ethnic group is characterized by a very unfavorable educational structure in comparison to the rest of the population — 40.8% of Roma have basic education, while 27.9% have primary education; only 0.5% have higher education.[253] The authors of the program concede that

---

251 See as well EC (2009).
252 This conclusion is supported in the program itself, see, e.g., NCCEDI (2010: 5).
253 In comparison, 25.6% of Bulgarians and 4.9% of Turks have completed higher education. The data are from the population census conducted in 2011, see NSI (2011). The primary (in general between ages 7 and 11 and grades 1 and 4) and basic education (ages 11 and 15, grades 5 and 8) are mandatory in Bulgaria.

despite the measures taken by the government, the segregated education (including the "secondary segregation" in ethnically mixed schools) *continues to be a particularly acute problem and that the number of school dropouts among the Roma children is very high* (NCCEDI 2010: 6).

The 2010 Framework Program outlines 19 "action priorities" in the sphere of education. The most important of them are (NCCEDI 2010: 7–8):

- inclusion into the educational system of all Roma children subject to mandatory education[254];
- establishing conditions for all Roma children, living in areas with ethnically mixed population, to study in ethnically mixed groups in kindergartens and classes in schools, as well as closure of the segregated schools that cannot provide that;
- terminating the practice to send healthy Roma children into "special schools" and removing the healthy Roma pupils from such schools[255];
- improving the quality of education in schools, which train exclusively Roma children;
- developing and implementing a comprehensive strategy to prevent dropouts from the education system and to reintegrate the ones who have already left;
- providing institutional support for the preservation and development of ethnic and cultural identity of Roma children through educational and training process (study of Romani language and Roma culture);
- preparing qualified teachers trained to work in multicultural environment;

---

[254] Until eighth grade.
[255] A large percent of the Roma children are sent to "special" schools for mentally retarded children and are included in "special" programs after being categorized as incapable to follow and complete the regular school programs. Thus the Roma children are denied the right to equal opportunities in education. The mechanism, which allows cultural specifics of Roma children and their unequal status in society to be defined as mental incapacity, is deeply discriminatory.

- incorporating of courses on intercultural education into university curricula;
- stimulating Roma children to continue their studies after they complete the mandatory education and providing (financial) support for them if needed; and
- creating conditions for early vocational guidance as well as career development.

Once again, the program does not specify *how* these measures should be implemented in practice; thus, it appears that they remain mostly into the realm of "good wishes." Since 2011, NCCEDI has become NCCEII. There were changes in the Rules of Organization and Proceedings of the institution (Gazette 2013). The most significant of them are as follows (NCCEII 2011: 1-2): the NCCEII coordinates, controls, and monitors the implementation of the National Action Plan for the initiative "Decade of Roma Inclusion 2005-2015" and the responsibilities of all state institutions according to their functional competence related to it; the president of NCCEII is the National Coordinator of the initiative "Decade of Roma Inclusion"; the Council includes a representative of the Minister in charge of management of the EU funds. Furthermore, NCCEII is, in general, responsible for preparation, submission, and approval of positions, analyses, reports, and other documents in the field of ethnic issues in relation to the participation of Bulgaria in the sessions of working groups and formations of the Council of the EU, the EC, the Council of Europe, the United Nations (UN), etc., and takes part in these meetings with its representatives. The Council consists of president, two vice-presidents, and members.[256] The president of the NCCEII is a deputy prime minister of Bulgaria.[257] Apart from the president, the Council includes 14 deputy ministers, the president of the National Statistical Institute, representatives of five state agencies, one representative of Directorate Monitoring of

---

256 See Gazette 2013: Art. 5 (1).
257 See Art. 5 (2).

Funds from the EU, the Bulgarian Academy of Sciences and the National Association of Municipalities, as well as 47 representatives of NGOs (Gazette 2013: Art. 5).

It is hard to see, in my opinion, the real benefits that these legislative amendments bring. As before, the main functions of the institution are *to coordinate* the actions of the ministries (e.g., the Ministry of Education and the Ministry of Health), which are responsible for the different branches of the integration policies, and *to consult* the government as a platform for expression of interests of minorities (in particular, the Roma) through the representatives of the NGOs. Unfortunately, while these prerogatives "look good" on paper, the reality is different. First, the Council, as before, does not have any substantial authority to enforce the implementation of the policies. The president of the Council *remains* a vice-president of the Republic of Bulgaria. Thus, second, the body is, in fact, viciously dependent on the political projects and ambitions of the majority. For this reason, representatives of the NGOs have described NCCEDI as "a political creature," justifying and covering up the inaction of the government toward the integration of the Roma (Kolev 2009). As in the NCCEDI, one of the vice-presidents of the Council is elected from the quota of the civil society. In spite of that, regrettably, in the former body the voices of the NGOs and civil society were often completely ignored. Thus, many NGOs, whose members were convinced that NCCEDI is a *causa perduta*, have refused to send their representatives to the institution (Kolev 2009). Nothing has been done to address these issues and *it is difficult to believe that the situation will "improve on its own."*

The new National Roma Integration Strategy (2012–2020) has been introduced by the government in 2012. The document is in line with the *National Reform Program of the Republic of Bulgaria (2011–2015)* and the *National Action Plan for the "Decade of Roma Inclusion 2005–2015"* (NCCEII 2012: 1–2). It incorporates the *Framework Program for Roma Integration in the Bulgarian Society 2010–2020* (ibid.: 2). The strategy applies an integrated targeted approach to the citizens of Roma background in vulnerable condition, which falls within the framework of a more general strategy for combating poverty and exclusion, and it does not preclude rendering support to disadvantaged persons from other ethnic groups (ibid.: 1). It adopts and integrates into a single strategy the objectives and measures contained in other government documents in the area of Roma integration, such as *Strategy for Educational Integration of the Children from Ethnic Minorities; Health Strategy for Disadvantaged Persons belonging to Ethnic Minorities, 2005–2015;* and *National Program for Improvement of the Housing of Roma, 2005–2015* (ibid.: 3).

The National Roma Integration Strategy is adopted for the period up to 2020 inclusive. Its implementation shall be carried out through Action Plan, divided into two periods. *The first period,* 2012–2014, ends with the completion of the implementation of the NAP-DRI, updated in 2011. According to the strategy, an overall analysis of the implementation during this period will be performed in connection with its completion (February 2, 2015). *The second period,* 2014–2020, shall cover and coincide with the next EU programming period for the operational programs to be implemented with the financial support and through the instruments of the EU. An interim review/updating of the Action Plan is foreseen and due in 2017, in order to ensure the efficiency and sustainability of the measures (ibid.: 4).[258]

The current status of the Roma community (in particular, in regard to housing, employment, education, and health care) is discussed in Section two of the Strategy. As a whole the analysis is objective. The authorities admit that *most of Roma continue to live in desperate conditions in spite of the integration policies.* The concentration of Roma in isolated neighborhoods "*has increased*[259] during the last 15 years both in the urban and rural areas"; a "significant part of the Roma residing in the cities, inhabit overpopulated neighborhoods [...] in a very poor condition, where the electricity supply is quite often done illegally or is nonexistent." Two-fifths of the Roma "still live in houses without water supply, three-fifths of the Roma

---

[258] The Strategy may be "extended, complemented or modified after 2020, depending on the achieved results, the existing political, social and economic realities and new challenges" (NCCEII 2012: 4).

[259] The emphasis is mine.

houses are not connected to the central sewer system, and four-fifths have no bathrooms inside" (NCCEII 2012: 6). Between 2001 and 2011, there has been a small increase of the Roma with higher education (from 0.2% to 0.5%).[260] However, the tendency of large number of Roma children remaining without education, dropping out of school at an early stage, or not enrolling at all remains (ibid.: 8). The analysis in the Strategy rightly points to *the direct link between education and employment, which was already emphasized in the present work*. The document states that the share of students in the Roma community is "extremely small" (ibid.: 7), it is:

> 7.3% of the economically inactive population, i.e. 4.4% of all Roma citizens above the age of fifteen. This low share of young people continuing their education after the age of fifteen *will determine the lower educational and qualification status of the Roma community in the long run, hence – the greater share of persons unemployed and dropping out of the labor market in the decades to come.*[261] (NCCEII 2012: 7)

As other policy documents that we already examined, the 2012 Strategy emphasizes that the integration of the Roma must be a "pro-active, two-way process" (ibid.: 10). *I believe that this approach is sound and pragmatic*. It means that Roma, as well as other groups in vulnerable position in the society, must not be merely the passive recipients of, for example, social benefits. *They have to make efforts themselves in order for integration policies to work and be successful*. The goal of the 2012 Strategy is to create conditions for integration of the Roma by ensuring equal opportunities and equal access to rights, goods, and services, by involving them in all public spheres and improving their quality of life, while observing the principles of equality and nondiscrimination (NCCEII 2012: 10). A positive moment in the Strategy is that it not only outlines, as usual, the priority areas (education, health care, housing conditions, employment, rule of law and nondiscrimination, culture, and media) but

---

260 According to the document, the success in this respect could be higher than this recorded during the census in 2011, because "many young people do not identify themselves as Roma after completing higher education" (NCCEII 2012: 7).
261 The emphasis is mine.

formulates *specific tasks* in each of them, and also stipulates *clearly defined objectives*.

For example, the implementation of the measures in the priority area of education must contribute to the reduction of the relative share of early leavers of the educational system by 11% and to the raise of the relative share of persons with higher education in the age group of 30–34 to 36% by 2020 (NCCEII 2012: 13); the steps undertaken in the field of employment should lead to 76% employment rate among the population aged 20–64 by 2020 (ibid.: 16). The optimization of the model of allocation of management responsibilities among the executive bodies in charge of the integration policies is also a significant change.[262] It is unequivocally stated that the key line ministries and authorities "*shall be responsible* for updating of the operational Roma integration documents in their respective areas, for the implementation of the planned measures, the monitoring, evaluation and reporting before NCCEII"[263] (NCCEII 2012: 18–19). *However it is not specified whether and what will be the sanctions when the responsibilities are not met.* The Strategy also attempts to improve the mechanisms of coordination with "the civil society structures" and to ensure the involvement of the local governments in the process of implementation[264] (ibid.: 20). The integration policies will be financed, as before (ibid.: 21), from the national budget and from foreign funds (mainly from the EU, through the Structural and Cohesion funds, and, to a much lower extent, through programs of the UN, the World Bank, the Council of Europe, etc.).

In spite of the criticisms, outlined above, *it has to be noted that the integration policies of Bulgarian governments led to certain positive results, which should not be neglected.* As far as the legal framework is concerned, of particular importance, and directly implementing the goals set in the 1999 Framework Program, are the *PADA*, adopted

---

262 NCCEII is the managing and coordinating institution, represented by its chairperson and assisted by the secretariat.
263 The emphasis is mine.
264 For example, through the establishment of advisory structures and mechanisms with the participation of the civil society.

in 2004,[265] as well as the national equality body — the Commission for Protection against Discrimination (CPAD), established under this act. Apart from the EU legislation in the field of human rights which Bulgaria must implement as a Member State, the BNA has also ratified the Framework Convention for the Protection of National Minorities in 1999.[266] Undoubtedly, the legislation changes *improved* the situation of minority ethnic groups. Nonetheless, there are multiple problematic issues, both in the legislation itself and in its implementation (Cholakov 2014a).[267] I outline these in detail in Section 3.2.

In the second half of November 2013, the government submitted to the EC unprecedentedly detailed "information" [268] (120 pages) on the country's progress in the priority areas defined in the National Roma Integration Strategy, 2012–2020. The document is divided into two main sections: implementation at national level (NCCEII 2014: 1–45) and at regional level (ibid.: 45–190). Here are some examples[269] that show that government policies *can bring real and tangible outcomes*. As far as *education* is concerned, "as a result of measures taken to prevent school dropout" the number of early school leavers has been significantly reduced — from 6,680 pupils in

---

265 This is the main antidiscrimination law, which transposes the EC antidiscrimination and gender equality directives (e.g., Directive 2000/43/EC and Directive 2000/78/EC). It is a single equality law universally banning discrimination on a range of grounds, and providing uniform standards of protection and remedies.

266 Of significance are also the ECHR (formally the Convention for the Protection of Human Rights and Fundamental Freedoms, drafted in 1950 by the then newly formed Council of Europe) and the case law of the European Court of Human Rights, which the convention established.

267 For an in-depth analysis of the national antidiscrimination legislation and international conventions, see Rechel (2008), Ilieva (2012), BHC (2012, 2013), Cholakov (2014a, 2014b). An excellent compendium of the antidiscrimination legislation in Bulgaria can be found in Berov (2009).

268 This is the original title of the document (although, essentially, this is a report), see NCCEII (2014).

269 The examples that follow are from the fields of education and employment. However, the documents also contain a detailed report on the measures and results in other priority areas such as housing, health care, rule of law, and non-discrimination.

2010 to 2,302 in 2012, and 2,122 in 2013 (ibid.: 4). These figures are, however, *somewhat difficult to interpret*, because they describe the total number of pupils. It is not stated how many of them belong to the Roma ethnic group. According to the document, Bulgaria has made significant progress in reducing the proportion of young people[270] between the age of 18 and 24 with less than secondary education[271] who were "outside" the educational system (by 6.6% for the last nine years). This share in 2001 was 20.5% and in 2010 – 13.9%, which, according to the document, is "below the European Union average value – 14.1%" (ibid.: 7).

With regard to *employment*, "until 2010, 69,389 people of Roma origin" have been included in various activities, aimed at the improvement of their skills and qualifications; 6,897 of them took part in literacy courses[272] and 8,299 in vocational training (NCCEII 2014: 18). In 2011, the plans to increase the competitiveness of the labor market and to employ 15,600 unemployed Roma "were fulfilled at 108.42%," or 16,914 persons "increased their competitiveness" and were employed (NCCEII 2014: 19). The Employment Agency periodically organizes and conducts specialized job fairs for which the target group are unemployed Roma.[273] The purpose of the fairs is to assist Roma by facilitating their access to information about job vacancies and providing direct contact and negotiation with employers. Six such fairs were organized in 2011 (ibid.: 19) – in Straldzha, Lom, Lukovit, Knezha, Chirpan, and Plovdiv (however, *only two job fairs were held in 2013*, ibid.: 21). The events were attended by 778 job seekers and 47 employers who announced 325 job vacancies. The number of persons who started work is 309 (NCCEII 2014: 19). In 2012, 21,663 Roma were included in various government programs for training and professional development.

---

270 Again, it is not clear how many of these are Roma pupils.
271 The secondary education in Bulgaria, usually, encompasses pupils who are between ages 15 and 19, and grades 9 and 12.
272 Established under the National Program "Literacy and Qualification of Roma" (NCCEII 2014: 18).
273 The Employment Agency has organized such job fairs for eight consecutive years. Forty job fairs were held for the period of 2006-2013; as a result 3,680 persons began work (NCCEII 2014: 21).

About 11,478 of them were employed (ibid.: 19). According to the report, the number of Roma, who participated in programs of this type in 2013 and were able to find a job, is even higher—12,292. Overall, the document gives a sharper image of the integration policies that addresses at least some of the questions and recommendations of the NGOs (e.g., OSI 2012) vis-à-vis the National Roma Integration Strategy. *Although the policies still leave a considerable room for improvement, the reported results provide grounds for cautious optimism.*

The new Strategy for Educational Integration of Children and Students from Ethnic Minorities (2015–2020) was adopted in 2015. According to the more recent data mentioned in this document (in comparison to these cited above), 42.1% of Roma have basic and 8.3% secondary education; 28.1% have primary education while the university graduates are only 0.5%; 21.1% have no education. There is some increase in the number of Roma with secondary and higher education in recent years. However, more than 23% of Roma children do not attend school.[274] The segregated kindergartens and schools remain.

As it is evident from the study, examined at the beginning of this book,[275] the collapse of the Yugoslav federation shows how the politicization of cultural identity in ethnically divided societies becomes a recipe for disaster when the pulse of institutions of central government is feeble. It is in this aspect that the ethnic model employed today in Bulgaria reveals *a striking resemblance* to the former SFRY. Once in a fragile state, it doesn't take long for the institutions of government to completely fail to control or render safe the treacherous repercussions of ethnic cleavages. While the administrative core of SFRY was gradually weakened under the pressure of ethnically defined entities and short-sighted reforms, *the abnormities in the operation of political institutions in Bulgaria tell the obscure and incomplete history of setbacks in the transition to democracy.* The economic recession has provoked the resurgence of populist radical

---

274 These data describe the situation in the mandatory education from 7 to 15 years.
275 See Section 1.2.

parties in many European states.[276] However, the deadlocks and severe shortcomings in the political process render Bulgaria and its ethnic model *particularly vulnerable*. When the political system is in crisis, ethnic minorities can easily become the scapegoat against which ethnic entrepreneurs skillfully direct and incite the marginalized, impoverished, and desperate members of society.

It is important to remember that the populism of radical leaders, the xenophobic manifests, or hate crimes against individuals or groups "whose only sin is that they are different," are *merely tokens, indicators revealing the faults in the work of institutions*. Therefore, *the main policy recommendation* which I would make in order that ethnic peace is preserved in Bulgaria is to heal institutions through combating corruption, ensuring the efficiency and impartiality of the judicial system and proceedings, drafting better regulations that guarantee the independence of the media, eradication of clientelism and political patronage over the appointments in civil service, and democratization of political parties and intraparty procedures through more transparent rules for their funding.

As far as the integration policies of Bulgarian governments are concerned, they show certain progress in comparison to the situation at the end of 1990s. However, the achievements, some of which were described above, are often disputed by the NGOs[277] on the grounds that they deliberately "set the bar too low." Most importantly, even after the recent amendments of its Rules for the Structure and Operation, the NCCEII is left again with predominantly consultative and coordination functions (Gazette 2013: Art. 1). Its prerogatives to hold responsible the institutions that delay or

---

276 For example, the Popular Association—Golden Dawn in Greece (Λαϊκός Σύνδεσμος—Χρυσή Αυγή), the Hungarian Jobbik—Movement for a Better Hungary (Jobbik Magyarországért Mozgalom), the French National Front (FN), the Dutch Party of Freedom (Partij voor de Vrijheid), the Finnish True Finns (Perussuomalaiset), the Italian Northern League (Lega Nord), Denmark's People's Party (Dansk Folkeparti, DF), the Freedom Party of Austria (FPÖ), the Alliance for the Future of Austria (BZÖ), the Sweden Democrats (Sverigedemokraterna, SD), the Progress Party in Norway (Framstegspartiet, FrP), and the Swiss People's Party (Schweizerische Volkspartei, SVP).
277 See, e.g., OSI (2012).

"derail" the implementation of integration policies need to be set out *clearly and unambiguously. The most urgent legislative changes must address this issue in particular.* It still appears that the relative acceleration and the huge multiplication of government efforts and programs, especially after the accession of the country to the EU in 2007, are predominantly a result of the continuing pressure from the European institutions and NGOs for reforms, instead of genuine commitment to improve the situation and implement the necessary measures.

3.2   The legislation and the judicial system

3.2.1   General framework for analysis

The institutions of the judiciary are political by nature.[278] At first glance, this is a paradox because the judicial system by definition must be independent.[279] However, on closer inspection, the political nature of the judiciary is a clear-cut reality which has *two sides*. First, its institutions are inevitably political not only in totalitarian regimes but also in liberal democracies because their modus operandi is based on constitution and laws,[280] which mirror the specific constellation of the interests of the political forces in the society. Courts' decisions, even when they are a manifestation of *bona voluntas* and do not purposefully distort the letter or/and the spirit of the law, can have groundbreaking political consequences.[281] *The other side* of the political nature of the judiciary is always present, albeit in different proportions. Unlike the first, legitimate side, this one is pathological. Here belong, for example, the vicious practices of manipulation of the appointments or of the election of the magistrates in order to have at hand the "support" of readily obedient partisans, the corruption of the officials in the judiciary for political

---

278 For a general theoretical analysis of the political "persona" of the judicial institutions see Gibson (2008: 514–34).
279 Constitution of the Republic of Bulgaria 1991: Art. 117 (2).
280 The constitution and the legislation are, of course, political institutions as well.
281 For example, the 2001 decision of the US Supreme Court in *Bush vs. Gore*, effectively "awarded" the presidency to George W. Bush.

and personal gain, or the cases of biased judgments favoring the powers that be.

As mentioned above,[282] corruption is a serious concern in Bulgaria. It affects the judicial system as well. In its progress report, released in July 2012, the EC found that acquittal rates were disproportionately high in corruption cases against senior government officials, and that the number of these cases declined sharply in 2011 after increases in 2009 and 2010 (Refworld 2013). The director of a new commission for the identification and seizure of criminal assets resigned in early 2012, citing insufficient political support.[283] According to the report of the EC, institutional and legal improvements in the judicial system have not led to practical gains in efficiency or accountability. The EU has noted ongoing flaws in the judicial appointment and disciplinary processes (Refworld 2013). The continuing "dependencies of the SAC in Bulgaria from the powerful politicians" (BHC 2013: 10) in 2012, the controversial nominations of judges for the Constitutional Court (in particular the "judge Markovska case"), the doubts voiced by some regarding the new chief prosecutor in the beginning of 2013, and last but not least the "Bulgarian Watergate" scandal from April 2013 (Mitov 2013) are indicative of the dimensions of the pathological side of the political nature of the judiciary system. If, as the facts do suggest, the judiciary in Bulgaria is regularly involved and misused in the political struggles, *it is safe to assume that the rights of the smaller ethnic groups will be particularly vulnerable, especially when they are not well represented in the political system.* The analysis of the antidiscrimination legislation, the relevant case law, and the functioning of the judiciary in Bulgaria must take into account the political context outlined above.

---

282 See Section 1.5.
283 See Refworld (2013). The Sofia-based NGO Center for the Study of Democracy estimated in June 2012 that an average of 150,000 bribes was paid in Bulgaria each month in 2011, see CSD (2012).

3.2.2 The PADA

3.2.2.1 *Purpose and concept*

Both the purpose and the scope of the PADA are much broader than those of Directive 2000/43/EC. The PADA, according to its Article 1, regulates "the protection against *all forms of discrimination* and shall contribute to its prevention." [284] In comparison, Directive 2000/43/EC, which sets only a minimum standard, aims to lay down a general framework for combating discrimination only on the protected grounds of racial and ethnic origin.[285] The PADA, which is the special antidiscrimination law in Bulgaria, bans discrimination on grounds of sex, race, national origin, ethnicity, human genome, nationality, origin, religion or faith, education, beliefs, political affiliation, personal or public status, disability, age, sexual orientation, family status, property status, or any other ground provided for by law or international treaty to which Bulgaria is a party (PADA[286] 2004: Art. 4 (1)).

The Act defines and prohibits direct and indirect discrimination, including discrimination by association and by presumption. *The direct discrimination* is defined as treating a person on protected grounds less favorably than another person is treated, has been treated, or would be treated in comparable circumstances.[287] *Indirect discrimination* occurs when a person is put, on the protected grounds, "in a less than favorable position compared to other persons through an apparently neutral provision, criterion or practice, unless this provision, criterion or practice are objectively justified in view of a legal aim [sic!] and the means of achieving this aim are appropriate and necessary" (PADA 2004: Art. 4 (3)).

The main problem in the Act, in this respect, is that the definition of indirect discrimination in it *is misleading and often judges confuse it with concealed direct discrimination*. While the intention of the lawmakers was to refer to protected grounds as characteristics defining

---

284 The emphasis is mine.
285 See Council Directive 2000/43/EC: Art. 1.
286 Protection against Discrimination Act.
287 Ibid.: Art. 4 (2).

the group that is put at a particular disadvantage, the result is that "a number of court and equality body decisions have read the phrase 'grounds of' as defining a causal link between an apparently neutral rule and the particular protected ground/s" (Ilieva 2012: 4, 23). In other words, this reading interprets "an apparently neutral" act as one that is de facto based on a particular ground but is not openly motivated by it. Therefore, indirect discrimination is understood, in this interpretation, as concealed direct discrimination. *The consequences from this misunderstanding of the concept are serious because the absolute ban on direct discrimination is then diluted in such reasoning by the general justification test that is valid only for indirect discrimination.*[288] The analysis of the decisions of the SAC in 2012 shows that it continues to define, erroneously, cases of direct discrimination as indirect (BHC 2013: 40). In addition, there is no legislative or judicial guidance on what constitutes a "legitimate aim." There are also some linguistic imperfections in the translation of the European law that are potentially problematic. For example, the principle of equal treatment is translated as the "*right* of equal treatment" and the term "legitimate aim" appears as "legal aim."

The antidiscrimination legislation in Bulgaria does not define terms like "racial and ethnic origin," "religion," or "belief." Although the courts, as well, have not defined "race" or "ethnicity," arguably they distinguish between them. It appears that an outdated conception of "race," which does not include "ethnic origin," is still in use. The implicit position of the judicial authorities and the CPAD is that discrimination against ethnic groups like the Roma and the Turks *is based on ethnicity rather than race* (Ilieva 2012: 18). The definition of "incitement to discrimination," including instructions to discriminate, under the PADA *is not compatible with the EU Directives* because it requires direct intent as an element, as well as for the perpetrator to be in a position to influence their addressee. The definition of "racial segregation" under the PADA *is also not compatible with the EU law* because it explicitly requires the state of

---

288 See Ilieva (2012: 5).

separation to be "forced." The implication seems to be "that the segregation may be "chosen," i.e., that segregated persons may have waived there right not to be discriminated" (ibid.: 9). This interpretation *contradicts* the case law of the European Court of Human Rights. The Court has consistently held in Roma segregation cases that no waiver of the right to nondiscrimination in this context is possible because it would conflict with an important public interest.[289] On a more positive note, the Bulgarian equality body has accepted that racial segregation might occur without coercion where separation is a result of objective tendencies. Unfortunately, the equality body has failed to use its power to start ex officio proceedings in number of cases of blatant discrimination such as the Roma segregation in education.[290]

3.2.2.2 *Scope*

Regarding the *personal scope*, nonnationals are protected from discrimination based on nationality only insofar as such discrimination is not based on the primary legislation (PADA 2014: Art. 3 (1), Art. 7 (1.1)). Executive and local government bodies, as well as private parties, are not allowed to treat nonnationals differently based on their nationality, unless the parliament has authorized such treatment by law. Associations of natural persons and legal persons are protected on the same basis as natural persons, where the former suffer discrimination on grounds of characteristics of their employees or members (ibid.: Art. 3 (2)). Legal residence is irrelevant to entitlement to antidiscrimination protection. The factual being within the territory of the Republic of Bulgaria is a sufficient condition for protection. Courts have interpreted the PADA as providing a basis to hold legal entities responsible for an act of discrimination by their employees.

As far as *the material scope* is concerned, the PADA *includes all fields under the EU Directives and even goes far beyond them*. As mentioned above, one of the most problematic issues is the segregation

---

289 See, e.g., D.H. v. Czech Republic, judgment of November 13, 2007; Sampanis v. Greece, judgment of June 5, 2008; Orsus v. Croatia, judgment of March 16, 2010.
290 Ilieva (2012: 9).

in education, in particular regarding the Roma. *The patterns of exclusion or segregation in education include* children at home or in the street with no access to education at all; separate schools for the Roma children in the ghettoes; children in separate classrooms in the public schools; children in remedial schools and in schools for juvenile delinquents where the Roma children are disproportionally represented (Ilieva 2012: 45). There have been some cases that bring forth the question of segregation in education. The attempts to eliminate discrimination in this field have been, as a whole, *unsuccessful*.

In *the European Roma Rights Centre v. Ministry of Education et al. case* the position of the Court of Appeal, which repealed the judgment of the Trial Court in Sofia, has been that the separation on ethnic grounds (in the particular school in question) is "not forced" because it is "not a consequence of factors outside of the students' will and did not occur against their will — it, therefore, did not result from legislation or administrative decision" (ibid.: 46). The court held that the students were enrolled in the school as a result of free will (theirs and their parents'). The housing situation of Roma is perceived by some as a clear case of discrimination.[291] As it was mentioned above, the majority of this ethnic group lives in ghettoes in dire conditions. For decades many local authorities have turned their backs on Romani housing and infrastructure needs, while consistently refusing to include Roma residential areas in urban planning and to regulate them.

3.2.2.3 Genuine and determining occupational requirements

Art. 7 (1.2) of the PADA provides for an exception for genuine and determining occupational requirements for all six grounds that is compatible with Art. 4 of Directive 2000/43 and Art. 4 (1) of Directive 2000/78. According to the text of the PADA the following shall not constitute discrimination: different treatment of persons based on "a characteristic related to the [protected] grounds [...]

---

[291] Cf. Ilieva (2012: 50).

where, by the reason of the nature of a particular occupation or activity, or of the conditions it is carried out in, such a characteristic constitutes an essential and determining occupational requirement, the aim is legal and the requirement does not exceed what is necessary to accomplish it" (PADA 2004: Art. 7). For example, the PADA permits, as an exception to the prohibition of discrimination, a different treatment on grounds of sex *with respect to an occupation carried out in a religious organization*, where, by reason of the nature of that occupation, or of the conditions it is carried out in, the sex of the employee is an essential and determining professional requirement in view of the nature of the organization, where the aim is legitimate and the requirement does not exceed what is necessary to achieve it (PADA 2004: Art. 7 (1.3)). The act allows as well for a different treatment of persons on grounds of religion/faith or sex *in religious education or training*, including training or education for the purposes of carrying out an occupation in a religious institution (ibid.: Art. 7: (1.4)).

3.2.2.4 *Positive action*

The PADA not only authorizes but requires positive action measures to create equal opportunities for disadvantaged groups. There are several provisions for positive action in the Act. More specifically, regarding the requirements of Directive 2000/43, these include measures for protection of the originality and identity of persons who belong to ethnic, religious, and linguistic minorities, and their right, individually or jointly with other members of their group, to preserve and develop their culture, to profess and practice their religion, or to use their language (PADA 2004: Art. 7 (1.15)); measures in the field of education and training ensuring the participation of persons who belong to the ethnic minorities, insofar as and while these measures are necessary (ibid.: Art. 7 (1.16)). The Act also places a duty on all authorities to take measures to equalize opportunities for disadvantaged groups, as well as to guarantee participation by ethnic minorities in education, whenever necessary to accomplish the objectives of the Act (ibid.: Art. 11 (1)). The authorities *must take such measures as priorities* for the benefit of victims of multiple discrimination (ibid.: Art. 11 (2)).

Under the PADA, employers have a duty to provide reasonable accommodation for religion/belief in terms of working hours and rest days, where "this would not lead to excessive difficulties [...] and where [it is possible] [...] to compensate for the possible adverse consequences on the [business]" (PADA 2004: Art. 13 (2)). In its Ruling No. 14 from 1992 the Constitutional Court stated that preferential treatment on constitutionally protected grounds, including race, ethnicity, sex, religion, or belief *is unconstitutional. Therefore, there is an apparent conflict between the norms of the PADA and the Constitution regarding the authorization for positive measures.* Still, as illustrated by the case law, this contradiction has not been used thus far to dispute the legality of positive discrimination. The principle of the supremacy of the EU law makes Ruling No.14 obsolete.

3.2.2.5 *Minimum requirements and protection of rights*

As far as the minimum requirements are concerned, there does not seem to be any regression; therefore, Art. 6 of Directive 2000/43 is correctly implemented. Two alternative methods exist for the enforcement of antidiscrimination rights: judicial proceedings before the general civil courts and specialized quasi-judicial proceedings before the independent equality body — the CPAD. Both methods are established in the PADA. A victim *is free to choose* between the two possibilities. The proceedings before the CPAD are listed in Chapter IV of the PADA. The proceedings are instituted on the basis of complaint by the affected persons; the initiative of the Commission; and communications from natural persons and legal persons, state and municipal authorities (PADA 2004: Art. 50). For prevention or termination of violations under PADA or other acts regulating equal treatment, the Commission applies the following compulsory administrative measures: mandatory instructions to employers and officials to eliminate violations and ceasing of the execution of unlawful decisions (ibid.: Art. 76). As far as judicial proceedings are concerned, any person whose rights under the

PADA or "other Acts regulating equal treatment have been violated may bring an action in the Regional Court" (ibid.: Art. 71 (1)). The respondent could be sentenced to terminate the violation and to restore the status quo ante the violation as well as to refrain from further violations.[292]

The judicial and the specialized quasi-judicial remedies are legally binding. Unlike the court, the equality body cannot order compensation to a victim. It is important to underline the fact that according to the PADA *the ending of an employment relationship makes no difference to bringing a claim*. For the judicial remedy the prescription period is *five years* and for the equality body *three years* after the violation was committed (PADA 2004: Art. 52 (1)). A positive element that makes both the court and the equality body procedures more accessible to the victims is that they are completely exempt from costs.[293] In conformity with Art. 7 (2) of Directive 2000/43, the Act postulates that trade unions as well as NGOs may bring action in court upon request from persons whose rights have been violated (ibid.: Art. 71 (3.2)). They can also join proceedings brought by victims in their support for which they do not formally need the complainant's consent.[294] In addition, in cases of multiple discrimination, trade unions and NGOs may bring an action in court on their own. Under the PADA, any entity or individual may bring proceedings before the CPAD without claiming victim status.

3.2.2.6 Burden of proof and victimization

Art. 9 of the PADA stipulates that *it is up to the respondent to prove that the principle of equal treatment has not been infringed once the claimant proves facts that may lead to a conclusion that discrimination has oc-*

---

[292] Ibid.: Art. 71 (1). Further clarification for the damages inflicted by state bodies and officials is given in Art. 74 (2). The relevant normative acts according to Chapter IV, Section II of the PADA are Code of Civil Procedure, Administrative Procedure Code, and the Act on the Liability Incurred by the State for Damage Inflicted on Citizens.
[293] Ibid.: Art. 53 and Art. 75 (2).
[294] Ibid.: Art. 71 (3.2).

curred. Therefore, the principle of burden of proof is correctly implemented in Art. 9 of the Act.[295] This principle applies to both judicial proceedings and proceedings before the equality body. It is uniformly applicable to all forms of discrimination, including harassment and victimization. Art. 5 of the PADA explicitly prohibits victimization as a form of discrimination. Victimization is defined as: (a) less favorable treatment of a person who has undertaken, or is presumed to have undertaken, or to undertake in the future any action for protection against discrimination; (b) less favorable treatment of a person, where a person associated with them has undertaken, or is presumed to have undertaken, or to undertake in the future any action for protection against discrimination; (c) less favorable treatment of a person who refused to discriminate.[296] Therefore protection is accorded to victimization both by presumption and by association. The definition of victimization is, as a whole, in conformity with the Directives. Still the understanding of victimization as "a less favorable treatment" rather than adverse treatment introduces the undue requirement for a comparator. From the point of view of the defense this "adds one more point to prove and makes the defense more onerous" (Ilieva 2012).

3.2.2.7 Dissemination of information and social dialogue

I have already outlined above the policies of government in promoting equality and nondiscrimination. Here I shall briefly outline mainly the steps undertaken by the CPAD and the Bulgarian Ombudsman regarding dissemination of information and social dialogue. The analysis below is essentially based on the Report for 2011 on the Measures to Combat Discrimination in Bulgaria (Ilieva 2012), prepared for the European Network of Legal Experts in the Non-Discrimination Field. In order to obtain a more objective assessment of the situation, *it is necessary to corroborate the findings of the report*

---

[295] As already mentioned, the Bulgarian translation is somewhat misleading, because the *"principle* of equal treatment" appears as the *"right* of equal treatment."

[296] See PADA 2004: additional provision § 1 (3).

with the help of other sources.[297] According to the Report (Ilieva 2012: 81) the information campaigns undertaken by the state *have been limited*. Only two bodies have taken such action — the CPAD and the National Council for Cooperation on Ethnic and Demographic Issues (NCCEDI)[298] within the Council of Ministers. The measures, which aimed at general awareness raising, were "insufficient and superficial" (ibid.: 81). The CPAD made a campaign broadcasted in the media and the NCCEDI organized conferences, disseminated brochures, and a survey questionnaire. The report claims that these measures did not have a community outreach dimension. The media that were involved in the campaign were the "mainstream ones that might be inaccessible to isolated communities, such as Roma" and the groups targeted by the seminars and the like have been "predominantly people from the mainstream — public officials, journalists and establishment-connected NGOs" (Ilieva 2012: 81).

In 2007, which was proclaimed as the European Year of Equal Opportunities, the Demographic Policy and Equal Opportunities Directorate[299] did some awareness raising in cooperation with the CPAD, the National Council for Cooperation on Ethnic and Demographic Issues and "selected establishment linked NGOs" (ibid.: 81). The report concludes that the campaign "failed to gain any meaningful visibility" (ibid.). The CPAD has signed a partnership agreement with one of the two principle trade unions. The practical aims of this agreement are unclear. There is no information as to whether the promotion of dialogue with employers, aimed at ensuring equality, is among its objectives. The Ombudsman initiated in 2008 an "expert council" with some NGOs. However, it is unlikely that this body will have real policy-shaping capabilities, because, according to Art. 2 of the Ombudsman Act, *the decisions of this office are not binding*. The CPAD, which has binding powers to enforce and evolve equality, "has not involved NGOs in cooperation or dialogue in any inclusive or meaningful way" (Ilieva 2012:

---

[297] See, e.g., Angelova (2001), Rechel (2008), and Kolev (2009).
[298] As explained above, currently the name of the institution is National Council for Cooperation on Ethnic and Integration Issues.
[299] Established within the Ministry of Labor and Social Policy.

82). The aforementioned Report further describes the contacts that the CPAD established with NGOs as "selective" and built on a "nontransparent basis"; the Commission is also "difficult and slow with NGOs in terms of providing them with access to its rulings and to statistical data about its cases" (ibid.: 82).

3.2.2.8 Equality body

The CPAD is the specialized body for prevention and protection against discrimination which ensures equality of opportunities (PADA 2004: Art. 40 (1)). The Commission exercises control over the implementation of and compliance with the PADA and other Acts regulating equal treatment. It has a legal personality; it is financed from the budget and presents an annual report for its activity to the National Assembly. The Commission consists of nine members of which at least four are jurists. The National Assembly elects five of its members, including the chairperson and the deputy chairperson. The Bulgarian president appoints four members. The members of the CPAD serve for a five-year term. A positive element is the requirement of the law that in the election or composition of the Commission "the principles of balanced participation of women and men and of persons which belong to ethnic minorities" must be respected (ibid.: Art. 41 (3)). It could be argued, however, that it is difficult to ensure in practice that the Commission is fully independent, as the law requires. As mentioned, the equality body is financed from the state budget. Therefore, *its operation is potentially susceptible to the decisions of the parliamentary majority and the policy of the government. Political dependencies can also stem from the fact that its members are selected by the parliament and the president.*

The national equality body deals with discrimination on all protected grounds. It has the mandate (ibid.: Art. 47): to hear complaints by victims and communications from third parties; to find discrimination by legally binding decisions; to impose financial sanctions; and to issue mandatory directions for compliance with the PADA or other Acts regulating equal treatment. It can initiate proceedings at its own discretion, in all fields and on all grounds, against any perpetrator. It can review and give opinions on draft legislation. The Commission takes decisions by a simple majority (ibid.: Art. 64 (1)). In accordance with the requirements of Art. 13 (2) of Directive 2000/43, the CPAD provides assistance to the victims of discrimination and has to carry out independent research and publish independent reports. It can also make recommendations to public authorities, including for legislative change (PADA 2004: Art. 47). The CPAD has standing to bring lawsuits in court and can intervene in court proceedings as an interested party. It is a quasi-judicial institution that takes binding decisions. The Commission's decisions are subject to judicial review by the SAC. In general, there has been an increase in the number of complaints lodged with the CAPD (see Table 7).

Table 7. Number of complaints lodged with the Commission for Protection Against Discrimination per year
Source: Equinet (2009), CPAD (2011), CPAD (2012), and Hristova (2014).

Year	2005	2006	2007	2008	2009	2010	2011	2012	2013
Complaints	26	279	566	673	967	777	846	823	860

In April 2010, the government attempted to reform the CPAD and introduced a bill to reduce the number of members of the Commission to five. Allegedly, the reasons behind the reform were financial. The draft legislation was astutely criticized by civil society organizations, human rights lawyers, and activists. As a concession to the protesters the government introduced another bill which aimed at reducing the members of the equality body to seven instead of five. The latter bill was adopted in July 2010 at first hearing in the parliament. However, since the nongovernmental organizations remained dissatisfied, the reform, at least in this respect, was blocked by the politicians.[300] It should be noted as well that, although the term of office of the members of the first CPAD expired in 2010 (they were appointed in 2005), the members de facto remained operational until mid-2012. In July 2012, the parliament and

---

300 There are however other revisions of the PADA. The most recent amendments date from February 15, 2013.

the president finally appointed new members to the CPAD. Their number has not changed and is still nine.

3.2.2.9 Compliance and sanctions

This is a problematic area. There are many national laws that have to be aligned with the PADA. These predate the main anti-discrimination law and provide for restrictions based on protected grounds without any justification test. Examples of such laws are the Judiciary Act (mental disability bar, Art. 162), the Academic Degrees and Titles Act (age bars, Art. 9), and the Defense and Armed Forces Act (age bars to employment, Art. 116, 127, 141–142). In addition, there is no coherence between the PADA and other, older, bans on discrimination in the legislation, including the Constitution.[301] According to the principle *lex specialis derogat legi generali*, the PADA in its quality as *lex specialis* should override general, or older or secondary legislation the provisions of which are in conflict with this law. Essentially, however under the Bulgarian legislation there is no specific mechanism to ensure that any conflicting norms are set aside, other than legislation before the courts or the equality body (Ilieva 2009: 107). The Constitutional Court is the only institution that is authorized to strike down conflicting norms under the primary legislation. For secondary legislation the remedy is judicial review proceedings before the SAC. Only a limited number of institutions, excluding the CPAD, can bring proceedings before the Constitutional Court. Nevertheless, there are efforts that aim to make the judicial system more coherent. For example, the Penal Code (PC) was amended in April 2010 and now includes specific enhanced penalties for racism and or xenophobia motivated murder (Penal Code 2015: Art. 116, subsection 11), and causing of bodily harm (ibid.: Art. 131, subsection 12). A new provision criminalizes acts of justifying, denying, or grossly denigrating crimes

---

301 The Constitutional Court has held that preferential treatment on constitutionally protected grounds, including race/ethnicity, sex, and religion/belief, is unconstitutional. This is the interpretation of the Court of Article 6 (2) of the Constitution. See Constitutional Court Ruling N14 of 1992.

against peace and humanity which create a risk of violence or hatred against individuals or racial, ethnic, national, and religious groups (ibid.: Art. 419a), as well as the instigation of such criminal acts.

Under the PADA, the CPAD can impose financial sanctions between the equivalents of EUR 125 – 1,250 (PADA 2004: Art. 78– 80). In principle, these amounts *should be dissuasive to the majority*. This conclusion is supported by the fact that the minimal wage per month in Bulgaria since January 1, 2016 (when it was increased), is merely EUR 214 (BGN 420), and the average salary is around EUR 478 (BGN 937, for December 2015).[302] The sanctions are not awarded to the victim as compensation. According to the most recent changes of the PADA, they will be used, from January 1, 2014, onward, to fund the budget of the equality body (PADA 2004: Art. 84). Where a breach is repeated the sanction is double (ibid.: Art. 81). The sanctions are uniformly applicable to all sections and fields, including the private and public sector, as well as the fields outside employment. In addition, the equality body can suspend the execution of employers' decisions in case these may lead to discrimination. However, the binding instructions (orders) of the equality body have been ignored many times. The body has no other powers in such cases, except to impose further fines (Ilieva and Simeonova 2010). The failure to comply with the decision of the courts or the equality body can lead to fines that go up to EUR 10,000 (ibid.: Art. 82). As mentioned above, the courts do not impose fines but only award compensation for damages. They may award any amount that they deem fair.

---

302 See NSI (2015). In comparison the average salary in the EU in 2015 was approximately EUR 1470.

3.3 Discrimination against Roma ethnic group: case studies

3.3.1 Segregation

One of the main challenges in front of the Roma community is *the segregation* to which it is subjected in housing and education. As mentioned, contrary to the case law of the ECtHR, the definition of segregation in the PADA requires that the state of separation "must be forced."[303] In a groundbreaking judgment from April 24, 2012, in *the Case of Yordanova and Others v. Bulgaria (Application no. 25446/06)* the ECtHR postulated that the planned eviction of Roma from their established settlement in "Batalova vodenica" district of Sofia would constitute a violation of the European Convention on Human Rights (ECHR).[304] More particularly, it violates Article 8 (1) which defends the need for respect for family life, home, and private life, as well as Article 46 (2) which requires the respondent — the Republic of Bulgaria to take measures to ensure proportionality when enforcing orders for recovery of public land.

The facts regarding the case are the following. The applicants are 23 members of the Roma community in the district, which consists of 250 people. The Roma settlement is situated on municipal land in Sofia, which was first occupied by Roma families in the 1960s. Their homes, which are built without authorization, are makeshift. There is no sewage or plumbing. According to the Court it is "undisputed that the applicants' homes do not meet the basic requirements of the relevant construction and safety regulations and could not be legalized without substantial reconstruction" (Case of Yordanova and Others v. Bulgaria: 1). When at the beginning of 1990s tension grew in Sofia between the Roma community

---

[303] "Racial segregation is the adoption of a legal act, the action or the non-action, which leads to the forced separation, isolation or partition of a person on the basis of his race, ethnicity, or color of skin," see PADA (2004): additional provision §1. 6.

[304] Formally, the Convention for the Protection of Human Rights and Fundamental Freedoms.

and its non-Roma neighbors, the issue of Roma settlements was widely debated and a number of leading politicians spoke of the need to empty the "Roma ghettos" in Sofia.[305] On September 17, 2005, the district mayor ordered the forcible removal of the applicants and their families. The domestic courts confirmed that that order was lawful and the mayor publicly stated that it was not possible to find alternative housing for the settlement's inhabitants, because "they had not been registered as people in need of housing and the municipality could not give them priority over others who had been on the waiting list for many years" (ibid.: 1).

The eviction was, however, stayed following intervention by the EP and the issue of an interim measure by the European Court of Human Rights under Rule 39 of its Rules. On the basis of Article 8 of the ECHR, the Court concluded that the applicants' expulsion from the makeshift houses "was liable to affect their lifestyle and social and family ties and so constituted interference with their right to respect for their homes, private lives and family lives" (ibid.: 2). While the order of the mayor had a valid foundation in domestic law and pursued the legitimate aims of securing the economic well-being of the country and protecting health and the rights of others, the government had not established that the impugned measures had been necessary in a democratic society. The authorities were in principle entitled to recover municipal land that was being occupied unlawfully, but they had tolerated the unlawful Roma settlement for several decades, thus allowing the applicants to build a community there. According to the ECtHR, the principle of proportionality:

> required that situations where a whole community and long period were concerned be treated as being entirely different from routine cases of removal of an individual from unlawfully occupied property. Under the relevant domestic law at the time, however, the municipal authorities had not been required to have regard to the various interests involved or consider proportionality and, relying on that legal framework, had given no reasons for the decision to expel the applicants other than to state that they occupied

---

305 Ibid.: 1. "The last offensive" against the settlement was launched at the time when Mr. Boyko Borisov (who subsequently became a Prime Minister of Bulgaria) was a mayor of Sofia.

the land unlawfully. The domestic courts had expressly refused to hear arguments based on proportionality and the length of time the applicants had occupied the land undisturbed. While it was undisputed that most of the applicants' houses did not meet basic sanitary and building requirements, the Government had not shown alternative methods of dealing with these problems,[306] nor had the authorities considered the risk of the applicants becoming homeless. Instead they had attempted to enforce the order in 2005 and 2006 regardless of the consequences. The Government had not shown that the land was urgently needed for the public need they had mentioned. Lastly, the authorities had refused to consider approaches specially tailored to the needs of the Roma community on the grounds that that would amount to discrimination against the majority population. That argument failed, however, to recognize the applicants' situation as an outcast community and socially disadvantaged group potentially in need of assistance to be able effectively to enjoy the same rights as the majority population. The underprivileged status of the applicants' group had to be a weighty factor in considering approaches to dealing with their unlawful settlement and, if their removal was necessary, in deciding on its timing, modalities and, if possible, arrangements for alternative shelter. This factor had not been taken into account in the present case. (Case of Yordanova and Others v. Bulgaria: 2)

Essentially, the 2005 removal order had been based on legislation and issued and reviewed under a decision-making procedure that did not require the examination of proportionality and did not offer safeguards against disproportionate interference. The ECtHR concluded unanimously that there is a violation of the Convention. Based on Article 46 of ECHR, the Court emphasized the need of amendments to the relevant domestic law and practice. It is essential to ensure that orders to recover public land or buildings, where liable to affect Convention-protected rights and freedoms, "should, even in cases of unlawful occupation, identify clearly the aims pursued, the individuals affected and the measures in place to secure proportionality" (Case of Yordanova and Others v. Bulgaria: 3). The individual measures required by the Court were either the repeal of the removal order of 2005 or its suspension pending measures to ensure that the authorities had complied with the Convention requirements, as clarified in the judgment. Additionally, the violation

---

306 For example, legalizing buildings where possible, constructing public sewage and water-supply facilities, and providing assistance to find alternative housing where eviction was necessary.

constituted sufficient just satisfaction for any nonpecuniary damage (Article 41). Despite the unequivocal and groundbreaking decision of the ECtHR,[307] in similar circumstances, the mayor of the town of Maglizh ordered on September 25, 2012, the eviction of 32 Roma houses. The inhabitants, about 150 people, were left in the streets without any provision for an alternative shelter (Hristov 2012).

Setting the segregation in housing aside, it has to be noted that *the Bulgarian government rejects emphatically the claims of its existence in the field of education*. In response to the Fourth Report of the European Commission against Racism and Intolerance (ECRI), published in 2009, the government reiterated that "there had never been a policy of school "segregation" — de jure or de facto — of Roma children in the national education system" (ECRI 2009: 49). While the government admitted that in some areas particular schools were attended predominantly by pupils of Roma origin, it explained this as "an unintended consequence" of the former administrative division of the school system. According to the rules valid for all children irrespective of their ethnic origin, admittance to any public school was linked administratively to the domicile of the family. In neighborhoods where the population was predominantly of Roma origin, this system produced schools, attended predominantly by pupils of Roma origin. The system "was abolished years ago and the authorities have taken special measures to rectify the situation. Therefore, the term 'segregation' (including '*de facto*') with respect to Roma children is inaccurate" (ibid.: 49). Furthermore, the Bulgarian government rejects the conclusions in Paragraph 43 of ECRI's report, mentioned above, according to which *less* financial and human resources are allocated for schools attended predominantly by pupils of Roma origin. According to the government, in the country exists "a uniform standard of maintenance per pupil," consequently the amount of the state subsidy that

---

[307] In a similar landmark decision, in the case of *Liliana Naidenova et al. v. Bulgaria* from November 14, 2012, the UN Human Rights Committee issued a permanent injunction preventing the forced eviction of the Dobri Zheliazkov community in Sofia, Bulgaria.

the schools receive depends exclusively on the numbers of pupils enrolled, and not on ethnicity (ECRI 2009: 54).

3.3.2 Use of excessive force by the police and lack of effective investigation

Analyses of the Bulgarian Helsinki Committee (BHC), the European Network against Racism, the Council of Europe, and other organizations (Refworld 2012) indicate that the police in Bulgaria have subjected Roma to:

- mistreatment;
- physical abuse;
- harassment;
- racially motivated discrimination;
- excessive use of force;
- ethnic profiling;
- arbitrary confiscation and/or destruction of property; and
- arbitrary detention.

According to surveys made by the BHC, which contain data that are not representative but still indicative of the situation in the country and comparable with the analyses produced by the organization in previous years, there is a slight decline in the use of force by the police in 2012 (see Table 8). Nonetheless, the levels of police violence remain *very high* and *most* of its victims belong to the Roma community. Several violations of Article 2 (more particularly the use of excessive force in an attempt to make lawful arrest and/or to prevent the escape of the person lawfully detained) and Article 14 (lack of effective investigation) of the ECHR demonstrate that the practices of some members of the Bulgarian civil and military police force regarding the members of the Roma community *indeed fall short of institutional racism*. The analysis of the following two cases supports this thesis.

Table 8. Use of force by the Bulgarian police by years (in percentages of the respondents)
Source: BHC 2013: 6.

Year/Circumstances	2010	2011	2012
Use of force during detention	26.2	27.1	24.6
Use of force in the police station	17.4	25.5	18

The applicant in *the Affaire Yotova c. Bulgarie (Requête no 43606/04)*,[308] a woman from Roma origin, was shot from a passing vehicle on July 13, 1999. After the timely medical intervention her life was saved but her left hand remained paralyzed and she was certified with 75% disability. Two days before the incident, there was a serious altercation in a night club between young Roma men from the same village as the applicant (Aglen, community of Lukovit), and a Bulgarian man (from the neighbor village of Pesterna). On the next day, July 12, 1999, the Bulgarian and several of his Bulgarian friends returned to the club in order to find the address of the Roma men and "took the law in their own hands" (ECtHR 2012b: 4, §18). The home of the applicant — Ms. Yolanda Yotova, was located in proximity to the house of one the Romani who took part in the brawl. The proceedings for an attempted murder commenced on July 14, 1999 (ibid.: 3, §15) but during the next two years were halted three times due to the impossibility to identify the perpetrator as well as the vehicle from which the shots were fired. According to the ECtHR, the authorities *did not take any steps in order to locate the weapon with which the crime was committed.* The Court emphasized particularly the disturbing fact that immediately after the incident a ballistic expertise was not conducted and that no gunshot residue probes were taken from the hands of the suspects (ibid.). Furthermore, the authorities never examined the (rather probable) racial motives of the suspects' actions.[309] In the view of all evidence and the facts regarding the case, the members of ECtHR decided unanimously that

---

308 The file of the case is only available in French, see ECtHR (2012b).
309 ECtHR (2012b: 24, §110): "dans la présente affaire, aucun effort n'a été fait pour enquêteur sur l'existence d'un éventuel motif raciste malgré l'existence d'éléments de preuves suffisamment concrets à cet régard. En particulier, les jeunes

there is a violation of Article 2 (procedural aspects) and Article 14 (in conjunction with Article 2) of the Convention. According to the judgment from October 23, 2012, the Bulgarian state has to pay the applicant EUR 12,000 for moral damages and EUR 3,770 to cover the costs related to the legal proceedings.

Similar to this case is that of *Nachova and Others v. Bulgaria (Application no. 43577/98)*. Two men of Roma origin—Mr. Angelov and Mr. Petkov, relatives of the applicants—were conscripts serving compulsory military service in an army division dealing with the construction of apartments. They escaped from the construction site and took refuge in the house of the grandmother of one of them. When a military police unit, commanded by Major G., attempted to arrest the two men, they tried to run away and were shot by G. after he had given them a warning to stop. Both men, who were unarmed, died on their way to hospital. One neighbor claimed that "several of the policemen had been shooting and that at one stage G. had pointed his gun at him in a brutal manner and had insulted him saying 'You damn Gypsies'" (ECtHR 2005: 1). The military investigation report concluded that G. had acted in accordance with the regulations and the military prosecutor accepted the conclusions and closed the investigation (ibid.: 1). The applicants' subsequent appeals were dismissed. The Grand Chamber of the ECtHR noted as a matter of grave concern that the regulations on the use of firearms by the military police in Bulgaria effectively had permitted lethal force to be used when arresting a member of the armed forces for even the most minor offence. There had been a general failure by Bulgaria to comply with its obligation under Article 2 of the ECHR to secure the right to life by putting in place an appropriate legal and administrative framework on the use of force and firearms by military police (ibid.: 2). The Grand Chamber stated that the authorities had failed to comply with their obligation to minimize the risk of loss of life since the arresting officers had been instructed to use all available means to arrest the two Roma

---

gens suspectés par les autorités n'ont jamais été interrogés sur leur attitude générale vis-à-vis le groupe ethnoculturel auquel appartenait la victim."

men, despite the fact that they were unarmed (ibid.: 2). In the circumstances of the case any resort to potentially lethal force was prohibited by Article 2, regardless of any risk that Mr. Angelov and Mr. Petkov might escape. In addition, the conduct of Major G., the officer who shot the victims, called for serious criticism in that he had used grossly excessive force.[310] The Court found a violation of the procedural aspects of Article 2 and questioned the effectiveness of the investigation conducted by the Bulgarian authorities[311]:

> [Their] failure to examine relevant matters in the file meant that there had been no strict scrutiny of all the material circumstances. A number of indispensable and obvious investigative steps had not been taken and the investigating authorities had ignored significant facts without seeking any proper explanation, preferring instead to accept Major G.'s statements and terminate the investigation. The investigator and the prosecutors had thus effectively shielded G. from prosecution.[312]

In addition to that, the Grand Chamber's judgment concluded that there was no adequate investigation of the possible racist motives of the arresting officers (Article 14, *procedural* aspects). It followed that the authorities had failed in their duty under Article 14 (together with Article 2), to take all possible steps to investigate whether or not discrimination may have played a role in the events. The Grand Chamber however did not find enough evidence in support of the claim that the killings were racially motivated. According to the Court, there was no violation of the *substantive* aspects of Article 14 taken together with Article 2.[313]

---

310 Other means could have been used to arrest the men. Although "he also carried a handgun, G. had chosen to use his automatic rifle and switched it to automatic mode making it impossible to take aim with any reasonable degree of precision. Lastly, there was no plausible explanation for the fact that Mr. Petkov had been wounded in the chest, and the possibility that he had turned to surrender at the last minute but had nevertheless been shot could not be excluded," see ECtHR (2005: 2).

311 A similar violation of Article 2 — the inadequate investigation of the death of a young Roma man (Mr. G. Gerasimov) — was found by the ECtHR in the Case of Dimitrova and others versus Bulgaria (Application no. 44862/04).

312 See ECtHR (2005: 2).

313 On the basis of Article 41, the Grand Chamber upheld the awards to the applicants in the amounts of EUR 25,000 and EUR 22,000, respectively, on all heads of damage. Additionally, the ECtHR made an award for costs.

3.3.3 Hate crimes

The ethnopolitical situation in Bulgaria rapidly deteriorated at the end of September 2011. Unprecedented acts of hatred against the Roma (BHC 2012: 33) ensued from the murder on September 23 in the village of Katunitsa of a 19-year-old Bulgarian. The victim was intentionally hit by a van driven by a Roma man, allegedly close to the shady Roma businessman Kiril Rashkov (aka "Tsar Kiro").[314] The perpetrator was arrested and sentenced on March 1, 2012, to 17 years in prison for premeditated murder. Additionally, Mr. Rashkov and his grandson were sentenced, respectively, to three and a half years, and to eight months, for threatening to kill a person who was close to the family of the victim. The murder in Katunitsa opened the floodgates of the largest and most vehement demonstrations and acts of violence incited by anti-Roma slogans from the beginning of the democratic changes in Bulgaria. The rallies took place in 14 towns and cities and lasted more than a week (Refworld 2012). In the protests, which were organized via Facebook and other social networks, took part "tens of thousands of activists of two ultra nationalistic and xenophobic political parties — Ataka and IMRO, as well as non-party extremists and football fans" (BHC 2012: 34). Protestors shouted racist slogans, including "Gypsies into glue!," "Turn the Gypsies into soap!," and "Death to the Gypsies!." Some protestors wore anti-Roma T-shirts (some of them distributed by the political party Ataka), with slogans such as "We do not want to live in a Gypsy state!." Others reportedly carried anti-Roma banners, with slogans such as "We don't want to pay for the Gypsies!" (Refworld 2012). During the events, the leader of Ataka, Mr. Volen Siderov, demanded the restoration of the death penalty (which was abolished in Bulgaria in 1998 when it was replaced with life imprisonment), the demolition of the "Roma ghettoes" and vouched to support prompt changes in the legislation with the aim to enshrine and defend the citizens' right to carry firearms in order to protect themselves and their property (BHC 2012: 33).

---

314 The demonstrations began in protest against the impunity of Rashkov and other criminal bosses in Bulgaria.

According to the BHC, it is indicative of the government's policy toward this ethnic group that the anti-Roma demonstrations were "tolerated" and that the police did not take any action to stop the protestors when they set on fire houses owned by Mr. Rashkov and damaged some of his vehicles (BHC 2012: 33). During the demonstrations several Romani were attacked and seriously injured and Roma property damaged.[315] Despite the bleak prognosis of the BHC, which suggested that because of the extremely sluggish legal procedures most of the offenders will probably remain unpunished, it has to be emphasized that there are facts which show that the authorities took the matter seriously. The chief public prosecutor at the time — Mr. Boris Velchev — ordered all signals of hate crimes (listed as offences in Articles 162 and 163 of the PC[316]), i.e., incitement to hatred on the grounds of ethnicity and religion, to be examined as fast as possible. At the beginning of 2012, there were 16 cases opened by the prosecution on these counts against participants in the rallies. Indeed, until mid-September 2012 there was only one person convicted,[317] but in these particular circumstances in which the authorities' actions are under the scrutinizing eye of the Bulgarian and European organizations defending human rights, the lack of faster results should not necessarily be interpreted as a by-product of prejudices toward the Roma or "the low motivation" of "the powers that be." There are no reasons to believe that the proceedings which do not deal with hate crimes will be faster.

Nonetheless, the stand of the SAC on instances of hate speech *continues to be controversial*. For example, in its *Decision 14426* from November 26, 2012, the Court did not accept that the aggressive

---

315 The UN Committee against Torture similarly voiced its concern that the police on several occasions did not prevent the destruction of Roma property during the riots (UN, December 14, 2011, para. 28). Agence France-Presse (AFP) notes that some protestors were armed with batons and knives and some tried to break into Roma neighborhoods, particularly in Varna (October 2, 2011).
316 See Penal Code (2016).
317 According to the BHC director, this was a person who started a Facebook group called "Kill the Gypsies." He was convicted for incitement of hatred and was fined. See Refworld (2012).

statement by the mayor of a village toward the woman partner of a Roma man ("Why do you live with these Gypsies?") constitutes harassment on the grounds of race (BHC 2013). According to the Court's judgment "the mere expression of a personal opinion in front of a third party *vis-à-vis* another person does not correspond to the criteria defining 'a discriminative attitude'," and "the existence of conflicts (between the parties) is not a sufficient reason for such conclusion be made" (BHC 2013: 40). However, in the case against Mr. Bojan Stankov-Rassate, the SAC confirmed that his statements against the refugees of African origin broadcasted on *Nova TV*[318] are a manifestation of racism and xenophobia. Essentially in the case against Rassate, the SAC adopted the position that "statements which include the dissemination of hate, spite, hostility and the [physical] elimination of people with different skin color are discrimination."[319] This wording is hardly congruent with the position of the SAC in the aforementioned Decision 14426.

The case studies, incorporated in the present work, indicate that *on number of occasions the rights of the Roma are not adequately protected by the legal institutions and even are violated by representatives of the very bodies that have the task to maintain justice and implement in the society the guiding principles of the liberal democracy*. It is tempting to divide the main issues, identified by this study, into two groups. In the first place, there are *procedural problems*, such as the continuing lack of coherence between the main antidiscrimination legislation and older acts; the difficulties that still some of the judges have to distinguish between direct and indirect discrimination; and the notorious sluggishness of the system, i.e., the "lack of effective remedy" for violations before the national authorities (European Convention on Human Rights 1950: Art. 13).[320]

Second, there are cases that reveal *criminal intent* (the forms of institutional racism manifested in the decisions/actions of judges, prosecutors, members of the police force, etc., along with the efforts

---

318 Нова телевизия, in English—"New Television," the second national private TV network in Bulgaria launched in 1994.
319 Ibid.: 41.
320 See as well Art. 6.

to cover tracks and perpetrators; the attempts to interfere in the work of the CPAD through political patronage and/or financial dependencies; the apparent and continuing segregation in housing and education; the impediments to the provision to goods and services, etc.). However, I believe that this distinction between "mechanical" faults or lacunae in the legal system and deliberate violations is misleading. The problems in the operation of the judicial institutions and the legislation *essentially mirror the same fact* — the general public is still not alarmed by discrimination against minority ethnic groups and does not perceive them as an issue worth of attention.

On the grounds of the analysis, the following general recommendations could be made. First, it is important and highly necessary to conduct additional training courses and seminars for legal professionals on the intricacies of European law in the field of anti-discrimination and protection of human rights. There is, second, a pressing need for amendments in the legislation in order to ensure a better coherence between the provisions and concepts related to the rights of the most vulnerable members of society, such as the persons who belong to ethnic minorities. Third, urgent steps must be taken to further strengthen the control over the law-enforcement agencies. Fourth, legislative changes must ensure that the equality body and the other government institutions that deal with the problems of discrimination steer clear of political dependencies. Fifth, government officials must allow that NGOs are much more involved in the tailoring of policies and strategies. Last, but not least, more efforts are needed in order to inform the members of society as a whole on the importance to combat and prevent intolerance, prejudice, and discrimination.

Conclusion:
A Story about Garbage Trucks

An author typically states the motives or the sources of inspiration for his work at the very beginning. Since one of my primary goals has been to keep the "narrative" as objective and impartial as possible, I decided to leave this personal note for the final pages of this book. My interest in the topic of ethnic relations and conflicts was sparked by a rather curious story which happened many years ago. I must have been in my early teens. It was shortly after the dramatic 1989 in which Bulgaria took an unexpected and radical political detour. I was walking with my granddad in a street at the heart of Sofia. We suddenly heard a lot of noise; there was a smoke, a smell of gasoline, some commotion, and an orange garbage truck which, unbeknownst to us had crawled behind us, stopped near the sidewalk... Thin, dark men in working outfits who shouted to each other in a loud voice, which sounded like gibberish to me, jumped out of the machine, and headed for the trash can. A well-dressed woman who walked near them covered her nose with disgust and hurriedly passed away... Without thinking, I made the same gesture. One of the men noticed that and turned his burning eyes toward me... "Please don't mind him," quickly said my granddad at the man and raised his hand as to protect me — "he is still a child." Then, my grandfather looked at me with reproach. He murmured sadly, staring at the truck which had already continued its boisterous way down the street: "they were like *slaves*" ... Obviously, he referred to the time of the communist regime.

    There were quite a few things that puzzled me about this story. Of course, I have seen similar trucks many times before in my childhood. But, first, not only did I not understand the "attitude" of my granddad but I was even somewhat offended by his timely "intervention" ... I remember the storm of thoughts in my head at the time: "why have compassion for *such* men ... after all, they are Gypsies ... *we all know* that they are dirty, stink and are at the lowest rung of the social ladder." I was also intrigued by the fact that my granddad used the word "slaves." "How is that possible?," I kept asking myself, "everyone knows that slavery has been abolished, certainly, it did not seize to exist only a few years ago and, at that, Bulgaria, a country which was liberated from the Turkish yoke at the end of the nineteenth century, had and maintained slaves?!"

Several decades have passed since then. Many of the garbage trucks, which have "matured" to even bigger clunkers or boneshakers, are of the same make and model as the ones years ago. And the vehicles are still exclusively operated by Roma men. Only their uniforms are different... The mystery which clouded the words of my granddad has been uncovered. But he was not entirely correct... *Slavery is not a thing of the past*. This ancient-old phenomenon has contemporary manifestations. Vulnerability to modern slavery is affected by a complex interaction of factors related to the presence or absence of "protection and respect for rights, physical safety and security, access to the necessities of life such as food, water and health care, and patterns of migration, displacement and conflict."[321] According to the Global Slavery Index (GSI), in 2016[322] there were 45.8 million people who were enslaved in the world.[323] The GSI was created on the basis of statistical testing which grouped twenty-four measures of vulnerability into four dimensions covering: civil and political protections; social health and economic rights; personal security; and refugee populations and conflict.[324] Although, as a region, it has the lowest prevalence of modern slavery in the world, "Europe remains a destination, and to a lesser extent, a source region for the exploitation of men, women and children in forced labor and commercial sexual exploitation."[325]

---

321 See GSI: Global Findings (2017).
322 All data from GSI quoted here are for 2016.
323 See GSI: Global Findings (2017).
324 Ibid.
325 GSI: Europe (2017).

According to the most recent Eurostat findings, EU citizens account for 65% of identified trafficked victims within Europe.[326] These individuals mostly originate from Eastern Europe, including Romania, Bulgaria, Lithuania and Slovakia."[327] Non-EU trafficked victims are predominantly from Nigeria, China, and Brazil (GSI: Europe 2017). Forced labor and commercial sexual exploitation remain the most commonly reported forms of modern slavery in Europe. The researchers who developed the GSI state that Roma, who are among most marginalized groups in Europe, are "particularly vulnerable to enslavement."[328] Due to poverty and lack of access to public services, "some Roma families resort to trafficking their own children, forced marriages or involving them in commercial sexual exploitation as a survival strategy" (GSI: Europe 2017). The GSI scholars cite Bulgaria as an example of a country in Europe where Roma children are potentially vulnerable to being sold or rented to other individuals for forced begging, and, in "some Roma communities" continues the practice of "bride kidnapping."[329] According to the GSI in 2016, the estimated number of people living in modern slavery in Bulgaria was 29,000.[330]

Now, without forgetting the disturbing facts that these data reveal, let us return to the results of the study to which this book is dedicated. Based on the analysis, *the second* of the three hypotheses[331] underlying the foundation of this work *has been partially confirmed*. It must be adjusted and supplemented in view of the varying degree of integration of the main minority ethnic groups. Unlike the Turks, Roma representation in the political institutions is feeble and almost imperceptible. Even in bodies such as the NCCEII, the role of NGOs that protect the rights of Roma is de facto often insignificant. Roma vote is dispersed, fragmented. Unlike the Turkish constituents, who until recently, before DOST entered the stage,

---

326 Ibid.
327 See GSI: Europe (2017).
328 Ibid.
329 Ibid.
330 GSI: Index — Bulgaria 2017.
331 See the Introduction.

were a "monopoly" of the MRF, a significant percentage of Roma vote in favor of other parties, the main players—GERB and BSP, in particular. As we saw, the latter, as well as the ethnic formations, *are in fact interested in keeping the Roma in the ghettoes, where they can be easily manipulated and used as an electoral resource. The instrument for that is the vicious interconnection between political brokers and organized crime.* As I have demonstrated, many of MRF's supporters, especially, have expressed doubts about the way in which their interests are "defended" by the party leadership. Therefore, if we transform the contents of the hypothesis in scientific conclusion, it will read the following: *the political system, so far, has been able to prevent serious conflicts, but the way it reflects the interests of the main minority ethnic groups, compared with the dominant (the ethnic Bulgarians), is unsatisfactory.*

The third hypothesis has to be rejected. A number of proofs have been brought in support of the view that the explosive alliance between political populism and extreme nationalism, which often is seen as the greatest threat for ethnic peace, is only a symptom of the disease, which actually should be treated. The disorder in question *is the sclerosis of the party and political system.* The lack of effectiveness of political institutions intermediaries in Bulgaria, the calling of which is to express the interests emerging in civil society, stems from the fact that they are, although to varying degrees, affected by nepotism and oligarchic tendencies. The distorted, perversive way in which parties and organizations "retranslate" the demands and expectations boiling in civil society is destructive for state institutions. This conclusion leads to *the first hypothesis which has been corroborated. The contemporary Bulgarian ethnic model is not a fixed political construct. It, however, did not evolve but, being organically connected to the trends and processes in the political system, mutated and deteriorated in the last decades. It, finally, turned into a chimera.* As the three stages of the development of this model, outlined above, reveal, the main ethnic party—the MRF—went from performer of balancing acts between the Socialists and the Right to a full-fledged partner in central government and, ultimately, to a persona non grata. Currently not only the PRR but the mainstream parties such as GERB and BSP refrain from working openly with the formation of Ahmed Dogan and Mustafa Karadaya. The ethnic relations are trapped. *On the one hand, the Bulgarian ethnic model is based on the institutionalization of ethnic cleavage that leads to the politicization of identity, and, on the other, the institutions, the function of which is to channel the aspirations of ethnic communities, are anemic and with problematic legitimacy. The ethnic peace has been entrusted to a defective mechanism. This is the most serious problem in the ethnic model built after 1989.*

Along with the conclusions that stem from the examination of the three main hypotheses, the project has led to other significant results. I outlined and analyzed the ways in which the Bulgarian institutions operate and interact in resolving ethnic conflicts. In other words, I "reverse engineered" the Bulgarian ethnic model. I highlighted not only the problems but also some improvements or "success stories," although the latter are rare. On the basis of the analysis, I drafted recommendations for the necessary institutional reforms. It will be redundant and unnecessary to repeat these here. Instead, I will limit myself to a shortlist which contains the three most pressing changes that have to be made as soon as possible.

First, the chief risk, as far as ethnic conflicts and national security are concerned, lies in bungled and mismanaged policies toward the Roma. The ghettoes can potentially shelter and nurture the radical ideas of false prophets. The integration of Roma must start from child's cradle, from kindergarten's door. It is imperative to complete the process of desegregation of schools.[332] Second, the passionate patriotic slogans that target the minorities and call for rapid and permanent "fixes," and I do not have in mind only the political messages of the PRR parties, must be cooled down with the help of pragmatic reasoning. In recent years, there has been an increasing pressure to amend the Electoral code in order to limit the voting rights of the Bulgarian citizens who live abroad, in particular those

---

332 See Dronzina et al. (2016) for alarming signs and patterns of radicalization of pupils from ethnic minorities observed in schools in Bulgaria.

in Turkey. Of course, the Bulgarian institutions cannot remain passive or stay indifferent[333] to the alleged attempts of the regime of Recep Tayyip Erdogan to interfere in the Bulgarian politics with the help of (ethnic) parties and organizations, such as Lyutvi Mestan's DOST and Orhan Ismailov's People's Party "Freedom and Dignity" — PPFD. However, the "logic" according to which, apparently, the government can have "issues" or "problems" with Bulgarian citizens, on the grounds of their ethnicity, religion, etc., is *deeply flawed*. Such mind-set contradicts the very pillars of the Constitution of July 13, 1991, the principle of popular sovereignty (Article 3) in particular.

Third, the reform of the party system, which continues to be mostly under the control of shady political engineers, cannot happen *without the active role of citizens themselves*. This holds true not only for the ethnic Bulgarians, but to Turks and Roma as well. To employ the classic distinction, the "subjective structure" in the composition of Bulgarian political culture appears to be a more important and influential element than the "participatory" [334] (Almond and Verba 1989). On the one hand, as electoral studies demonstrate, there are many Bulgarians who continuously refuse to go to the polls. On the other, those who vote appear to often suffer from a sui generis "cognitive dissonance." The record low confidence in institutions such as the Popular Assembly (in the last years the trust in the parliament fluctuates around 15% of the respondents) shows that many constituents deceive themselves in believing that the politicians who they support possess the necessary qualities to lead, only to quickly become disillusioned. As Fyodor Dostoyevsky noted, a "man who lies to himself, and believes his own lies, becomes unable to recognize truth, either in himself or in

---

333 Although it does not mention particular countries, parties, or names, the latest annual report of State Agency "National Security" (ДАНС) warns of such attempts; see SANS (2017). However, the Bulgarian President Rumen Radev clearly stated that the actions of the regime of Erdogan toward Bulgaria "are unacceptable." See "Radev: The interference of Turkey in Bulgaria is a fact" (2017).

334 And especially the culture of the "dominant ethnic group" — the ethnic Bulgarians.

anyone else, and ends up losing respect for himself and for others" (Dostoyevski 2002: 44). Bulgarians, it seems to me, are inherently prone to be obedient to the powers that be or to the self-proclaimed "elites." *The ability to resist any undemocratic deviations is essential to the existence of a vibrant and vigorous civil society, without which the Bulgarian political and party system will remain in their unenviable state.*

What does the future hold for the ethnic relations and conflicts in Bulgaria? First, given the high risk of terrorist attacks as well as the prevailing attitudes among the ethnic Bulgarians, who appear to become less and less tolerant toward country's large minorities such as Roma and Turks, the support for the PRR will remain strong. It is possible that it will increase *even further*. I do not share the view that the disappointing results for the "United Patriots" in the snap elections of 2017, in which they obtained almost 69,000 votes fewer than Ataka and NFSB received in 2014, are a signal that the mainstream parties managed to stop the triumphant march of the PRR. The collaboration with the parties of the status quo usually takes its toll on the antisystem formations. Nonetheless, even if the "destiny" of the "United Patriots," who after the snap elections in 2017 received key positions in the third Office of Boyko Borisov, confirms this trend and the formations in the coalition go separate ways and/or the public support for them greatly diminishes, we can rest assured that this type of "ideas" will quickly find new preachers and enthusiastic proponents.

Second, the strength and role of the PRR will continue to depend on those of ethnic parties and vice versa. In the snap election of 2017, the MRF has lost 170,000 votes in comparison to 2014. This is a very significant "chunk" of its electoral support. DOST, which worked in coalition with NPFD, has managed to capture most of the votes of Bulgarian Turks who live abroad (i.e., in Turkey, but not only there). Therefore, the strategy of Erdogan's regime *was partially successful*. The future of DOST depends on the fate and whim of Turkey's current political leaders—it appears that this political formation is a project in which they have invested a lot. The outcome of the Turkish Referendum on the proposed 18 constitutional amendments held on April 16, 2017, untied Erdogan's hands for transition to an executive presidency and a presidential system.³³⁵ Although the Referendum was won by a small margin (51.41% vs. 48.59%)³³⁶ by the governing Justice and Development Party and Nationalist Movement Party, which proposed the amendments, and the opposition prevailed in many large cities (Istanbul, Ankara, Izmir, Adana, Antalya, etc.), it is indisputable that Turkey is drifting far away from the ideals and the political legacy of Mustafa Kemal Atatürk (Bechev 2017). The Referendum demonstrated that the country is divided. Erdogan has lost the support of the more educated, wealthier members of the society, the new "bourgeoisie" based in the cities (Aydıntaşbaş 2017). More importantly, although Bulgarian Muslims "do not have radical political attitudes" the majority of them—49% *approve of regime of Erdogan*, only 19% disapprove, and "the trust in Turkey" among them is increasing and is 69% (Alpha Research 2017).³³⁷ In a nutshell, the doctrine of neo-Ottomanism promoted by Erdogan will continue to be employed by the Bulgarian PRR in order to vindicate its very existence and daily "actions." The other side of the coin, of course, is that the longer the "Untied Patriots" or similar parties are behind country's steering wheel, the ethnic formations will have scarecrows to which they can comfortably point and which they will use relentlessly in order to mobilize and discipline their constituencies. The "plans" of some PRR parties such as Ataka, which maintain close relations with the

---

335 It should be remembered, however, that the legislative amendments which will allow this to take place will enter into force only after the presidential and parliamentary elections in November 2019. Still, the immediate ramification of the Referendum is the extension of the state of emergency by three months. The state of emergency, in itself, gives substantial powers to the President Erdogan (Aydıntaşbaş 2017). Erdogan's promise to reinstate the death penalty would end any hopes that Turkey will join the EU.

336 The opposition, as well as many local and foreign political observers, has disputed the outcome of the Referendum. According to Asli Aydıntaşbaş, "this was perhaps the most imbalanced and unfair electoral environment in Turkey since a post-coup referendum held by the military generals in 1982" (Aydıntaşbaş 2017).

337 Seventy-two percent of the Turkish citizens in Bulgaria voted "No" in the Referendum, however, note that only 17% of them went to the polls.

regime of Vladimir Putin,[338] will be also contingent on the policies of the Kremlin, and more particularly on its hybrid war strategies and tactics.

Third, in the foreseeable future, *the state of the economy will continue to work in favor of demagogues and ethnic entrepreneurs.* Although in the last years the economic conditions in Bulgaria are improving, if we take into consideration a key indicator such as the amount of net monthly income,[339] the country is still at the rear of the EU. As the collapse of the Central Cooperative Bank (Corpbank) in 2014 demonstrated,[340] the banking sector remains a hostage and a victim of the battles of criminalized political "elites." The legacy of weak supervision[341] in this sector has not been overcome. Actions are still needed in order to remove the weaknesses uncovered during the stress tests of the banking system.[342] Other significant issues are the great firm indebtedness, gray economy, undeclared labor,[343] and the insurmountable corruption. Numerous studies, some of which were quoted in this book, reveal that the majority of Bulgarians continue to oppose the measures of positive discrimination benefiting minorities. At the same time, 63% of the Muslims in Bulgaria have declared that they receive an average monthly income per capita

---

338 Scholars like Ognyan Minchev claim that Russia has other, rather surprising (given Kremlin's support for Ataka), Trojan horses on the Bulgarian political stage—such as the ethnic party MRF. See Minchev (2016).

339 The "Borisov 3" Government has promised to increase the minimal wage to 650 leva (approximately 332 Euro) by the end of its term (i.e., until 2021). This amount is still very low, compared to the EU average.

340 At the end of November 2013, Corpbank was the fourth largest bank in Bulgaria in terms of assets, third in terms of net profit, and first in terms of deposit growth. After it collapsed in 2014 during the Office of Mr. Plamen Oresharski, Corpbank's board was accused of operating a Ponzi scheme. Its license was revoked by the Bulgarian National Bank. Mr. Tsvetan Vasilev, the chairman of Corpbank, fled the country and as of the end of 2016 faces extradition proceeding in Serbia.

341 I am referring, of course, to the collapse of the banking system during the Office of Mr. Zhan Videnov (1995-1997).

342 Including banking and nonbanking supervision as well as obstacles in the procedures for insolvency.

343 The percentage of bad credits is a two-digit number, unlike the average European level. State enterprises with the biggest debt are those in the energy sector.

which is less than 250 leva[344] – approximately 128 Euro, and 74% of the "Muslims in the ghettoes"[345] receive less than 100 leva or 51 Euro (Alpha Research 2017). Although further data analyses are necessary in order to prove conclusively the correlation between the rise of populism and economic decline (Mudde 2007), it is indisputable that institutional weakness is a major obstacle to prosperity (Fukuyama 2004a). *The public resistance against positive discrimination measures will continue to be weaponized by ethnic entrepreneurs notwithstanding to which camp they belong – to the one of the ethnic parties, to that of the populist radical right/left or to the political mainstream.*

One thing is certain. Politicized ethnicity will remain a preferred instrument for propaganda and mobilization on the Balkan Peninsula. Bulgaria will not stand out as an exception. What Bulgarians can and should aspire to do instead, is to keep violence which emerges in between societal cleavages at bay. Otherwise, it will erupt and mercilessly destroy the political system and its institutions. It is imperative to understand and appreciate how invaluable and fragile ethnic peace is. Indeed, as Laozi pointed out in *Tao Te Ching*, "a journey of a thousand kilometers begins with a single step."[346] And, in order to obtain that understanding, we can start by exposing the puppeteers who thrive on instigating ethnic strife, who capitalize on keeping ethnic communities in the state of obedient pawns, toy soldiers or a glass menagerie, used in their countless games. We can commence by taking down the masks of ethnic entrepreneurs.

---

344 While the country average is 35%, see Alpha Research (2017).
345 Most of the "Muslims in the Ghettoes" are Roma.
346 See Laozi (2016: chapter 64).

References

"Ahmed Bashev: No Romani were settled in Garmen, their number increased due to the high birthrate" (2015), available from: http://www.dnevnik.bg (webpage accessed on February 23, 2016), [in Bulgarian].

Ahmed, D. (2008) "Name, Renaming and Double Identity (Bulgarian Turks during the so Called 'Revival Process,' 1984–1989)," *Sociological Problems*, 1–2 (2003): 167–78, [in Bulgarian].

"Ahmed Dogan: 'I allocate funding in the state'" (2009), available from: http://www.mediapool.bg (webpage accessed on March 25, 2016), [in Bulgarian].

"Ahmed Musa Ahmed got two years in prison for preaching radical Islam" (2015), available from: http://www.mediapool.bg (webpage accessed on March 25, 2016), [in Bulgarian].

Aleksandrova, N. (2011) "What hides behind the Roma court Meshere," available from: http://dariknews.bg (webpage accessed on March 25, 2016), [in Bulgarian].

Almond, G., Verba, S. (1989) *The Civic Culture: Political Attitudes and Democracy in Five Nations* (Newbury Park, CA: Sage Publications).

"'Alpha Research': Campaigning for local elections is becoming a direct marketing" (2015), available from: http://www.dnevnik.bg (webpage accessed on February 18, 2016), [in Bulgarian].

Alpha Research (2008) "MRF—An Inside Look" (data from in-depth interviews and a representative quantitative survey among 560 potential voters of MRF in the regions of Blagoevgrad, Dobrich, Kardzhali, Silistra, Targovishte, Shumen, Haskovo, held between August 8–20, 2008, available from: http://alpharesearch.bg (webpage accessed on March 25, 2016), [in Bulgarian].

Alpha Research (2009) "Social-Demographic Portrait of the Voters in the EU Parliament Elections," available from: http://alpharesearch.bg (webpage accessed on March 25, 2016), [in Bulgarian].

Alpha Research (2013) "Public Attitudes—December 2013," available from: http://alpharesearch.bg (webpage accessed on March 25, 2016), [in Bulgarian].

Alpha Research (2014) "Public Attitudes, January 2014—Electoral Turmoil after the Start of ABV," available from: http://alpharesearch.bg (webpage accessed on March 25, 2016), [in Bulgarian].

Alpha Research (2015a) "Public Evaluation of the Work of the Parliament," June 2015, available from: http://alpharesearch.bg (webpage accessed on June 24, 2015), [in Bulgarian].

Alpha Research (2015b) "National Representative Survey," November 10–18, 2015, available from: http://www.dnevnik.bg (webpage accessed on March 25, 2017), [in Bulgarian].

Alpha Research (2016) "Public Attitudes: September 2016," available from: http://alpharesearch.bg (webpage accessed on March 25, 2017), [in Bulgarian].

Alpha Research (2017) "Main Results of the Project 'Attitudes among the Muslims in Bulgaria,'" available from: http://alpharesearch.bg (webpage accessed on April 6, 2017), summary available from: http://www.dnevnik.bg, [in Bulgarian].

Altermatt, U. (1998) *Ethnonationalism in Europe* (Sofia: GALIKO Press), [in Bulgarian].

Anderson, B. (2006) *Imagined Communities: Reflections on the Origin and Spread of Nationalism*, revised and extended edition (London: Verso).

Angelov, V. (2010) *The Protest Actions of Turks in Bulgaria (January–May 1989)*, 2nd edition (Sofia: Self-published).

Angelova, K. (2001) "Whatever Happened to the Framework Program for the Integration of Roma?," *Objective, Journal of the Bulgarian Helsinki Committee* 70: 7.

Aresnova, D., Kertikov, K. (2002) "The Bulgarian Ethnic Model and the Constitutional Crisis in Macedonia," Part I, Balkans'21, 1/2003, [in Bulgarian].

Aresnova, D., Kertikov, K. (2003) "The Bulgarian Ethnic Model and the Constitutional Crisis in Macedonia," Part II, Balkans'21, 2/2003, [in Bulgarian].

Arts, W., Gelissen, J. (2002) "Three Worlds of Welfare Capitalism or More?" *Journal of European Social Policy* 12 (2): 137–58.

Asenov, A. (2007) "Dogan—five years earlier," available from: http://www.capital.bg (webpage accessed on March 25, 2016), [in Bulgarian].

Auty, Ph. (1970) *Tito: A Biography* (New York: McGraw-Hill Book Company).

Avramov, I. et al. (2009) *The Bulgarian Parliament and the Transition* (Sofia: Ciela Press), [in Bulgarian].

Avramov, K. (2015) "The Bulgarian Radical Right Marching up from the Margins," in *Transforming the Transformation*, M. Minkenberg, ed. (London: Routledge), pp. 299–318.

Avramov, R. (2007) *The Communal Capitalism*, vol. 3 (Sofia: Foundation "Bulgarian Science and Culture," Centre for Liberal Strategies), [in Bulgarian].

Avramov, R. (2017) *Economics of "Revival Process"* (Sofia: Centre for Advanced Study), [in Bulgarian].

Aydıntaşbaş, A. (2017) "Turkish Referendum: Erdogan Home but Not Yet Dry," European Council on Foreign Relations, available from http://www.ecfr.eu (webpage accessed on April 20, 2017).

Azar, E. (1990) *The Management of Protracted Social Conflict* (Aldershot: Dartmouth).

Baeva, I. (2011) "The Consequences of the Revival Process and the 'Bulgarian ethnic model' Today," in *The Bulgarian Ethnic Model: Political Mythologem or a Problematic Reality*, K. Kertikov, ed. (Sofia: Avangard Prima), pp. 65–80, [in Bulgarian].

Banchev, B. (2009) *Bulgaria and the Yugoslav Crisis 1989–1995* (Sofia: University of St. Kliment Ohridski Press), [in Bulgarian].

Bar Zohar, M. (1998) *Beyond Hitler's Grasp. The Heroic Rescue of Bulgaria's Jews* (Holbrook: Adams Media Corporation).

Bechev, D. (2017) "No Hope in Turkey," available from: http://blogs.lse.ac.uk (webpage accessed on April 20, 2017).

Bedrov, I. (2014) "Did Anyone Understand What Happened in Pazardzhik?," available from: http://www.dw.com (webpage accessed on March 25, 2016), [in Bulgarian].

Berov, Hr. (2009) *State and Confessions: Normative Regulation of Religion and the Religious Communities in Bulgaria* (Sofia: Ciela Press), [in Bulgarian].

Bezlov, T. (2007a) "Roma and Crime: Police Statistics and Realities," Part 1, available from: http://www.capital.bg (webpage accessed on March 25, 2016), [in Bulgarian].

Bezlov, T. (2007b) "Roma and Crime: Police Statistics and Realities," Part 2, available from: http://www.capital.bg (webpage accessed on March 25, 2016), [in Bulgarian].

Bezlov, T. (2007c) "Roma and Crime: Police Statistics and Realities," Part 3, available from: http://www.capital.bg (webpage accessed on March 25, 2016), [in Bulgarian].

Bezlov, T. (2007d) "Roma and Crime: Police Statistics and Realities," Part 4, available from: http://www.capital.bg (webpage accessed on March 25, 2016), [in Bulgarian].

Bezlov, T. (2007e) "Roma and Crime: Police Statistics and Realities," Part 5, available from: http://www.capital.bg (webpage accessed on March 25, 2016), [in Bulgarian].

Bezlov, T. (2007f) "Roma and Crime: Police Statistics and Realities," Part 6, available from: http://www.capital.bg (webpage accessed on March 25, 2016), [in Bulgarian].

Bezlov, T. (2007g) *Organized Crime in Bulgaria: Markets and Trends* (Sofia: Center for the Study of Democracy), [in Bulgarian].

Bezlov, T., Gounev, P. (2012a) "Bulgaria: Corruption and Organized Crime in Flux," in *Corruption and Organized Crime in Europe: Illegal Partnerships*, P. Gounev and V. Ruggiero, eds. (London: Routledge), pp. 15-31.

Bezlov, T., Gounev, P. (2012b) "Corruption and Criminal Markets," in *Corruption and Organized Crime in Europe: Illegal Partnerships*, P. Gounev and V. Ruggiero, eds. (London: Routledge), pp. 69-92.

Bezlov, T., Gounev, P. (2012c) "Organised Crime, Corruption and Public Bodies," in *Corruption and Organized Crime in Europe: Illegal Partnerships*, P. Gounev and V. Ruggiero, eds. (London: Routledge), pp. 95-107.

Bhalla, S. (1994) "Freedom and Economic Growth: A Virtuous Cycle?," paper presented at the South Asia Seminar, Center for International Affairs, Harvard University, February 1994.

BHC (2011) *Human Rights in Bulgaria in 2010, Annual Report of the Bulgarian Helsinki Committee* (Sofia: Bulgarian Helsinki Committee), available from: http://www.bghelsinki.org (webpage accessed on February 25, 2014), [in Bulgarian].

BHC (2012) *Human Rights in Bulgaria in 2011, Annual Report of the Bulgarian Helsinki Committee* (Sofia: Bulgarian Helsinki Committee), available from: http://www.bghelsinki.org (webpage accessed on February 25, 2014), [in Bulgarian].

BHC (2013) *Human Rights in Bulgaria in 2012, Annual Report of the Bulgarian Helsinki Committee* (Sofia: Bulgarian Helsinki Committee), available from: http://www.bghelsinki.org (webpage accessed on February 25, 2014), [in Bulgarian].

Bobbio, N. (1994) "Rechts und Links: Zum Sinn einer politischen Unterscheidung," *Blätter für deutsche und internationale Politik* 39 (5): 543–9.

Bojilov, Y. ed. (2016) *Radicalism and the Young* (Sofia: Elestra), [in Bulgarian].

Bookman, M. (1994) "War and Peace: The Divergent Breakups of Yugoslavia and Czechoslovakia," *Journal of Peace Research* 31 (2), (May): 175–88.

Bosakov, V. (2004) "Profiles of Islam in Bulgaria. Ethnic and Religious Identification in the Manifestation of "Otherness," *Sociological Problems*, 1–2: 354–75, [in Bulgarian].

Bosakov, V. (2006) "The Bulgarian Ethnic Model, Constructing a Foundation for Its Interpretation and Exploration)," *Worlds in Sociology* (Sofia: St. Kliment Ohridski), pp. 471–81, [in Bulgarian].

Bose, S. (1995), "State Crises and Nationalities Conflict in Sri Lanka and Yugoslavia," *Comparative Political Studies* 28 (1), (April:): 87–117.

Bozukova, M. (2011) "The State is Losing 700 Million Leva/Pa because of Roma Unemployment," available from: http://www.mediapool.bg (webpage accessed on March 25, 2016), [in Bulgarian].

Buccus, Imr. (2011) "Political Tolerance on the Wane in South Africa," SA Reconciliation Barometer, available from: http://reconciliationbarometer.org (webpage accessed on June 7, 2013).

Bugajski, J. (1995) *Ethnic Politics in Central and Easter Europe* (New York: The Centre for Strategic and International Studies).

Butterfield, H. (1951) *History and Human Relations* (Collins).

Case of Yordanova and Others v. Bulgaria (Application no. 25446/06), European Court of Human Rights, available from: http://www.echr.coe.int (webpage accessed on February 25, 2014), [in Bulgarian].

Caseli, F., Coleman, W. (2012) "On the Theory of Ethnic Conflict," available from: http://personal.lse.ac.uk (webpage accessed on February 25, 2014).

CDDAABCSS (2007) Decision No. 14 from September 4, 2007 of Commission for Disclosure of Documents and Announcing Affiliation of Bulgarian Citizens with the State Security and the Intelligence Services of the Bulgarian People's Army, available from: http://bg.wikisource.org (webpage accessed on March 13, 2014), [in Bulgarian].

Central Commission on Elections (2013) Elections for Bulgarian National Assembly, May 12, 2013, available from: http://results.cik.bg/ (webpage accessed on January 4, 2014), [in Bulgarian].

Cerami, Al. (2013) *Permanent Emergency Welfare Regimes in Sub-Saharan Africa: the Exclusive origins of Dictatorship and Democracy* (Palgrave Macmillan).

Cerami, Al., Wagué, A. (2013), "Africa," in *The Routledge Handbook of the Welfare State*, B. Greve, ed. (London: Routledge).

"'Chart of the Day: The parties retain electoral support'; the public confidence in the Government is decreasing" (2016), available from: http://www.capital.bg (webpage accessed on October 14, 2016).

Cholakov, P. (2013a) "The Bulgarian Ethnic Model and the End of the 'End of History,'" in *Bulgarian National Values, Statics and Dynamics in the Process of European Integration*, K. Kertikov, ed. (Sofia: Institute for the Study of Societies and Knowledge, BAS), pp. 253–64, [in Bulgarian].

Cholakov, P. (2013b) "The Institutional Approach to Ethnic Conflicts and Its Significance for Bulgaria," in *Ethnic Dimensions of Social Integration*, V. Zlatanova, ed. (Sofia: Omda), available from: http://www.omda.bg/ (webpage accessed on October 14, 2016), [in Bulgarian].

Cholakov, P. (2013c) "Ethnic Relations, Conflicts and Security: The Bulgarian Ethnic Models," *Papers Presented at the National Conference under the Auspice of the President of Bulgaria "National Security: Current Problems, Questions and Solutions," Sofia, Bulgaria, 21–22 October 2013* (Sofia: Sofia Security Forum), [in Bulgarian].

Cholakov, P. (2014a) "Contemporary Ethnopolitical Conflicts in Bulgaria: Legal Dimensions," *Sociological Problems* (Special Issue 2014): 131–50.

Cholakov, P. (2014b) "Canalizing Ethnopolitical Conflicts in Bulgaria: The Role of Legislation and Judicial System," in *Intégration et Voisinage Européens*, dirigée par Radovan Gura et Gilles Rouet (Paris: L'Harmattan, Collection Local & Global), pp. 77–100.

Cholakov, P. (2015) "Is the 'Bulgarian Ethnic Model' Doomed?" in *Reshaping Politics and Ideology: In Bulgaria, Europe and the World*, M. Mirchev, ed. (Sofia: University of National and World Economy), pp. 200–11, [in Bulgarian].

Cholakov, P. (2016a) "The Genesis of Populist Radical Right in Bulgaria," in *Political Science Facing the Global and National Challenges at the Beginning of the Twenty-first Century*, G. Iankov, ed. (Sofia: University of National and World Economy), pp. 289–96, [in Bulgarian].

Cholakov, P. (2016b) "The Ethnic Underclass: The Paper Tower of Roma Integration in Bulgaria," *Sociological Problems* (Special Issue 2016): 152–72.

Cholakov, P. (2017a) "The Bulgarian Populist Radical Right: Origins, Characteristics, Tendencies," in *Party Systems, Political Order and Constitutional Reforms: Experiences and Perspectives*, R. Zheleva, ed. (Skopje–Sofia: BAS Press), pp. 113–26, [in Bulgarian].

Cholakov, P. (2017b) "The Populist Radical Right in Bulgaria: Representatives, Origins, Ideology, Future Perspectives," *Political Studies*, [in Bulgarian], in print.

Christman, H. M. ed. (1970) *The Essential Tito* (New York: St. Martin's Press).

CIA (2014) *World Factbook 2014 – Population Growth (2014 Estimates)*, available from: https://www.cia.gov (webpage accessed on May 11, 2015).

CIA (2015) *World Factbook 2015*, available from: https://www.cia.gov (webpage accessed on June 8, 2015).

Constitution of Republic of Bulgaria (1991), available from: http://www.parliament.bg (webpage accessed on December 4, 2017).

Coser, L. (1968) *Continuities in the Study of Social Conflict* (New York: The Free Press).

Council Directive 2000/43/EC Implementing the principle of equal treatment between persons irrespective of racial or ethnic origin (2000).

Council Directive 2000/78/EC Establishing a general framework for equal treatment in employment and occupation (2000).

CPAD (2011) *Annual Report of the Commission for Protection against Discrimination* (CPAD), 2010, [in Bulgarian].

CPAD (2012) *Annual Report of the Commission for Protection against Discrimination* (CPAD), 2011, [in Bulgarian].

Crawford, B., Lipschutz, R. eds. (1998) *The Myth of Ethnic Conflict: Politics, Economics and "Cultural Violence"* (Berkeley, CA: University of California Press).

Crush, J., Pendleton, W. (2004). "Regionalizing Xenophobia? Citizen Attitudes to Immigration and Refugee Policy in Southern Africa" (South African Migration Project, Migration Policy Institute), available from: http://www.queensu.ca (webpage accessed on December 20, 2012).

CSD (2012) *CSD Brief No 35, Corruption and Anti-corruption in Bulgaria 2011–2012* (in Bulgarian), available from http://www.csd.bg (webpage accessed on April 24, 2013).

Cvii, C. (1993) "Who's to Blame for the War in Ex-Yugoslavia?," *World Affairs* 156 (2), (Fall): 72–80.

Dahrendorf, R. (1959) *Class and Class Conflict in Industrial Society* (Stanford: Stanford University Press).

Dahrendorf, R. (2007) *The Modern Social Conflict: The Politics of Liberty*, 2nd edition (New Brunswick, NJ: Transaction Publishers).

Dainov, E. (2013) *The Barbarians: The Rule of GERB (2009-2013)* (Sofia: Milenium).

Daskalov, R. (2005) *Bulgarian Society 1878-1939*, v. 1 and v. 2 (Sofia: Gutenberg), [in Bulgarian].

Dawson, J. (2014) *Cultures of Democracy in Serbia and Bulgaria* (Ashgate).

Denitch, B. (1994) *Ethnic Nationalism: The Tragic Death of Yugoslavia* (Minneapolis: University of Minnesota Press).

Denton, G. et al. (2003) *Political Participation of Roma in Bulgaria* (Sofia: National Democratic Institute of the USA), [in Bulgarian].

Detrez, R., Segaert, B. (2008) *Europe and the Historical Legacies in the Balkans* (Brussels: P.I.E. Peter Lang).

Dimitrov, V. (2001) *Bulgaria: The Uneven Transition* (London: Routledge).

Dimitrova, V. (2015) "Pickpockets from Ignatievo candidates for local government," available from: http://novanews.novatv.bg (webpage accessed on February 18, 2016), [in Bulgarian].

Dogan: "we have a circle of companies—they fund us, we help them" (2005), available from: http://www.mediapool.bg (webpage accessed on March 25, 2016), [in Bulgarian].

Dostoyevski, F. (2002) *The Brothers Karamazov*, transl. by Richard Pevear and Larissa Volokhonsky (New York: Farrar, Straus and Giroux).

Dronzina, T. (2004) *Ethnic Conflicts and Identities: The Challenges of the Balkans to United Europe* (Sofia: Kota Press), [in Bulgarian].

Dronzina, T. ed. (2007) *Ethnic Conflicts, Minorities and the New European Identity* (Sofia: Europartners Press), [in Bulgarian].

Dronzina, T. et al. (2016) "Radicalization and Bulgarian Schools," in *Radicalism and the Young*, Y. Bojilov, ed. (Sofia: Elestra), pp. 31-38, [in Bulgarian].

EC (2004) *2004 Regular Report on Bulgaria's Progress towards Accession* (Brussels: European Commission).

EC (2009) *Vademecum: 10 Common Basic Principles of Roma Inclusion of the Council of Ministers of the EU* (Brussels: European Commission), available from http://www.coe.int (webpage accessed on February 25, 2014).

ECRI (2009) *Observations on ECRI Fourth Report on Bulgaria (2009)*.

ECtHR (2005) *Nachova and Others v. Bulgaria, Judgement of the Grand Chamber of the ECtHR from 6.07.2005, Information Note on the Court's case-law No. 77* (Legal Summary).

ECtHR (2012a) *Case of Yordanova and Others v. Bulgaria* (25446/06), (Legal Summary).

ECtHR (2012b) *Affaire Yotova c. Bulgarie* (Requête no 43606/04), Arrêt, 23 octobre 2012, available from: http://hudoc.echr.coe.int (webpage accessed on April 4, 2013).

Eminov, A. (1997) *Turkish and Other Muslim Minorities of Bulgaria* (New York: Routledge).

Engström, J. (2009) *Democratization and the Prevention of Violent Conflict* (Farnham: Ashgate).

Engström, J. (2014) *Democratization and the Prevention of Violent Conflict in Southeast Europe: The Cases of Bulgaria and Republic of Macedonia*, PhD thesis (Michigan: Proquest).

Equinet (2009) Interview with Mr. Kemal Euyp, Chairman of the Commission for Protection against Discrimination, given for EQUINET (European Network of Equality Bodies), available from: http://www.equineteurope.org/ (webpage accessed on December 11, 2009).

Esping-Andersen, G. (1993) *The Three Worlds of Welfare Capitalism* (Princeton: Princeton University Press).

European Convention on Human Rights (1950) (formally the Convention for the Protection of Human Rights and Fundamental Freedoms).

Eurostat (2012) "One out of six employees in the EU27 was a low-wage earner in 2010." Eurostat, December 20, 2012, available from: http://ec.europa.eu/eurostat (webpage accessed on December 20, 2012).

Fenger, H. G. M. (2007) "Welfare Regimes in Central and Eastern Europe: Incorporating Post-communist Countries in a Welfare Regime Typology," *Contemporary Issues and Ideas in Social Sciences* 3 (2):1–30.

Flere, S. (1991) "Explaining ethnic Antagonism in Yugoslavia," *European Sociological Review* 7 (N3) (special edition on Eastern Europe).

Fotev, G. (1994) *The Other Ethnos* (Sofia: Marin Drinov Press), [in Bulgarian].

Framework Convention for Protection of National Minorities (1995), electronic version of Council of Europe publication, available from: https://rm.coe.int (webpage accessed on December 4, 2017), [in Bulgarian].

Fukuyama, Fr. (1992) *The End of History and the Last Man* (New York: The Free Press).

Fukuyama, Fr. (2004a) "The Imperative of State-building," *Journal of Democracy* 15 (2): 17–31.

Fukuyama, Fr. (2004b) *State-Building: Governance and World Order in the 21st Century* (New York: Cornell University Press).

Fukuyama, Fr. (2006) *America at the Crossroads: Democracy, Power, and the Neoconservative Legacy* (New Haven, CT: Yale University Press).

Fukuyama, Fr. (2008) *Falling Behind: Explaining the Development Gap between Latin America and the United States* (Oxford: Oxford University Press).

Fukuyama, Fr. (2012) "The Future of History: Can Liberal Democracy Survive the Decline of the Middle Class?," *Foreign Affairs*, January/February.

Fukuyama, Fr. (2013) "What is Governance," CGD Working Paper 314 (Washington: Centre for Global Development).

Gallup (2014a) "Political and Economic Index—January 2014," available from: http://www.gallup-international.bg (webpage accessed on February 17, 2014), [in Bulgarian].

Gallup (2014b) "Political and Economic Index—February 2014," available from: http://www.gallup-international.bg (webpage accessed on February 21, 2014), [in Bulgarian].

Gallup (2015) "At the End of the Decade of Roma Inclusion: Symptoms of Permanent Exclusion, representative survey," survey conducted June 26–July 2, 2015, available from: http://www.gallup-international.bg/ (webpage accessed on July 30, 2015), [in Bulgarian].

Ganev, V. I. (2004) "History, Politics, and the Constitution: Ethnic Conflict and Constitutional Adjudication in Postcommunist Bulgaria," *Slavic Review* 63 (1) (Spring): 66–89.

Garabedian, A. (2007) *Border and Ethno-national Conflicts in Central and Southeastern Europe*, papers from scientific conference, June 12–13, 2007 (Sofia: Institute for Balkan Studies, BAS), [in Bulgarian].

Gazette (1995) Rules for the Structure and Organization of the National Council on Social and Demographic Issues, Gazette No. 57 from June 23, 1995, [in Bulgarian].

Gazette (1997) Rules for the Structure and Organization of the Work of the National Council on Ethnic and Demographic Issues at the Council of Ministers, Gazette No. 118 from December 10, 1997, [in Bulgarian].

Gazette (2004) *Decree No. 333 of the Council of Ministers of 10 December 2004 Establishing a National Council for Cooperation on Ethnic and Demographic Issues at the Council of Ministers and to Adopt Regulations for Its Operation*, Gazette No. 110 from December 17, 2004, [in Bulgarian].

Gazette (2013) Rules for the Structure and Operation of the National Council for Cooperation on Ethnic and Integration Issues at the Council of Ministers, Gazette No. 107, December 13, 2013.

Geertz, Cl. (1973) *The Interpretation of Cultures* (New York: Basic Books).

Gelner, E. (1983) *Nations and Nationalism* (Ithaca: Cornell University Press).

Genov, N. ed. (2004) *Ethnic Relations in South Eastern Europe* (Berlin-Sofia: Friedrich-Ebert-Stiftung, Free University Berlin).

Genov, N. ed. (2005) *Ethnicity and Educational Policies in South Eastern Europe* (Berlin-Sofia: Friedrich-Ebert-Stiftung, Free University Berlin).

Georgieva, V. (2011) "Tsar Kiro only fined once in twenty-two years," available from: http://www.trud.bg (webpage accessed on March 25, 2016), [in Bulgarian].

Gibson, J. L. (2008) "Judicial Institutions," in *The Oxford Handbook of Political Institutions*, R.A.W. Rhodes, S.A. Binder, and B.A. Rockman, eds. (Oxford: Oxford University Press), pp. 514–34.

Geiselmann, Ch., Karamelska, T. (2010) "Here They Called Us Turks, in Turkey They Called Us Infidels." A Biographical Approach to Ethnic Identity," *Sociological Problems* XLII–II: 120–40.

Gligorov, V. (1995) "What If They Will Not Give Up? Civil War in the Former Yugoslavia," *East European Politics and Societies* 9 (3) (Fall): 499–513.

Gocheva, P. (1991) *MRF: In the Shadows and in the Light* (Sofia: Impress), [in Bulgarian].

Grekova, M. (2008) "Integration of Roma in Bulgarian Society: Deeds and Documents (1999–2007)," *Sociological Problems* (Special Volume on Roma Inclusion: Policies and Science Perspectives): 103–36, [in Bulgarian].

Grekova, M. (2010) "Children of Roma Origin in Secondary Education: Integrated and Segregated Schools," *Year-book of University of Sofia "St. Kl. Ohridski," Department of Sociology*, vol. 102, [in Bulgarian].

Grosby, St. (1994). "The Verdict of History: The Inexpungeable Tie of Primordiality—A Response to Eller and Coughlan," *Ethnic and Racial Studies* 17 (1): 164–71.

GSI: Europe (2017), available from: http://www.globalslaveryindex.org (webpage accessed on April 21, 2017).

GSI: Global Findings (2017), available from: http://www.globalslaveryindex.org (webpage accessed on April 21, 2017).

GSI: Index—Bulgaria (2017), available from: http://www.globalslaveryindex.org (webpage accessed on April 21, 2017).

Gulubov, A. (2008) "The Decade of Roma Inclusion: Integrity, Efficacy and Quality of the Public Policies," *Sociological Problems* XXXX-I: 24-35, [in Bulgarian].

Gurr, T. (1991) *Peoples Verses States: Minorities at Risk in the New Century* (Sofia: Voenno Izdatelstvo), [in Bulgarian].

Gurr, T. (1993) *Minorities at Risk: A Global View of Ethnopolitical Conflicts* (Washington DC: US Institute of Peace Press).

Hechter, M. (2000) *Containing Nationalism* (New York: Oxford University Press).

Herz, J. (1950) "Idealist Internationalism and the Security Dilemma," *World Politics* 2 (2): 171-201.

Herz, J. (1959) *Political Realism and Political Idealism* (Chicago: University of Chicago Press).

Higgins, R. (1993) "The New United Nations and Former Yugoslavia," *International Affairs* 69 (3) (July): 465-84.

Hinkova, S. (1998) *The Case of Yugoslavia: Ethnic Conflicts in South Eastern Europe* (Sofia: Kritika and Humanism), [in Bulgarian].

Hopken, U. (2000) *The Policy toward Minorities in Bulgaria* (Sofia: International Centre for the Problems of Minorities and Cultural Cooperation), [in Bulgarian].

Horowitz, D. L. (1985) *Ethnic Groups in Conflict* (Berkley: University of California Press).

Hristov, Hr. (2012) "Is the Demolition of the Roma Houses in Maglizh a Pre-election PR?" (in Bulgarian), available from: http://www.bghelsinki.org (webpage accessed on April 15, 2013).

Hristova, Hr. (2014) "The Number of Complaints Lodged in the Commission for Protection against Discrimination Have Increased," available from: http://sever.bg (webpage accessed on March 19, 2014), [in Bulgarian].

Huntington, S. (2011) *The Clash of Civilizations and the Remaking of World Order* (New York: Simon and Schuster).

Hutchinson, J., Smith, A. eds. (1996) *Ethnicity* (Oxford: Oxford University Press).

Ignazi, P. (2003) *Extreme Right Parties in Western Europe* (Oxford: Oxford University Press).

Ilieva, M. (2009) *Report on Measures to Combat Discrimination, Directives 2000/43/EC and 2000/78/EC: Country Report 2008 on Bulgaria (State of Affairs up to 31 December 2008)*, available from: http://www.non-discrimination.net (webpage accessed on April 22, 2013).

Ilieva, M. (2012) *Report on Measures to Combat Discrimination, Directives 2000/43 EC and 2000/78 EC, Country Report 2011 (State of Affairs up to 1st January, 2012)*, available from: http://www.non-discrimination.net (webpage accessed on April 22, 2013).

Ilieva, M., Simeonova, D. (2010) *Study on Equality Bodies Established under Directives 2000/43/EC, 2004/113/EC and 006/54/EC (VT/2009/012), BULGARIA, April 2010: Focus Group Discussion with Equality Body members and staff.*

Indzhov, M. (2017) "A Revival Process in Spanish Fashion," available from: https://clubz.bg (webpage accessed on October 5, 2017), [in Bulgarian].

Is the Bulgarian "division time" coming back? (2012), available from: http://www.dw.com (webpage accessed on March 25, 2016), [in Bulgarian].

Ivanov, M. I. (2008) "On the Policy of Social Inclusion towards the Roma," *Sociological Problems*, XXXX–I: 66–83, [in Bulgarian].

Jervis, R. (1976) *Perception and Misperception in International Politics* (Princeton N.J.: Princeton University Press).

Kabakchieva, P. (2006) "Populism and the Fear of Modernity," *Worlds in Sociology* (Sofia: University of St. Kliment Ohridski Press), [in Bulgarian].

Kabakchieva, P. (2008) "The Openness to the World and the Fear of the Alien," *State of Society* (Sofia Open Society Institute), pp. 75–95, [in Bulgarian].

Kalinova, E., Baeva, I. (2001) *The Bulgarian Transitions 1939–2001* (Sofia: Paradigma), [in Bulgarian].

Kanev, K. (2003) *The First Steps: An Evaluation of the Nongovernmental Desegregation Projects in Six Bulgarian Cities. An External Evaluation Report to the Open Society Institute* (Budapest: OSI).

Kaplan, R. (1993) *Balkan Ghosts: A Journey through History* (New York: St. Martin's Press).

Karasimeonov, G. (1997) *Politics and Political Institutions* (Sofia: University of St. Kliment Ohridski Press), [in Bulgarian].

Karasimeonov, G. (2000) *The Political Parties* (Sofia: Gorex Press), [in Bulgarian].

Karasimeonov, G. (2010) *The Party System in Bulgaria*, 3rd edition (Sofia: Nik), [in Bulgarian].

Karasimeonov, G., Lyubenov, M. (2007) "Internal Party Democracy in Bulgaria: Trends and Perspectives," in *Reshaping the Broken Image of Political Parties. Internal Party Democracy in South Eastern Europe*, G. Karasimeonov, ed. (Sofia: Gorex Press), pp. 70–101.

Katz, S., Mair, P. (1995) "Changing Models of Party Organization and Party Democracy: the Emergence of the Cartel Party," *Party Politics*, 1995, 1, 5. Online version, available from: http://ppq.sagepub.com (webpage accessed on February 15, 2014).

Kaufmann, D., Kraay, A., Mastruzzi, M. (2010) *The Worldwide Governance Indicators: Methodology and Analytical Issues*, available from: http://info.worldbank.org (webpage accessed on June 6, 2013).

Kertikov, K. (1991) "Le probleme etnonational en Bulgarie (1944–1991)," *Bulgarian Quarterly* I, (3): 81–91.

Kertikov, K. (1992) "Le probleme etnonational en Bulgarie," /Suite/, *Bulgarian Quarterly*, II (I): 74–88.

Kertikov, K. (2003) "The Bulgarian Ethnosociology — Some Working Concepts" (Part 2), "Balkans "21," 5/2003, available from: http://www.balkans21.org (webpage accessed on February 16, 2014), [in Bulgarian].

Kertikov, K. (2011) "The Bulgarian Ethnic "Models" in the Context of the European Values," in *Bulgarian National Values, Statics and Dynamics in the Process of European Integration*, K. Kertikov, ed. (Sofia: Institute for the Study of Societies and Knowledge, BAS), pp. 46–64, [in Bulgarian].

Kertikov, K. et al. (1990) *The Ethnic Conflict in Bulgaria – in 1989* (Sofia: Profizdat), [in Bulgarian].

Kolev, D. (2009) "National Council on Cooperation on Ethnic and Demographic Issues (NCEDDI): Can It Start Working?," available from: http://www.bghelsinki.org (webpage accessed on February 15, 2014).

Koritarov, G. (2016) "Interview with Leonid Reshetnikov," November 24, 2016, *Svobodna zona*, available from: https://www.youtube.com (webpage accessed on April 15, 2017).

Kostova, D. (2017) "MRF Is Suffering but It's Not Only DOST's Fault," available from: http://www.webcafe.bg (webpage accessed on April 15, 2017).

Koštunica, V. (1998) "The Constitution and the Federal State," in *Jugoslavija. A Fractured Federalism,* Dennison Rusinow, ed. (Washington: The Wilson Center Press), pp. 78–92.

Krasteva, A. ed. (1998) *Communities and Identities in Bulgaria* (Sofia: Petekston Press), [in Bulgarian].

Krasteva, A. (1999) *Communities, Discourse and Power* (Sofia: Petekston Press), [in Bulgarian].

Krasteva, A. (2015) "Religion, Politics, and Nationalism in Postcommunist Bulgaria: Elastic (Post)Secularism," *Nationalism and Ethnic Politics* 21 (4): 422–45.

Krasteva, A., Lazaridis, G. (2016) "FAR RIGHT: Populist Ideology, 'Othering' and Youth," in *Populism, Media and Education*, Maria Ranieri, ed. (Abingdon and New York: Routledge).

Laozi (2016) *Tao Te Ching* (CreateSpace Independent Publishing Platform).

Law on Confessions (Republic of Bulgaria) (2002).

Levy, J., Kagan, R., John Zysman, J. (1995) "The Twin Restorations: The Political Economy of the Reagan and Thatcher 'Revolutions'," unpublished manuscript (Berkeley, October).

Lieberman, E., Singh, P. (2012) "The Institutional Origins of Interethnic Violence," available from: https://evanlieberman.files.wordpress.com (webpage accessed on March 30, 2016).

Lijphart, A. (1968) *The Politics of Accommodation. Pluralism and Democracy in the Netherlands* (Berkeley: University of California Press).

Lijphart, A. (1977) *Democracy in Plural Societies: A Comparative Exploration* (New Haven: Yale University Press).

Lijphart, A. (1994) *Electoral Systems and Party Systems: A Study of Twenty-Seven Democracies, 1945–1990* (Oxford: Oxford University Press).

Lijphart, A. (1999) *Patterns of Democracy: Government Forms and Performance in Thirty-Six Countries* (New Haven, CT: Yale University Press).

Limenopoulou, K. (2004) "The Politics of Ethnic Identity in the Balkans in a Post Communist Power Vacuum" (Hellenic Foundation for European and Foreign Policy), available from: http://www.css.ethz.ch (webpage accessed on October 3, 2017).

Lyubenov, M. (2011) *The Bulgarian Party System: Grouping and Structuring of Party Preferences, 1990-2009* (Sofia: St. Kliment Ohridski), [in Bulgarian].

Mair, P. (1998) *Party System Change: Approaches and Interpretations* (Oxford: Oxford University Press).

Makariev, P. (1999) "Promoting Inter-ethnic Dialogue in Bulgaria," in *Creating Democratic Societies: Values and Norms*, Pl. Makariev, A. Blasko, and A. Davidov, eds. (Washington, DC: The Council for Research in Values and Philosophy), pp. 239-56.

Makariev, P. (2017) *The Public Legitimacy of Minority Claims. A Central/Eastern European Perspective* (New York: Routledge).

Man set himself on fire in Radnevo (2013), available from: http://www.dnes.bg (webpage accessed on March 25, 2016), [in Bulgarian].

Mantarova, A. (2002) "Ethnic Aspects of Crime in Bulgaria and Macedonia," Balkans'21 (electronic journal), 2002, 1, available from: http://www.balkans21.org (webpage accessed on March 6, 2017), [in Bulgarian].

Mantarova, A., Zaharieva, M. (2007) "Ethnic Relations: Toleration and Distances," in *Eurointegration and Sustainable Development* (Sofia: Friedrich Ebert Foundation), pp. 123-40, [in Bulgarian].

March, J., Olsen, J. (2008) "Elaborating the New Institutionalism," *Oxford Handbook of Political Institutions* (Oxford: Oxford University Press), pp. 3-20.

McGarry, J., O'Leary, B. (1993) *The Politics of Ethnic Conflict Regulation* (Abingdon: Routledge).

Mearsheimer, J., Pape, R. (1993) "The Answer," *New Republic*, June 14, 1993.

"Mestan: the Election Code is a Continuation of the Revival Process" (2016), available from: http://www.clubz.bg (webpage accessed on May 4, 2016).

Metodieva, M. et al. (2012) *Report on Public Policies for the Integration of Roma in Bulgaria and the Main Problems Standing in Front of the Socio-economic Inclusion of the Roma Community (Part of the EUINCLUSIVE Project – Transfer of Data and Exchange of Good Practices between Romania, Bulgaria, Spain and Italy, regarding the Inclusion of the Roma)* (Sofia: Open Society Institute).

Michels, R. (2001) *Political Parties: A Sociological Study of the Oligarchical Tendencies of Modern Democracy* (Kitchener: Batoche Books).

Mihalev, I. (2005) "An Unemployed Roma Male Holds the Record of Due VAT," available from: http://www.capital.bg (webpage accessed on March 6, 2017), [in Bulgarian].

Miller, L. (1975) *Bulgaria during the Second World War* (Stanford: Stanford University Press).

Minchev, K. (2009) *The Bloody End of Yugoslavia* (Sofia: Paradigma), [in Bulgarian].

Minchev, O. (2016) "Ognyan Minchev: Dogan Is the Biggest Winner: A 'Patriot' and Dressed All in White," available from: http://www.mediapool.bg (webpage accessed on March 25, 2016), [in Bulgarian].

"Minka Kapitanova: Ahmed Bashev personally incited Roma in Garmen" (2015), available from: https://www.24chasa.bg (webpage accessed on September 18, 2015), [in Bulgarian].

Mirchev, M. (2011) "The Bulgarian Ethnic Model: A Social and Civilizational Result," in *The Bulgarian Ethnic Model: Political Mythologem or a Problematic Reality*, K. Kertikov, ed. (Sofia: Avangard Prima), pp. 206–40, [in Bulgarian].

Mirchev, M. (2017) "The Inconclusive Elections and the Revolution Against 'Bulgarian Ethnic Model'," available from: http://pogled.info (webpage accessed on April 11, 2017), [in Bulgarian].

Miris (2001) *Ethnic Composition of the Population in Bulgaria*, available from: http://miris.eurac.edu (webpage accessed on March 25, 2016), [in Bulgarian].

Mitev, P. (1994) "Relations of Compatibility and Incompatibility in the Everyday Life of Christians and Muslims in Bulgaria," *Relations of Compatibility and Incompatibility between Christians and Muslims in Bulgaria* (Sofia).

Mitev, P. (2005) "The Bulgarian Ethnic Model and the Bulgarian Paradoxes," paper presented at a round table held at Radisson Hotel, Sofia, January 26, 2005 [in Bulgarian].

Mitov, B. (2013) "The total scheme of illegal eavesdropping in Ministry of Interior largely confirmed," available from: http://www.mediapool.bg (webpage accessed on February 17, 2014), [in Bulgarian].

Mizov, M. (2003) *The Roma in the Social Space* (Sofia: Paradigma), [in Bulgarian].

Mizov, M. ed. (2008) *Social Stratification and Social Conflicts in Contemporary Bulgaria* (Sofia: Centre for Historical and Political Analyses), [in Bulgarian].

Mizov, M. (2010) *Ahmed Dogan and the Bulgarian Ethnic Model* (Sofia: Zemia), [in Bulgarian].

MRF (2006) *Program Declaration Adopted at the 6th National conference of MRF* [in Bulgarian].

MRF (2009) *Program Declaration Adopted at the 7th National conference of MRF* [in Bulgarian].

MRF (2017) *Statute of the MRF*, available from: http://www.dps.bg (webpage accessed on April 3, 2017), [in Bulgarian].

Mudde, C. (2007) *Populist Radical Right Parties in Europe* (Cambridge: Cambridge University Press).

Nazurska, Zh. (1999) *The Bulgarian State and Its Minorities, 1879–1885* (Sofia: LIK), [in Bulgarian].

NCCEDI (2005) *National Action Plan Roma Inclusion Decade 2005–2015*, available from: http://www.nccedi.government.bg (webpage accessed on February 17, 2014).

NCCEDI (2006) *Action Plan for the Implementation of the Framework Program for Equal Integration of Roma in Bulgarian Society for 2006*, available from: http://www.nccedi.government.bg (webpage accessed on February 23, 2014), [in Bulgarian].

NCCEDI (2010) *Framework Program for Integration of Roma in Bulgarian Society, 2010–2020*, available from: http://www.nccedi.government.bg (webpage accessed on February 23, 2014).

NCCEII (2011) *Report of the National Council for Cooperation on Ethnic and Integration Issues of the Council of Ministers for 2011*, available from: http://www.nccedi.government.bg (webpage accessed on February 17, 2014), [in Bulgarian].

NCCEII (2012) *National Roma Integration Strategy of the Republic of Bulgaria, 2012–2020*, available from: http://www.nccedi.government.bg (webpage accessed on February 17, 2014).

NCCEII (2014) *Information submitted by the Republic of Bulgaria on the Progress in the Implementation of the National Strategy of Republic of Bulgaria for Roma Integration, 2012–2020*, available from: http://www.nccedi.government.bg (webpage accessed on February 25, 2014), [in Bulgarian].

NCEDI (1999) *Framework Program for Equal Integration of Roma in Bulgarian Society*], available from: http://www.nccedi.government.bg (webpage accessed on February 17, 2014), [in Bulgarian].

NCEDI (2003) *Action Plan for the Implementation of the Framework Program for Equal Integration of Roma in Bulgarian Society, for the Period of 2003–*

2004, available from: http://www.nccedi.government.bg (webpage accessed on February 17, 2014), [in Bulgarian].

Nedelcheva, T. (2002) "Transformations in Bulgarian Identity and the Image of Macedonia," Balkans'21, 1/2002, available from: http://www.balkans21.org (webpage accessed on February 19, 2014), [in Bulgarian].

Nedelcheva, T. (2003) "Ethnic, National and Cultural Identity," Balkans'21, 3/2003, available from: http://www.balkans21.org (webpage accessed on February 19, 2014), [in Bulgarian].

Nedelcheva, T. (2004) *Identity and Time* (Sofia: Marin Drinov Press), [in Bulgarian].

Nedelcheva, T. (2007) "European Minority Identities," in *European Integration and Sustainable Development*, A. Mantarova and M. Zaharieva, eds. (Sofia: Friedrich Ebert), pp. 111–22, [in Bulgarian].

Nedelcheva, T. (2010) "National Identity of Bulgarian Muslims," Balkans'21, 7/2010, [in Bulgarian].

Nedelcheva, T. (2011) "Possible Borderline Situations for the Bulgarian Ethnic Model," in *The Bulgarian Ethnic Model: Political Mythologem or a Problematic Reality*, K. Kertikov, ed. (Sofia: Avangard Prima), pp. 81–96, [in Bulgarian].

Nedelcheva, T., Topalova, V. eds. (2010) *Essays on Ethnosociology* (Sofia: Askoni), [in Bulgarian].

NSI (2011) *Population Census 2011: Results*, available from: http://www.nsi.bg/census2011 (webpage accessed on February 17, 2014).

NSI (2014) *Average Monthly Wages and Salaries in 2014*, National Statistical Institute, see http://www.nsi.bg (webpage accessed on June 24, 2015).

NSI (2015) "Average salary in Bulgaria in 2015," available from: http://www.nsi.bg (webpage accessed on March 25, 2016), [in Bulgarian].

Nuttal, S. (1994) "The EC and Yugoslavia: Deus ex Machina or Machina sine Deo?," *Journal of Common Market Studies* 32 (3) (September): 11–26.

Offnews.bg (2016) "Karakachanov Will Fight the Tsiganization and Islamization of Bulgaria," available from: http://offnews.bg (webpage accessed on February 3, 2017).

Ombudsman Act (2004) (Bulgaria), [in Bulgarian].

OSI (2002) *Monitoring the EU Accession Process: Minority Protection*, Vol. I, *An Assessment of Selected Policies of Candidate States* (Budapest, New York: Open Society Institute).

OSI (2012) *Review of EU Framework Roma National Integration Strategies (NRIS)*, compiled by B. Rorke (Open Society Institute).

Osipov, A. (2013) "Non-Territorial Autonomy during and after Communism: In the Wrong or Right Place?," *Journal on Ethnopolitics and Minority Issues in Europe*.

Pamporov, A. (2008) "Something old, Something New, Something about the Neighbours—The Bulgarian Ethnic Model through the Prism of Social Distances," *State of Society, 2008*, (Sofia: Open Society Institute), [in Bulgarian].

Pamporov, A. (2012) "Social Distances in Bulgaria in 2008-2012 Period," available from: http://www.bghelsinki.org (webpage accessed on August 10, 2016) (Sofia: Bulgarian Helsinki Committee), [in Bulgarian].

Pamporov, A. (2016) "Feeding the Hatred in the Neighborhood," *Policies*, No. 2, available from: http://politiki.bg (webpage accessed on August 10, 2016) (Sofia: Open Society Institute), [in Bulgarian].

Pavlov, Y. (2014) "What coalition will govern us?," analysis in the Bulgarian National Television's broadcast "The Day Begins," October 29, 2014, available from: http://bnt.bg (webpage accessed on November 14, 2014), [in Bulgarian].

Pavlowitch, S. (1994) "Who Is Balkanizing Whom? The Misunderstandings between the Debris of Yugoslavia and an Unprepared West," *Daedalus* 123 2 (Spring): 203-24.

Penal Code (2016), available from: http://www.vks.bg (webpage accessed on May 2, 2016), [in Bulgarian].

Personal Data Protection Act (2002), available from: https://www.cpdp.bg (webpage accessed on May 2, 2016), (in Bulgarian).

Peši, V. (1996) "Serbian Nationalism and the Origins of the Yugoslav Crisis," *Peaceworks*, No. 8 (Washington, D.C.: U.S. Institute of Peace).

Petkova, K. (2013) "The Discrimination Based on Ethnic Origin: Reality and Dimensions," in *Ethnic Dimensions of Social Integration*, V. Zlatanova, ed. (Sofia: Omda), available from: http://www.omda.bg/ (webpage accessed on May 2, 2016), [in Bulgarian].

Petrova, G. (2009) "Social-Demographic Portrait of the Voters in the Parliamentary Elections in 2009," available from: http://alpharesearch.bg (webpage accessed on May 2, 2016), [in Bulgarian].

Podchasov, N. (2016) "Bulgarian Surprise" ["Болгарский сюрприз"], available from: https://riss.ru (webpage accessed on April 19, 2017), [in Russian].

Popivanov, B. (2015) *Changing Images of the Left in Bulgaria: an Old-and-New Divide* (Stuttgart: ibidem Press).

Popper, K. (1994) *The Poverty of Historicism* (Abingdon: Routledge).

Popper, K. (2013) *The Open Society and Its Enemies*, new one volume edition (Princeton: Princeton University Press).

Poppetrov, N. ed. (2009) *Socially Left, Nationalism—Forward. Programmatic and Organizational Documents of Bulgarian Authoritarian Nationalist Formations* (Sofia: Publishing House "Gutenberg"), [in Bulgarian].

Protection against Discrimination Act (2004), [in Bulgarian].

"Quote of the Day: 'If someone spent his whole day in the ghetto drinking beer and listening to chalga—his pension is not going to be increased'" (2017), available from: http://www.dnevnik.bg (webpage accessed on April 19, 2017), [in Bulgarian].

"Radev: The interference of Turkey in Bulgaria is a fact and this is unacceptable" (2017) Nova TV, available from: https://nova.bg (webpage accessed on April 19, 2017).

Raichev, A., Stoichev, K. (1998) *What Happened?* (Sofia: Trud), [in Bulgarian].

Ramet, S.P. (2006) *The Three Yugoslavias: State-Building and Legitimation, 1918–2005* (Indiana: Indiana University Press).

Ramsbotham, Ol., Woodhouse, T., Miall, H. (2011) *Contemporary Conflict Resolution*, 3rd edition (Cambridge: Polity Press).

Rechel, B. (2004) "A Journey into "Virtual Reality?" Elite Interviews in Bulgaria," paper presented at the Annual Conference of the Centre for Russian and East-European Studies, University of Birmingham, June 11–13, 2004, Cumberland Lodge, Windsor Great Park.

Rechel, B. (2007) "The Bulgarian Ethnic Model: Reality or Ideology?," *Europe-Asia Studies* 59 (7): 1201–15.

Rechel, B. (2008) "The Failure of the Measures aimed at the Integration of Minorities," *Sociological Problems* (Special Volume on Roma Inclusion: Policies and Science Perspectives): 84–102, [in Bulgarian].

Refworld (2012) "Bulgaria: Violence against Roma, including by extremist groups; state protection and treatment by police (2008–2012)," available from http://www.unhcr.org (webpage accessed on April 10, 2013).

Refworld (2013) *Freedom in the World 2013 — Bulgaria*, 10 April 2013, available from: http://www.refworld.org (webpage accessed on April 24, 2013).

Reporters Without Borders (2017) *2017 World Press Freedom Index*, available from: https://rsf.org (webpage accessed on April 26, 2017).

Republic of Bulgaria (2003) *Report Submitted by Bulgaria Pursuant to Article 25, Paragraph 1 of the Framework Convention for the Protection of National Minorities, April 9, 2003* (Strasbourg: Council of Europe).

Rhodes, R.A.W. et al. eds. (2008) *The Oxford Handbook of Political Institutions* (Oxford: Oxford University Press).

Rief, D. (1994) *Slaughterhouse: Bosnia and the Failure of the West* (New York: Simon and Schuster).

"Roma in Garmen prepare for national protest" (2015), available from: http://www.dnevnik.bg (webpage accessed on February 18, 2016), [in Bulgarian].

Room, G., ed. (1995) *Beyond the Threshold. The Measurements and Analyses of Social Exclusion* (Bristol: Policy Press).

Roth, J. (2013) "Bulgarian media power and the powerlessness of democracy," available from: http://www.dw.de (webpage accessed on March 13, 2014), [in Bulgarian].

Rusinov, R. (2001) "The Bulgarian Framework Program for the Equal Integration of Roma: participation in the policy making process," *Roma Rights Journal*, 2001 (2-3), available from: http://www.errc.org (webpage accessed on December 4, 2017).

Rusinow, D. (1985), "Nationalities Policy and the 'National Question,'" in *Yugoslavia in the 1980s*, Pedro Ramet, ed. (Boulder: Westview).

SANS (2017) *Year Report of State Agency "National Security" for 2016*, available from: http://www.dans.bg (webpage accessed on April 19, 2017), [in Bulgarian].

Shermerhorn, R. (1996) "Ethnicity and Minority groups," in *Ethnicity*, J. Hutchinson and A. Smith, eds. (Oxford: Oxford University Press).

Siderov, V. (2007) *My Battle for Bulgaria* (Sofia: "Boomerang").

Siderov, V. (2011) *Fundamentals of Bulgarianism* (Sofia: "Ataka").

Silber, L., Little, A. (1991) *Yugoslavia: Death of a Nation* (New York: TV Books).

Smilov, D. (2006) "Early Warning: Rising Populism and Its Impact," in *The Bridge: Bimonthly Review of European Integration in South East Europe and the Mediterranean*, Issue 3, 04 (2006): 92-94.

Smilov, D. (2007) "Populism, Liberal Democracy and the Rule of Law," *Forum Analytica*, 8 (Spring), Special Issue on Populism: 46–8.

Smilov, D. (2008) "The Parties and the Frustrated Democracy," in *State of Society*, 2008 (Sofia: Open Society Institute), pp. 34–61, [in Bulgarian].

Smilov, D., Vaysova, L. (2013) # *The Protest. Analyses and Positions in the Bulgarian Press. Summer 2013* (Sofia: Iztok-Zapad Press), [in Bulgarian].

Smith, Ant. (1986) "Conflict and Collective Identity: Class, Ethnie and Nation," in *International Conflict Resolution: Theory and Practice*, E. Azar, J. Burton, eds. (Sussex: Wheatsheaf Books).

Smith, M.G. (1969) "Institutional and Political Conditions of Pluralism," in *Pluralism in Africa*, Leo Kuper and M.G. Smith, eds. (Berkeley and Los Angeles: University of California Press), pp. 27–65.

Spasov, S. (2013) "Plamen Goranov — Varna's Jan Palch," available from: http://www.capital.bg (webpage accessed on March 22, 2016).

Stain, M. (1968) "Federal Political Systems and Federal Societies," *World Politics* 20 (4): 721–47.

Stoyanov, St. (2009) "Ataka — a party of the province's disenchantment with the transition to democracy," available from: http://alpharesearch.bg (webpage accessed on April 21, 2017), [in Bulgarian].

Stoychev, S. (2016) *Controlled Voting in Bulgaria: Threats to Human Security* (Sofia: IRIS).

"The 'Big excursion' and the collapse of assimilation" (2013), available from: www.dnevnik.bg (webpage accessed on April 21, 2017), [in Bulgarian].

"The protest ended peacefully in Garmen" (2015), available from: http://www.vesti.bg (webpage accessed on February 18, 2016).

"The protests start to turn into a civil disobedience" (2013), available from: http://www.mediapool.bg (webpage accessed on March 25, 2016), [in Bulgarian].

"The Roma Meshere elected its boss" (2013), available from: http://btvnovinite.bg (webpage accessed on March 25, 2016), [in Bulgarian].

Titmus, R. (1950) *Problems of Social Policy* (London: HMSO).

Todorov, A. (2005) "Postcommunist Cleavages," in *Conflicts, Confidence, Democracy*, A. Krasteva and A. Todorov, eds. (Sofia: NBU Press), pp. 132–39, [in Bulgarian].

Todorov, A. (2010) *Citizens, Parties, Elections: Bulgaria 1879–2009* (Sofia: Iztok-Zapad), [in Bulgarian].

Todorov, A. (2012) "The Far Right in Bulgaria" (Sofia: Friedrich Ebert).

Todorov, V. (2002) "The Conflict in Macedonia: Hypotheses of Its Development," Balkans'21, 1/2002, available from http://www.balkans21.org, (webpage accessed on March 25, 2016), [in Bulgarian].

Todorov, Tzv. (2001) *The Fragility of Goodness. Why Bulgaria's Jews Survived the Holocaust* (London: Weidenfeld & Nicolson).

Todorova, E. (2002) "Transforming Post-Communist Countries' Welfare System: The Role of the State and the Civil Society," in *Sociological Problems*, Special Issue 2002: 185–96.

Todorova, E. (2008) "The Social Policy in the Transition Period and the Labor Market in Bulgaria," *Labor Market Magazine*, May 2008.

Todorova, M. (1992) "Ethnicity, Nationalism, and the Communist Legacy in Eastern Europe," *East European Politics and Societies* 7 (1): 135–55.

Tomova, I. (2006) "Ethnicity and Social Exclusion, the Roma in the Post-communist Period," in *Worlds in Sociology: A Compendium in Honor of Professor Georgy Fotev*, P. Boyadjieva et al., eds. (Sofia: University of St. Kliment Ohridski Press), pp. 537–60, [in Bulgarian].

Tomova, I. (2011) "Stereotypes and Prejudices about the Roma in the Press," available from: http://www.bghelsinki.org (webpage accessed on 25 February 2014), [in Bulgarian].

Tomova, I., Nikolova, S. (2011) *In the Mirror of Difference: Health Status of the Roma and Access to Healthcare* (Sofia: Marin Drinov), [in Bulgarian].

Transparency International (2013) *Corruption Perception Index for 2012*, available from: http://cpi.transparency.org (webpage accessed on February 17, 2014).

Transparency International (2014) *Corruption Perception Index for 2013*, available from: http://cpi.transparency.org (webpage accessed on February 17, 2014).

Transparency International (2015) *Corruption Perception Index for 2014*, available from: http://cpi.transparency.org (webpage accessed on February 17, 2015).

Transparency International (2016) *Corruption Perception Index for 2015*, available from: http://www.transparency.org (webpage accessed on June 24, 2017).

Transparency International (2017) *Corruption Perception Index for 2016*, available from: http://www.transparency.org (webpage accessed on June 24, 2017).

Traub, J. (2015) "The Regression of Victor Orban," *Foreign Policy*, October 21, 2015, available from: http://foreignpolicy.com (webpage accessed on April 25, 2017).

"Trial of suspected Bulgarian 'hate preachers' begins" (2012), available from: http://www.euronews.com (webpage accessed on September 18, 2015).

Twenty Items of the Agenda of Ataka Party (2009), available from: www.ataka.bg (webpage accessed on March 21, 2017), [in Bulgarian].

"Valeri Simeonov prefers a sea battle with Russia over a wave of immigrants" (2016), available from: http://btvnovinite.bg (webpage accessed on March 21, 2017), [in Bulgarian].

Van Den Berghe, P. (1978) *The Ethnic Phenomenon* (New York: Praeger).

Vanhanen, T. (1991) *Politics of Ethnic Nepotism. India as an Example* (New Delhi: Sterling Publishers Private Ltd.).

Vasilev, Il. (2016) "Novorossia on the Balkans?," Part 1, *Bulgaria Analytica*, available from: http://bulgariaanalytica.org (webpage accessed on February 18, 2016), [in Bulgarian].

Vodopivec, P. (1992) "Slovenes and Yugoslavia, 1918–1991," *East European Politics and Societies* 6 (3) (Fall): 220–42.

Volen Siderov on Bulgaria becoming a "Gypsy State" (2013), available from: http://www.youtube.com (webpage accessed on June 3, 2013), [in Bulgarian].

Vucovic, G. (1997) *Ethnic Cleavages and Conflict: the Sources of National Cohesion and Integration. The Case of Yugoslavia*, (London: Ashgate).

Weber, M. (1994) "The Profession and Vocation of Politics," in *Max Weber: Political Writings*, P. Lassman and R. Speirs, eds. (Cambridge: Cambridge University Press), pp. 309–69.

Weber, M. (2003) *Political Writings* (Cambridge: Cambridge University Press).

Whitehead, L. (1995) "Political Democratization and Economic Liberalization," paper presented at the Southern California Seminar on Political and Economic Liberalization, University of Southern California, Los Angeles, January 30, 1995.

"Who Is Kiril Rashkov—Tsar Kiro?" (2011), available from: http://dariknews.bg (webpage accessed on February 18, 2016), [in Bulgarian].

"Will EU Entry Shrink Bulgaria's Population Even More?" (2006). Deutsche Welle. December 26, 2006, available from: http://www.dw.de (webpage accessed on March 25, 2016).

Woodward, S. (1995) *Balkan Tragedy: Chaos and Dissolution after the Cold War* (Washington, D.C.: Brookings).

World Bank (1997) *World Development Report 1997: The State in a Changing World* (New York: Oxford University Press).

World Bank (2009) *Gini Index (World Bank estimate)*, available from: http://data.worldbank.org (webpage accessed on May 4, 2015).

World Bank (2015) *Worldwide Governance Indicators*, available from: http://info.worldbank.org (webpage accessed on April 18, 2015).

Zhecheva, K. (2007) "Ataka between nationalism and populism," *Political Studies*, No. 3 (2007): 49–68, [in Bulgarian].

Zimmerman, W. (1995) "The Last Ambassador: A Memoir of the Collapse of Yugoslavia," *Foreign Affairs* 74 (2) (March–April): 2–21.

Zlatanova, V. ed. (2013) *Ethnic Dimensions of Social Integration* (Sofia: Omda), [in Bulgarian].

Zografova, I. (1996) "Interethnic Attitudes and Social Distances," *Sociological Problems* 2: 55–65, [in Bulgarian].

SOVIET AND POST-SOVIET POLITICS AND SOCIETY

Edited by Dr. Andreas Umland

ISSN 1614-3515

1 Андреас Умланд (ред.)
Воплощение Европейской
конвенции по правам человека в
России
Философские, юридические и
эмпирические исследования
ISBN 3-89821-387-0

2 Christian Wipperfürth
Russland – ein vertrauenswürdiger
Partner?
Grundlagen, Hintergründe und Praxis
gegenwärtiger russischer Außenpolitik
Mit einem Vorwort von Heinz Timmermann
ISBN 3-89821-401-X

3 Manja Hussner
Die Übernahme internationalen Rechts
in die russische und deutsche
Rechtsordnung
Eine vergleichende Analyse zur
Völkerrechtsfreundlichkeit der Verfassungen
der Russländischen Föderation und der
Bundesrepublik Deutschland
Mit einem Vorwort von Rainer Arnold
ISBN 3-89821-438-9

4 Matthew Tejada
Bulgaria's Democratic Consolidation
and the Kozloduy Nuclear Power Plant
(KNPP)
The Unattainability of Closure
With a foreword by Richard J. Crampton
ISBN 3-89821-439-7

5 Марк Григорьевич Меерович
Квадратные метры, определяющие
сознание
Государственная жилищная политика в
СССР. 1921 – 1941 гг
ISBN 3-89821-474-5

6 Andrei P. Tsygankov, Pavel
A.Tsygankov (Eds.)
New Directions in Russian
International Studies
ISBN 3-89821-422-2

7 Марк Григорьевич Меерович
Как власть народ к труду приучала
Жилище в СССР – средство управления
людьми. 1917 – 1941 гг.
С предисловием Елены Осокиной
ISBN 3-89821-495-8

8 David J. Galbreath
Nation-Building and Minority Politics
in Post-Socialist States
Interests, Influence and Identities in Estonia
and Latvia
With a foreword by David J. Smith
ISBN 3-89821-467-2

9 Алексей Юрьевич Безугольный
Народы Кавказа в Вооруженных
силах СССР в годы Великой
Отечественной войны 1941-1945 гг.
С предисловием Николая Бугая
ISBN 3-89821-475-3

10 Вячеслав Лихачев и Владимир
Прибыловский (ред.)
Русское Национальное Единство,
1990-2000. В 2-х томах
ISBN 3-89821-523-7

11 Николай Бугай (ред.)
Народы стран Балтии в условиях
сталинизма (1940-е – 1950-е годы)
Документированная история
ISBN 3-89821-525-3

12 Ingmar Bredies (Hrsg.)
Zur Anatomie der Orange Revolution
in der Ukraine
Wechsel des Elitenregimes oder Triumph des
Parlamentarismus?
ISBN 3-89821-524-5

13 Anastasia V. Mitrofanova
The Politicization of Russian
Orthodoxy
Actors and Ideas
With a foreword by William C. Gay
ISBN 3-89821-481-8

14   Nathan D. Larson
Alexander Solzhenitsyn and the
Russo-Jewish Question
ISBN 3-89821-483-4

15   Guido Houben
Kulturpolitik und Ethnizität
Staatliche Kunstförderung im Russland der neunziger Jahre
Mit einem Vorwort von Gert Weisskirchen
ISBN 3-89821-542-3

16   Leonid Luks
Der russische „Sonderweg"?
Aufsätze zur neuesten Geschichte Russlands im europäischen Kontext
ISBN 3-89821-496-6

17   Евгений Мороз
История «Мёртвой воды» – от страшной сказки к большой политике
Политическое неоязычество в постсоветской России
ISBN 3-89821-551-2

18   Александр Верховский и Галина Кожевникова (ред.)
Этническая и религиозная интолерантность в российских СМИ
Результаты мониторинга 2001-2004 гг.
ISBN 3-89821-569-5

19   Christian Ganzer
Sowjetisches Erbe und ukrainische Nation
Das Museum der Geschichte des Zaporoger Kosakentums auf der Insel Chortycja
Mit einem Vorwort von Frank Golczewski
ISBN 3-89821-504-0

20   Эльза-Баир Гучинова
Помнить нельзя забыть
Антропология депортационной травмы калмыков
С предисловием Кэролайн Хамфри
ISBN 3-89821-506-7

21   Юлия Лидерман
Мотивы «проверки» и «испытания» в постсоветской культуре
Советское прошлое в российском кинематографе 1990-х годов
С предисловием Евгения Марголита
ISBN 3-89821-511-3

22   Tanya Lokshina, Ray Thomas, Mary Mayer (Eds.)
The Imposition of a Fake Political Settlement in the Northern Caucasus
The 2003 Chechen Presidential Election
ISBN 3-89821-436-2

23   Timothy McCajor Hall, Rosie Read (Eds.)
Changes in the Heart of Europe
Recent Ethnographies of Czechs, Slovaks, Roma, and Sorbs
With an afterword by Zdeněk Salzmann
ISBN 3-89821-606-3

24   Christian Autengruber
Die politischen Parteien in Bulgarien und Rumänien
Eine vergleichende Analyse seit Beginn der 90er Jahre
Mit einem Vorwort von Dorothée de Nève
ISBN 3-89821-476-1

25   Annette Freyberg-Inan with Radu Cristescu
The Ghosts in Our Classrooms, or: John Dewey Meets Ceauşescu
The Promise and the Failures of Civic Education in Romania
ISBN 3-89821-416-8

26   John B. Dunlop
The 2002 Dubrovka and 2004 Beslan Hostage Crises
A Critique of Russian Counter-Terrorism
With a foreword by Donald N. Jensen
ISBN 3-89821-608-X

27   Peter Koller
Das touristische Potenzial von Kam''janec'-Podil's'kyj
Eine fremdenverkehrsgeographische Untersuchung der Zukunftsperspektiven und Maßnahmenplanung zur Destinationsentwicklung des „ukrainischen Rothenburg"
Mit einem Vorwort von Kristiane Klemm
ISBN 3-89821-640-3

28   Françoise Daucé, Elisabeth Sieca-Kozlowski (Eds.)
Dedovshchina in the Post-Soviet Military
Hazing of Russian Army Conscripts in a Comparative Perspective
With a foreword by Dale Herspring
ISBN 3-89821-616-0

29 *Florian Strasser*
    Zivilgesellschaftliche Einflüsse auf die
    Orange Revolution
    Die gewaltlose Massenbewegung und die
    ukrainische Wahlkrise 2004
    Mit einem Vorwort von Egbert Jahn
    ISBN 3-89821-648-9

30 *Rebecca S. Katz*
    The Georgian Regime Crisis of 2003-
    2004
    A Case Study in Post-Soviet Media
    Representation of Politics, Crime and
    Corruption
    ISBN 3-89821-413-3

31 *Vladimir Kantor*
    Willkür oder Freiheit
    Beiträge zur russischen Geschichtsphilosophie
    Ediert von Dagmar Herrmann sowie mit
    einem Vorwort versehen von Leonid Luks
    ISBN 3-89821-589-X

32 *Laura A. Victoir*
    The Russian Land Estate Today
    A Case Study of Cultural Politics in Post-
    Soviet Russia
    With a foreword by Priscilla Roosevelt
    ISBN 3-89821-426-5

33 *Ivan Katchanovski*
    Cleft Countries
    Regional Political Divisions and Cultures in
    Post-Soviet Ukraine and Moldova
    With a foreword by Francis Fukuyama
    ISBN 3-89821-558-X

34 *Florian Mühlfried*
    Postsowjetische Feiern
    Das Georgische Bankett im Wandel
    Mit einem Vorwort von Kevin Tuite
    ISBN 3-89821-601-2

35 *Roger Griffin, Werner Loh, Andreas
    Umland (Eds.)*
    Fascism Past and Present, West and
    East
    An International Debate on Concepts and
    Cases in the Comparative Study of the
    Extreme Right
    With an afterword by Walter Laqueur
    ISBN 3-89821-674-8

36 *Sebastian Schlegel*
    Der „Weiße Archipel"
    Sowjetische Atomstädte 1945-1991
    Mit einem Geleitwort von Thomas Bohn
    ISBN 3-89821-679-9

37 *Vyacheslav Likhachev*
    Political Anti-Semitism in Post-Soviet
    Russia
    Actors and Ideas in 1991-2003
    Edited and translated from Russian by Eugene
    Veklerov
    ISBN 3-89821-529-6

38 *Josette Baer (Ed.)*
    Preparing Liberty in Central Europe
    Political Texts from the Spring of Nations
    1848 to the Spring of Prague 1968
    With a foreword by Zdeněk V. David
    ISBN 3-89821-546-6

39 *Михаил Лукьянов*
    Российский консерватизм и
    реформа, 1907-1914
    С предисловием Марка Д. Стейнберга
    ISBN 3-89821-503-2

40 *Nicola Melloni*
    Market Without Economy
    The 1998 Russian Financial Crisis
    With a foreword by Eiji Furukawa
    ISBN 3-89821-407-9

41 *Dmitrij Chmelnizki*
    Die Architektur Stalins
    Bd. 1: Studien zu Ideologie und Stil
    Bd. 2: Bilddokumentation
    Mit einem Vorwort von Bruno Flierl
    ISBN 3-89821-515-6

42 *Katja Yafimava*
    Post-Soviet Russian-Belarussian
    Relationships
    The Role of Gas Transit Pipelines
    With a foreword by Jonathan P. Stern
    ISBN 3-89821-655-1

43 *Boris Chavkin*
    Verflechtungen der deutschen und
    russischen Zeitgeschichte
    Aufsätze und Archivfunde zu den
    Beziehungen Deutschlands und der
    Sowjetunion von 1917 bis 1991
    Ediert von Markus Edlinger sowie mit einem
    Vorwort versehen von Leonid Luks
    ISBN 3-89821-756-6

44 *Anastasija Grynenko in Zusammenarbeit mit Claudia Dathe*
Die Terminologie des Gerichtswesens der Ukraine und Deutschlands im Vergleich
Eine übersetzungswissenschaftliche Analyse juristischer Fachbegriffe im Deutschen, Ukrainischen und Russischen
Mit einem Vorwort von Ulrich Hartmann
ISBN 3-89821-691-8

45 *Anton Burkov*
The Impact of the European Convention on Human Rights on Russian Law
Legislation and Application in 1996-2006
With a foreword by Françoise Hampson
ISBN 978-3-89821-639-5

46 *Stina Torjesen, Indra Overland (Eds.)*
International Election Observers in Post-Soviet Azerbaijan
Geopolitical Pawns or Agents of Change?
ISBN 978-3-89821-743-9

47 *Taras Kuzio*
Ukraine – Crimea – Russia
Triangle of Conflict
ISBN 978-3-89821-761-3

48 *Claudia Šabić*
"Ich erinnere mich nicht, aber L'viv!"
Zur Funktion kultureller Faktoren für die Institutionalisierung und Entwicklung einer ukrainischen Region
Mit einem Vorwort von Melanie Tatur
ISBN 978-3-89821-752-1

49 *Marlies Bilz*
Tatarstan in der Transformation
Nationaler Diskurs und Politische Praxis 1988-1994
Mit einem Vorwort von Frank Golczewski
ISBN 978-3-89821-722-4

50 *Марлен Ларюэль (ред.)*
Современные интерпретации русского национализма
ISBN 978-3-89821-795-8

51 *Sonja Schüler*
Die ethnische Dimension der Armut
Roma im postsozialistischen Rumänien
Mit einem Vorwort von Anton Sterbling
ISBN 978-3-89821-776-7

52 *Галина Кожевникова*
Радикальный национализм в России и противодействие ему
Сборник докладов Центра «Сова» за 2004-2007 гг.
С предисловием Александра Верховского
ISBN 978-3-89821-721-7

53 *Галина Кожевникова и Владимир Прибыловский*
Российская власть в биографиях I
Высшие должностные лица РФ в 2004 г.
ISBN 978-3-89821-796-5

54 *Галина Кожевникова и Владимир Прибыловский*
Российская власть в биографиях II
Члены Правительства РФ в 2004 г.
ISBN 978-3-89821-797-2

55 *Галина Кожевникова и Владимир Прибыловский*
Российская власть в биографиях III
Руководители федеральных служб и агентств РФ в 2004 г.
ISBN 978-3-89821-798-9

56 *Ileana Petroniu*
Privatisierung in Transformationsökonomien
Determinanten der Restrukturierungs-Bereitschaft am Beispiel Polens, Rumäniens und der Ukraine
Mit einem Vorwort von Rainer W. Schäfer
ISBN 978-3-89821-790-3

57 *Christian Wipperfürth*
Russland und seine GUS-Nachbarn
Hintergründe, aktuelle Entwicklungen und Konflikte in einer ressourcenreichen Region
ISBN 978-3-89821-801-6

58 *Togzhan Kassenova*
From Antagonism to Partnership
The Uneasy Path of the U.S.-Russian Cooperative Threat Reduction
With a foreword by Christoph Bluth
ISBN 978-3-89821-707-1

59 *Alexander Höllwerth*
Das sakrale eurasische Imperium des Aleksandr Dugin
Eine Diskursanalyse zum postsowjetischen russischen Rechtsextremismus
Mit einem Vorwort von Dirk Uffelmann
ISBN 978-3-89821-813-9

60 Олег Рябов
    «Россия-Матушка»
    Национализм, гендер и война в России XX века
    С предисловием Елены Гощило
    ISBN 978-3-89821-487-2

61 Ivan Maistrenko
    Borot'bism
    A Chapter in the History of the Ukrainian Revolution
    With a new introduction by Chris Ford
    Translated by George S. N. Luckyj with the assistance of Ivan L. Rudnytsky
    ISBN 978-3-89821-697-5

62 Maryna Romanets
    Anamorphosic Texts and Reconfigured Visions
    Improvised Traditions in Contemporary Ukrainian and Irish Literature
    ISBN 978-3-89821-576-3

63 Paul D'Anieri and Taras Kuzio (Eds.)
    Aspects of the Orange Revolution I
    Democratization and Elections in Post-Communist Ukraine
    ISBN 978-3-89821-698-2

64 Bohdan Harasymiw in collaboration with Oleh S. Ilnytzkyj (Eds.)
    Aspects of the Orange Revolution II
    Information and Manipulation Strategies in the 2004 Ukrainian Presidential Elections
    ISBN 978-3-89821-699-9

65 Ingmar Bredies, Andreas Umland and Valentin Yakushik (Eds.)
    Aspects of the Orange Revolution III
    The Context and Dynamics of the 2004 Ukrainian Presidential Elections
    ISBN 978-3-89821-803-0

66 Ingmar Bredies, Andreas Umland and Valentin Yakushik (Eds.)
    Aspects of the Orange Revolution IV
    Foreign Assistance and Civic Action in the 2004 Ukrainian Presidential Elections
    ISBN 978-3-89821-808-5

67 Ingmar Bredies, Andreas Umland and Valentin Yakushik (Eds.)
    Aspects of the Orange Revolution V
    Institutional Observation Reports on the 2004 Ukrainian Presidential Elections
    ISBN 978-3-89821-809-2

68 Taras Kuzio (Ed.)
    Aspects of the Orange Revolution VI
    Post-Communist Democratic Revolutions in Comparative Perspective
    ISBN 978-3-89821-820-7

69 Tim Bohse
    Autoritarismus statt Selbstverwaltung
    Die Transformation der kommunalen Politik in der Stadt Kaliningrad 1990-2005
    Mit einem Geleitwort von Stefan Troebst
    ISBN 978-3-89821-782-8

70 David Rupp
    Die Rußländische Föderation und die russischsprachige Minderheit in Lettland
    Eine Fallstudie zur Anwaltspolitik Moskaus gegenüber den russophonen Minderheiten im „Nahen Ausland" von 1991 bis 2002
    Mit einem Vorwort von Helmut Wagner
    ISBN 978-3-89821-778-1

71 Taras Kuzio
    Theoretical and Comparative Perspectives on Nationalism
    New Directions in Cross-Cultural and Post-Communist Studies
    With a foreword by Paul Robert Magocsi
    ISBN 978-3-89821-815-3

72 Christine Teichmann
    Die Hochschultransformation im heutigen Osteuropa
    Kontinuität und Wandel bei der Entwicklung des postkommunistischen Universitätswesens
    Mit einem Vorwort von Oskar Anweiler
    ISBN 978-3-89821-842-9

73 Julia Kusznir
    Der politische Einfluss von Wirtschaftseliten in russischen Regionen
    Eine Analyse am Beispiel der Erdöl- und Erdgasindustrie, 1992-2005
    Mit einem Vorwort von Wolfgang Eichwede
    ISBN 978-3-89821-821-4

74 Alena Vysotskaya
    Russland, Belarus und die EU-Osterweiterung
    Zur Minderheitenfrage und zum Problem der Freizügigkeit des Personenverkehrs
    Mit einem Vorwort von Katlijn Malfliet
    ISBN 978-3-89821-822-1

75 Heiko Pleines (Hrsg.)
Corporate Governance in postsozialistischen Volkswirtschaften
ISBN 978-3-89821-766-8

76 Stefan Ihrig
Wer sind die Moldawier?
Rumänismus versus Moldowanismus in Historiographie und Schulbüchern der Republik Moldova, 1991-2006
Mit einem Vorwort von Holm Sundhaussen
ISBN 978-3-89821-466-7

77 Galina Kozhevnikova in collaboration with Alexander Verkhovsky and Eugene Veklerov
Ultra-Nationalism and Hate Crimes in Contemporary Russia
The 2004-2006 Annual Reports of Moscow's SOVA Center
With a foreword by Stephen D. Shenfield
ISBN 978-3-89821-868-9

78 Florian Küchler
The Role of the European Union in Moldova's Transnistria Conflict
With a foreword by Christopher Hill
ISBN 978-3-89821-850-4

79 Bernd Rechel
The Long Way Back to Europe
Minority Protection in Bulgaria
With a foreword by Richard Crampton
ISBN 978-3-89821-863-4

80 Peter W. Rodgers
Nation, Region and History in Post-Communist Transitions
Identity Politics in Ukraine, 1991-2006
With a foreword by Vera Tolz
ISBN 978-3-89821-903-7

81 Stephanie Solywoda
The Life and Work of Semen L. Frank
A Study of Russian Religious Philosophy
With a foreword by Philip Walters
ISBN 978-3-89821-457-5

82 Vera Sokolova
Cultural Politics of Ethnicity
Discourses on Roma in Communist Czechoslovakia
ISBN 978-3-89821-864-1

83 Natalya Shevchik Ketenci
Kazakhstani Enterprises in Transition
The Role of Historical Regional Development in Kazakhstan's Post-Soviet Economic Transformation
ISBN 978-3-89821-831-3

84 Martin Malek, Anna Schor-Tschudnowskaja (Hrsg.)
Europa im Tschetschenienkrieg
Zwischen politischer Ohnmacht und Gleichgültigkeit
Mit einem Vorwort von Lipchan Basajewa
ISBN 978-3-89821-676-0

85 Stefan Meister
Das postsowjetische Universitätswesen zwischen nationalem und internationalem Wandel
Die Entwicklung der regionalen Hochschule in Russland als Gradmesser der Systemtransformation
Mit einem Vorwort von Joan DeBardeleben
ISBN 978-3-89821-891-7

86 Konstantin Sheiko in collaboration with Stephen Brown
Nationalist Imaginings of the Russian Past
Anatolii Fomenko and the Rise of Alternative History in Post-Communist Russia
With a foreword by Donald Ostrowski
ISBN 978-3-89821-915-0

87 Sabine Jenni
Wie stark ist das „Einige Russland"?
Zur Parteibindung der Eliten und zum Wahlerfolg der Machtpartei im Dezember 2007
Mit einem Vorwort von Klaus Armingeon
ISBN 978-3-89821-961-7

88 Thomas Borén
Meeting-Places of Transformation
Urban Identity, Spatial Representations and Local Politics in Post-Soviet St Petersburg
ISBN 978-3-89821-739-2

89 Aygul Ashirova
Stalinismus und Stalin-Kult in Zentralasien
Turkmenistan 1924-1953
Mit einem Vorwort von Leonid Luks
ISBN 978-3-89821-987-7

90 *Leonid Luks*
Freiheit oder imperiale Größe?
Essays zu einem russischen Dilemma
ISBN 978-3-8382-0011-8

91 *Christopher Gilley*
The 'Change of Signposts' in the Ukrainian Emigration
A Contribution to the History of Sovietophilism in the 1920s
With a foreword by Frank Golczewski
ISBN 978-3-89821-965-5

92 *Philipp Casula, Jeronim Perovic (Eds.)*
Identities and Politics During the Putin Presidency
The Discursive Foundations of Russia's Stability
With a foreword by Heiko Haumann
ISBN 978-3-8382-0015-6

93 *Marcel Viëtor*
Europa und die Frage nach seinen Grenzen im Osten
Zur Konstruktion ‚europäischer Identität' in Geschichte und Gegenwart
Mit einem Vorwort von Albrecht Lehmann
ISBN 978-3-8382-0045-3

94 *Ben Hellman, Andrei Rogachevskii*
Filming the Unfilmable
Casper Wrede's 'One Day in the Life of Ivan Denisovich'
Second, Revised and Expanded Edition
ISBN 978-3-8382-0044-6

95 *Eva Fuchslocher*
Vaterland, Sprache, Glaube
Orthodoxie und Nationenbildung am Beispiel Georgiens
Mit einem Vorwort von Christina von Braun
ISBN 978-3-89821-884-9

96 *Vladimir Kantor*
Das Westlertum und der Weg Russlands
Zur Entwicklung der russischen Literatur und Philosophie
Ediert von Dagmar Herrmann
Mit einem Beitrag von Nikolaus Lobkowicz
ISBN 978-3-8382-0102-3

97 *Kamran Musayev*
Die postsowjetische Transformation im Baltikum und Südkaukasus
Eine vergleichende Untersuchung der politischen Entwicklung Lettlands und Aserbaidschans 1985-2009
Mit einem Vorwort von Leonid Luks
Ediert von Sandro Henschel
ISBN 978-3-8382-0103-0

98 *Tatiana Zhurzhenko*
Borderlands into Bordered Lands
Geopolitics of Identity in Post-Soviet Ukraine
With a foreword by Dieter Segert
ISBN 978-3-8382-0042-2

99 *Кирилл Галушко, Лидия Смола (ред.)*
Пределы падения – варианты украинского будущего
Аналитико-прогностические исследования
ISBN 978-3-8382-0148-1

100 *Michael Minkenberg (ed.)*
Historical Legacies and the Radical Right in Post-Cold War Central and Eastern Europe
With an afterword by Sabrina P. Ramet
ISBN 978-3-8382-0124-5

101 *David-Emil Wickström*
Rocking St. Petersburg
Transcultural Flows and Identity Politics in the St. Petersburg Popular Music Scene
With a foreword by Yngvar B. Steinholt
Second, Revised and Expanded Edition
ISBN 978-3-8382-0100-9

102 *Eva Zabka*
Eine neue „Zeit der Wirren"?
Der spät- und postsowjetische Systemwandel 1985-2000 im Spiegel russischer gesellschaftspolitischer Diskurse
Mit einem Vorwort von Margareta Mommsen
ISBN 978-3-8382-0161-0

103 *Ulrike Ziemer*
Ethnic Belonging, Gender and Cultural Practices
Youth Identitites in Contemporary Russia
With a foreword by Anoop Nayak
ISBN 978-3-8382-0152-8

104 Ksenia Chepikova
‚Einiges Russland' - eine zweite
KPdSU?
Aspekte der Identitätskonstruktion einer
postsowjetischen „Partei der Macht"
Mit einem Vorwort von Torsten Oppelland
ISBN 978-3-8382-0311-9

105 Леонид Люкс
Западничество или евразийство?
Демократия или идеократия?
Сборник статей об исторических дилеммах
России
С предисловием Владимира Кантора
ISBN 978-3-8382-0211-2

106 Anna Dost
Das russische Verfassungsrecht auf dem
Weg zum Föderalismus und zurück
Zum Konflikt von Rechtsnormen und
-wirklichkeit in der Russländischen Föderation
von 1991 bis 2009
Mit einem Vorwort von Alexander Blankenagel
ISBN 978-3-8382-0292-1

107 Philipp Herzog
Sozialistische Völkerfreundschaft,
nationaler Widerstand oder harmloser
Zeitvertreib?
Zur politischen Funktion der Volkskunst
im sowjetischen Estland
Mit einem Vorwort von Andreas Kappeler
ISBN 978-3-8382-0216-7

108 Marlène Laruelle (ed.)
Russian Nationalism, Foreign Policy,
and Identity Debates in Putin's Russia
New Ideological Patterns after the Orange
Revolution
ISBN 978-3-8382-0325-6

109 Michail Logvinov
Russlands Kampf gegen den
internationalen Terrorismus
Eine kritische Bestandsaufnahme des
Bekämpfungsansatzes
Mit einem Geleitwort von
Hans-Henning Schröder
und einem Vorwort von Eckhard Jesse
ISBN 978-3-8382-0329-4

110 John B. Dunlop
The Moscow Bombings
of September 1999
Examinations of Russian Terrorist Attacks
at the Onset of Vladimir Putin's Rule
Second, Revised and Expanded Edition
ISBN 978-3-8382-0388-1

111 Андрей А. Ковалёв
Свидетельство из-за кулис
российской политики I
Можно ли делать добро из зла?
(Воспоминания и размышления о
последних советских и первых
послесоветских годах)
With a foreword by Peter Reddaway
ISBN 978-3-8382-0302-7

112 Андрей А. Ковалёв
Свидетельство из-за кулис
российской политики II
Угроза для себя и окружающих
(Наблюдения и предостережения
относительно происходящего после 2000 г.)
ISBN 978-3-8382-0303-4

113 Bernd Kappenberg
Zeichen setzen für Europa
Der Gebrauch europäischer lateinischer
Sonderzeichen in der deutschen Öffentlichkeit
Mit einem Vorwort von Peter Schlobinski
ISBN 978-3-89821-749-1

114 Ivo Mijnssen
The Quest for an Ideal Youth in
Putin's Russia I
Back to Our Future! History, Modernity, and
Patriotism according to *Nashi*, 2005-2013
With a foreword by Jeronim Perović
Second, Revised and Expanded Edition
ISBN 978-3-8382-0368-3

115 Jussi Lassila
The Quest for an Ideal Youth in
Putin's Russia II
The Search for Distinctive Conformism in the
Political Communication of *Nashi*, 2005-2009
With a foreword by Kirill Postoutenko
Second, Revised and Expanded Edition
ISBN 978-3-8382-0415-4

116 Valerio Trabandt
Neue Nachbarn, gute Nachbarschaft?
Die EU als internationaler Akteur am Beispiel
ihrer Demokratieförderung in Belarus und der
Ukraine 2004-2009
Mit einem Vorwort von Jutta Joachim
ISBN 978-3-8382-0437-6

117 **Fabian Pfeiffer**
Estlands Außen- und Sicherheitspolitik I
Der estnische Atlantizismus nach der
wiedererlangten Unabhängigkeit 1991-2004
Mit einem Vorwort von Helmut Hubel
ISBN 978-3-8382-0127-6

118 **Jana Podßuweit**
Estlands Außen- und Sicherheitspolitik II
Handlungsoptionen eines Kleinstaates im
Rahmen seiner EU-Mitgliedschaft (2004-2008)
Mit einem Vorwort von Helmut Hubel
ISBN 978-3-8382-0440-6

119 **Karin Pointner**
Estlands Außen- und Sicherheitspolitik III
Eine gedächtnispolitische Analyse estnischer
Entwicklungskooperation 2006-2010
Mit einem Vorwort von Karin Liebhart
ISBN 978-3-8382-0435-2

120 **Ruslana Vovk**
Die Offenheit der ukrainischen
Verfassung für das Völkerrecht und
die europäische Integration
Mit einem Vorwort von Alexander
Blankenagel
ISBN 978-3-8382-0481-9

121 **Mykhaylo Banakh**
Die Relevanz der Zivilgesellschaft
bei den postkommunistischen
Transformationsprozessen in mittel-
und osteuropäischen Ländern
Das Beispiel der spät- und postsowjetischen
Ukraine 1986-2009
Mit einem Vorwort von Gerhard Simon
ISBN 978-3-8382-0499-4

122 **Michael Moser**
Language Policy and the Discourse on
Languages in Ukraine under President
Viktor Yanukovych (25 February
2010–28 October 2012)
ISBN 978-3-8382-0497-0 (Paperback edition)
ISBN 978-3-8382-0507-6 (Hardcover edition)

123 **Nicole Krome**
Russischer Netzwerkkapitalismus
Restrukturierungsprozesse in der
Russischen Föderation am Beispiel des
Luftfahrtunternehmens "Aviastar"
Mit einem Vorwort von Petra Stykow
ISBN 978-3-8382-0534-2

124 **David R. Marples**
'Our Glorious Past'
Lukashenka's Belarus and
the Great Patriotic War
ISBN 978-3-8382-0574-8 (Paperback edition)
ISBN 978-3-8382-0675-2 (Hardcover edition)

125 **Ulf Walther**
Russlands "neuer Adel"
Die Macht des Geheimdienstes von
Gorbatschow bis Putin
Mit einem Vorwort von Hans-Georg Wieck
ISBN 978-3-8382-0584-7

126 **Simon Geissbühler (Hrsg.)**
Kiew – Revolution 3.0
Der Euromaidan 2013/14 und die
Zukunftsperspektiven der Ukraine
ISBN 978-3-8382-0581-6 (Paperback edition)
ISBN 978-3-8382-0681-3 (Hardcover edition)

127 **Andrey Makarychev**
Russia and the EU
in a Multipolar World
Discourses, Identities, Norms
With a foreword by Klaus Segbers
ISBN 978-3-8382-0629-5

128 **Roland Scharff**
Kasachstan als postsowjetischer
Wohlfahrtsstaat
Die Transformation des sozialen
Schutzsystems
Mit einem Vorwort von Joachim Ahrens
ISBN 978-3-8382-0622-6

129 **Katja Grupp**
Bild Lücke Deutschland
Kaliningrader Studierende sprechen über
Deutschland
Mit einem Vorwort von Martin Schulz
ISBN 978-3-8382-0552-6

130 **Konstantin Sheiko, Stephen Brown**
History as Therapy
Alternative History and Nationalist
Imaginings in Russia, 1991-2014
ISBN 978-3-8382-0665-3

131 **Elisa Kriza**
Alexander Solzhenitsyn: Cold War
Icon, Gulag Author, Russian
Nationalist?
A Study of the Western Reception of his
Literary Writings, Historical Interpretations,
and Political Ideas
With a foreword by Andrei Rogatchevski
ISBN 978-3-8382-0589-2 (Paperback edition)
ISBN 978-3-8382-0690-5 (Hardcover edition)

132　Serghei Golunov
　　The Elephant in the Room
　　Corruption and Cheating in Russian
　　Universities
　　ISBN 978-3-8382-0570-0

133　Manja Hussner, Rainer Arnold (Hgg.)
　　Verfassungsgerichtsbarkeit in
　　Zentralasien I
　　Sammlung von Verfassungstexten
　　ISBN 978-3-8382-0595-3

134　Nikolay Mitrokhin
　　Die "Russische Partei"
　　Die Bewegung der russischen Nationalisten in
　　der UdSSR 1953-1985
　　Aus dem Russischen übertragen von einem
　　Übersetzerteam unter der Leitung von Larisa Schippel
　　ISBN 978-3-8382-0024-8

135　Manja Hussner, Rainer Arnold (Hgg.)
　　Verfassungsgerichtsbarkeit in
　　Zentralasien II
　　Sammlung von Verfassungstexten
　　ISBN 978-3-8382-0597-7

136　Manfred Zeller
　　Das sowjetische Fieber
　　Fußballfans im poststalinistischen
　　Vielvölkerreich
　　Mit einem Vorwort von Nikolaus Katzer
　　ISBN 978-3-8382-0757-5

137　Kristin Schreiter
　　Stellung und Entwicklungspotential
　　zivilgesellschaftlicher Gruppen in
　　Russland
　　Menschenrechtsorganisationen im Vergleich
　　ISBN 978-3-8382-0673-8

138　David R. Marples, Frederick V. Mills
　　(eds.)
　　Ukraine's Euromaidan
　　Analyses of a Civil Revolution
　　ISBN 978-3-8382-0660-8

139　Bernd Kappenberg
　　Setting Signs for Europe
　　Why Diacritics Matter for
　　European Integration
　　With a foreword by Peter Schlobinski
　　ISBN 978-3-8382-0663-9

140　René Lenz
　　Internationalisierung, Kooperation
　　und Transfer
　　Externe bildungspolitische Akteure in der
　　Russischen Föderation
　　Mit einem Vorwort von Frank Ettrich
　　ISBN 978-3-8382-0751-3

141　Juri Plusnin, Yana Zausaeva, Natalia
　　Zhidkevich, Artemy Pozanenko
　　Wandering Workers
　　Mores, Behavior, Way of Life, and Political
　　Status of Domestic Russian Labor Migrants
　　Translated by Julia Kazantseva
　　ISBN 978-3-8382-0653-0

142　David J. Smith (eds.)
　　Latvia – A Work in Progress?
　　100 Years of State- and Nation-Building
　　ISBN 978-3-8382-0648-6

143　Инна Чувычкина (ред.)
　　Экспортные нефте- и газопроводы
　　на постсоветском пространстве
　　Анализ трубопроводной политики в свете
　　теории международных отношений
　　ISBN 978-3-8382-0822-0

144　Johann Zajaczkowski
　　Russland – eine pragmatische
　　Großmacht?
　　Eine rollentheoretische Untersuchung
　　russischer Außenpolitik am Beispiel der
　　Zusammenarbeit mit den USA nach 9/11 und
　　des Georgienkrieges von 2008
　　Mit einem Vorwort von Siegfried Schieder
　　ISBN 978-3-8382-0837-4

145　Boris Popivanov
　　Changing Images of the Left in
　　Bulgaria
　　The Challenge of Post-Communism in the
　　Early 21st Century
　　ISBN 978-3-8382-0667-7

146　Lenka Krátká
　　A History of the Czechoslovak Ocean
　　Shipping Company 1948-1989
　　How a Small, Landlocked Country Ran
　　Maritime Business During the Cold War
　　ISBN 978-3-8382-0666-0

147　Alexander Sergunin
　　Explaining Russian Foreign Policy
　　Behavior
　　Theory and Practice
　　ISBN 978-3-8382-0752-0

148   Darya Malyutina
      Migrant Friendships in
      a Super-Diverse City
      Russian-Speakers and their Social
      Relationships in London in the 21st Century
      With a foreword by Claire Dwyer
      ISBN 978-3-8382-0652-3

149   Alexander Sergunin, Valery Konyshev
      Russia in the Arctic
      Hard or Soft Power?
      ISBN 978-3-8382-0753-7

150   John J. Maresca
      Helsinki Revisited
      A Key U.S. Negotiator's Memoirs
      on the Development of the CSCE into the
      OSCE
      With a foreword by Hafiz Pashayev
      ISBN 978-3-8382-0852-7

151   Jardar Østbø
      The New Third Rome
      Readings of a Russian Nationalist Myth
      With a foreword by Pål Kolstø
      ISBN 978-3-8382-0870-1

152   Simon Kordonsky
      Socio-Economic Foundations of the
      Russian Post-Soviet Regime
      The Resource-Based Economy and Estate-
      Based Social Structure of Contemporary
      Russia
      With a foreword by Svetlana Barsukova
      ISBN 978-3-8382-0775-9

153   Duncan Leitch
      Assisting Reform in Post-Communist
      Ukraine 2000–2012
      The Illusions of Donors and the Disillusion of
      Beneficiaries
      With a foreword by Kataryna Wolczuk
      ISBN 978-3-8382-0844-2

154   Abel Polese
      Limits of a Post-Soviet State
      How Informality Replaces, Renegotiates, and
      Reshapes Governance in Contemporary
      Ukraine
      With a foreword by Colin Williams
      ISBN 978-3-8382-0845-9

155   Mikhail Suslov (ed.)
      Digital Orthodoxy in the Post-Soviet
      World
      The Russian Orthodox Church and Web 2.0
      With a foreword by Father Cyril Hovorun
      ISBN 978-3-8382-0871-8

156   Leonid Luks
      Zwei „Sonderwege"? Russisch-
      deutsche Parallelen und Kontraste
      (1917-2014)
      Vergleichende Essays
      ISBN 978-3-8382-0823-7

157   Vladimir V. Karacharovskiy, Ovsey I.
      Shkaratan, Gordey A. Yastrebov
      Towards a New Russian Work Culture
      Can Western Companies and Expatriates
      Change Russian Society?
      With a foreword by Elena N. Danilova
      Translated by Julia Kazantseva
      ISBN 978-3-8382-0902-9

158   Edmund Griffiths
      Aleksandr Prokhanov and Post-Soviet
      Esotericism
      ISBN 978-3-8382-0903-6

159   Timm Beichelt, Susann Worschech
      (eds.)
      Transnational Ukraine?
      Networks and Ties that Influence(d)
      Contemporary Ukraine
      ISBN 978-3-8382-0944-9

160   Mieste Hotopp-Riecke
      Die Tataren der Krim zwischen
      Assimilation und Selbstbehauptung
      Der Aufbau des krimtatarischen
      Bildungswesens nach Deportation und
      Heimkehr (1990-2005)
      Mit einem Vorwort von Swetlana
      Czerwonnaja
      ISBN 978-3-89821-940-2

161   Olga Bertelsen (ed.)
      Revolution and War in
      Contemporary Ukraine
      The Challenge of Change
      ISBN 978-3-8382-1016-2

162   Natalya Ryabinska
      Ukraine's Post-Communist
      Mass Media
      Between Capture and Commercialization
      With a foreword by Marta Dyczok
      ISBN 978-3-8382-1011-7

163 Alexandra Cotofana,
James M. Nyce (eds.)
Religion and Magic in Socialist and Post-Socialist Contexts I
Historic and Ethnographic Case Studies of Orthodoxy, Heterodoxy, and Alternative Spirituality
With a foreword by Patrick L. Michelson
ISBN 978-3-8382-0989-0

164 Nozima Akhrarkhodjaeva
The Instrumentalisation of Mass Media in Electoral Authoritarian Regimes
Evidence from Russia's Presidential Election Campaigns of 2000 and 2008
ISBN 978-3-8382-1013-1

165 Yulia Krasheninnikova
Informal Healthcare in Contemporary Russia
Sociographic Essays on the Post-Soviet Infrastructure for Alternative Healing Practices
ISBN 978-3-8382-0970-8

166 Peter Kaiser
Das Schachbrett der Macht
Die Handlungsspielräume eines sowjetischen Funktionärs unter Stalin am Beispiel des Generalsekretärs des Komsomol Aleksandr Kosarev (1929-1938)
Mit einem Vorwort von Dietmar Neutatz
ISBN 978-3-8382-1052-0

167 Oksana Kim
The Effects and Implications of Kazakhstan's Adoption of International Financial Reporting Standards
A Resource Dependence Perspective
With a foreword by Svetlana Vlady
ISBN 978-3-8382-0987-6

168 Anna Sanina
Patriotic Education in Contemporary Russia
Sociological Studies in the Making of the Post-Soviet Citizen
With a foreword by Anna Oldfield
ISBN 978-3-8382-0993-7

169 Rudolf Wolters
Spezialist in Sibirien
Faksimile der 1933 erschienenen ersten Ausgabe
Mit einem Vorwort von Dmitrij Chmelnizki
ISBN 978-3-8382-0515-1

170 Michal Vít,
Magdalena M. Baran (eds.)
Transregional versus National Perspectives on Contemporary Central European History
Studies on the Building of Nation-States and Their Cooperation in the 20th and 21st Century
With a foreword by Petr Vágner
ISBN 978-3-8382-1015-5

171 Philip Gamaghelyan
Conflict Resolution Beyond the International Relations Paradigm
Evolving Designs as a Transformative Practice in Nagorno-Karabakh and Syria
With a foreword by Susan Allen
ISBN 978-3-8382-1057-5

172 Maria Shagina
Joining a Prestigious Club
Cooperation with Europarties and Its Impact on Party Development in Georgia, Moldova, and Ukraine 2004–2015
With a foreword by Kataryna Wolczuk
ISBN 978-3-8382-1084-1

173 Alexandra Cotofana,
James M. Nyce (eds.)
Religion and Magic in Socialist and Post-Socialist Contexts II
Baltic, Eastern European, and Post-USSR Case Studies
With a foreword by Anita Stasulane
ISBN 978-3-8382-0990-6

174 Barbara Kunz
Kind Words, Cruise Missiles, and Everything in Between
The Use of Power Resources in U.S. Policies towards Poland, Ukraine, and Belarus 1989–2008
With a foreword by William Hill
ISBN 978-3-8382-1065-0

175 Eduard Klein
Bildungskorruption in Russland und der Ukraine
Eine komparative Analyse der Performanz staatlicher Antikorruptionsmaßnahmen im Hochschulsektor am Beispiel universitärer Aufnahmeprüfungen
Mit einem Vorwort von Heiko Pleines
ISBN 978-3-8382-0995-1

176   Markus Soldner
      Politischer Kapitalismus im
      postsowjetischen Russland
      Die politische, wirtschaftliche und mediale
      Transformation in den 1990er Jahren
      Mit einem Vorwort von Wolfgang Ismayr
      ISBN 978-3-8382-1222-7

177   Anton Oleinik
      Building Ukraine from Within
      A Sociological, Institutional, and Economic
      Analysis of a Nation-State in the Making
      ISBN 978-3-8382-1150-3

178   Peter Rollberg,
      Marlene Laruelle (eds.)
      Mass Media in the Post-Soviet World
      Market Forces, State Actors, and Political
      Manipulation in the Informational
      Environment after Communism
      ISBN 978-3-8382-1116-9

179   Mikhail Minakov
      Development and Dystopia
      Studies in Post-Soviet Ukraine and Eastern
      Europe
      With a foreword by Alexander Etkind
      ISBN 978-3-8382-1112-1

180   Aijan Sharshenova
      The European Union's Democracy
      Promotion in Central Asia
      A Study of Political Interests, Influence, and
      Development in Kazakhstan and Kyrgyzstan
      in 2007–2013
      With a foreword by Gordon Crawford
      ISBN 978-3-8382-1151-0

181   Andrey Makarychev,
      Alexandra Yatsyk (eds.)
      Boris Nemtsov and Russian Politics
      Power and Resistance
      With a foreword by Zhanna Nemtsova
      ISBN 978-3-8382-1122-0

182   Sophie Falsini
      The Euromaidan's Effect
      on Civil Society
      Why and How Ukrainian Social Capital
      Increased after the Revolution of Dignity
      With a foreword by Susann Worschech
      ISBN 978-3-8382-1131-2

183   Andreas Umland (ed.)
      Ukraine's Decentralization
      Challenges and Implications of the Local
      Governance Reform after the Euromaidan
      Revolution
      ISBN 978-3-8382-1162-6

184   Leonid Luks
      A Fateful Triangle
      Essays on Contemporary Russian, German
      and Polish History
      ISBN 978-3-8382-1143-5

185   John B. Dunlop
      The February 2015 Assassination of
      Boris Nemtsov and the Flawed Trial
      of his Alleged Killers
      An Exploration of Russia's "Crime of the 21st
      Century"
      With a foreword by Vladimir Kara-Murza
      ISBN 978-3-8382-1188-6

186   Vasile Rotaru
      Russia, the EU, and the Eastern
      Partnership
      Building Bridges or Digging Trenches?
      ISBN 978-3-8382-1134-3

187   Marina Lebedeva
      Russian Studies of International
      Relations
      From the Soviet Past to the Post-Cold-War
      Present
      With a foreword by Andrei P. Tsygankov
      ISBN 978-3-8382-0851-0

188   George Soroka,
      Tomasz Stepniewski (eds.)
      Ukraine after Maidan
      Revisiting Domestic and Regional Security
      ISBN 978-3-8382-1075-9

189   Petar Cholakov
      Ethnic Entrepreneurs Unmasked
      Political Institutions and Ethnic Conflicts in
      Contemporary Bulgaria
      ISBN 978-3-8382-1189-3

190   A. Salem, G. Hazeldine,
      D. Morgan (eds.)
      Higher Education in Post-Communist
      States
      Comparative and Sociological Perspectives
      ISBN 978-3-8382-1183-1

ibidem.eu